LAURENCE E. MOREHOUSE
Ph.D., F.A.C.S.M.

Professor of Physical Education,
University of California at Los Angeles

PHILIP J. RASCH
C.C.T., Ph.D., F.A.C.S.M.

Assistant Professor of Physical Medicine and Rehabilitation
College of Osteopathic Physicians and Surgeons

W. B. SAUNDERS COMPANY

Philadelphia   1958   London

Scientific

Basis of

Athletic

Training

Preface

The study of the athlete in competition affords a unique opportunity to elucidate the factors which affect maximum human performance. Since peak performance is achieved only by the disregard of both comfort and caution, the athlete's bold reach to excel may expose him to the possibility of an injury which will thwart his effort. The problems of preparing an athlete for maximum performance, of shielding him from possibly damaging sequelae, and of restoring him to maximum performance should injury occur are the subjects of this book.

This text is concerned with the preparation of the athlete for competition, the protection of the athlete from injuries, the etiology, examination and first aid care of the injured athlete, and the rehabilitation of the athlete following injury. The actual diagnosis, treatment and prognosis of injuries, which are adequately discussed in medical literature, are not taken up here.

The contents are broad in scope so as to be useful in various sports. The principles of conditioning and of prevention and care of injuries apply to both the novice athlete and the champion. The problems of women, children and older adults in athletics have received special consideration.

The writers are grateful to the authors and publishers who have given permission to reproduce their material, the sources of which are acknowledged in the text.

Gene A. Logan, M.S., R.P.T., F.A.C.S.M., gave freely of his exten-sive knowledge regarding acceptable training room design, methods and procedures. In addition, he created the preliminary sketches used to illustrate techniques of athletic bandaging.

The section on protective features of various materials in the chapter on Protection from Impact Forces was compiled from technical reports and laboratory records kindly furnished by Herman Roth, A.M. The chapter on Behavioral Factors in Athletics was read critically by John Nidever, M.S.

Original photography was performed by Fred Swartz, A.S.M.P. Myron Gerber obligingly served as his subject. The entire manu-script was read by Harvey E. Billig, Jr., M.D., F.I.C.S., F.A.C.S.M., and by William W. W. Pritchard, D.O., D.Sc., A.O.C.P.M.R., both of whom made numerous helpful suggestions, many of which were freely incorporated into the text.

LAURENCE E. MOREHOUSE
PHILIP J. RASCH

April, 1958

Contents

CHAPTER I

Historical Introduction

Our knowledge of the training of athletes is derived from four sources: (1) traditional beliefs and practices; (2) archeological findings; (3) writings of historians; and (4) scientific investigation.

Traditional Beliefs and Practices

It may be surmised that many of the traditional beliefs and practices which civilized man uses today to improve his athletic performance stem from those which his primitive ancestors employed to increase their chances of survival. Much of the corpus of man's information concerning the training of athletes and the care of athletic injuries is millennia old.

To our primitive food-hunting ancestors survival itself was largely a matter of developing physical skills and of training their bodies to make effective use of these skills under the arduous conditions of the life of the hunter. The hunter could not permit minor injuries to keep him from the chase, or to prevent his flight from the beasts who were hunting him. He had to find methods of caring for injuries which would enable him to maintain his readiness to meet the rigors of his environment. His urgent need for means of speeding recovery impelled him to search for methods of promoting more rapid healing.

The shaman, or medicine man, was considered a member of the

1

learned profession, since he was generally the custodian of whatever bits of scientific information the tribe possessed. He not only used herbs and heat, but sought to control natural processes by spells and other magical means acquired through long professional training. As the population of the earth increased and tribes contended for hunting grounds, fishing rights, hot springs or other good things of nature, the methods of training and care of injuries originally developed for the hunter came to be an important part of the training and care of the warrior.

Archeological Findings

The findings of the archeologists suggest that boxing, wrestling and other forms of athletics were highly developed in the days of the dynastic kings of Egypt. A stone slab on which were the figures of two pugilists and a cast bronze figurine of two wrestlers dating from about the same period were found in the ruins of a temple at Kyafaje, near Bagdad, in Iraq. Although the methods which the trainers of those days used to achieve a high level of performance are not revealed, it may be assumed that the athletes were systematically trained.

To the north of Egypt was the island home of the great sea kings of Crete. The Hagia Triada vase (c. 1600 B.C.) found in their palace at Knossos depicts both boxers and wrestlers. The boxers appear to be wearing a close-fitting helmet, their hands are padded and there are guards on their forearms. This is the earliest known illustration of the protective headguards and gloves worn by boxers. Also of interest are the various pictures of gymnastic feats in which both boys and girls are shown seizing a bull by the horns, somersaulting to his back and then to the ground, where they appear to be aided by an assistant.

Writings of Historians

Ancient Greece. Much of the Cretan culture spread across the Mediterranean Sea to ancient Hellas, and here are found the first written records of training regimens. In Hellas four great athletic contests were held at regular intervals: the Olympian, Isthmian, Pythian and Nemean festivals. Of these the greatest were the Olympian games, first held some time prior to 776 B.C., probably in honor of the dead. Competitors were expected to spend ten

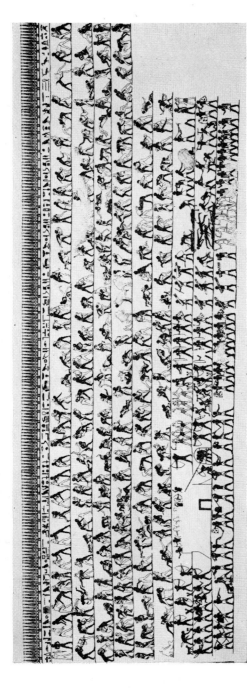

Figure 1. Mural illustrating the high degree of training achieved in athletic activities about 2000 B.C. It was found in nearly intact condition in the funerary chapel of Baket at Beni Hasan, Egypt. (Percy E. Newberry, *Beni Hasan*, Part II. London: Egypt Exploration Society, 1893.)

months in hard training. At the games a training table was provided, with cheese, figs and wheat bread as the principal items. Fried and boiled foods and cold drinks were prohibited. Abstinence from wine was customary. Light conversation at meals was encouraged as an aid to the digestion. There was an upper age limit of 35 and women were banned both as participants and as spectators, with the exception of the priestesses of Demeter. Hippodamia finally set up women's Olympic Games, called the Heraea.

In the earliest games the contestants wore loincloths, but in 720 B.C., after Orsippus of Megara lost his cloth during a race which he won, the other contestants decided that his victory was due to the fact that he was not hindered by this garment. Thereafter all athletes competed nude. Eventually a widow named Callipateira slipped into the games as the trainer of her son. Her joyful abandon at his victory led to the discovery of her sex. Her life was spared because her father, brother and son were Olympic victors, but thereafter trainers were also required to appear nude.[1]

Two conflicting views of athletics developed among the Hellenes. The Spartans held them as valuable solely as a part of military training; the Athenians considered them not only a means of training soldiers, but also necessary to develop beauty and harmony of body and spirit. Socrates (c. 470 B.C.–399 B.C.), himself a distinguished warrior, reproved the unathletic young Epigenes for his failure to train in these words:

... do you suppose that an ill condition of body is more salutary and advantageous than a good condition? Or do you despise the benefits secured by a good state of the body: Yet the lot which falls to those who have their bodies in good condition is exactly the reverse of that which falls to those who have them in ill condition; for those who have their bodies in a good state are healthy and strong ... for be well assured that neither in any other contest, nor in any affair whatever, will you at all come off the worse because your body is better trained than that of other men; since the body must bear its part in whatever men do, and in all the services required from the body, it is of the utmost importance to have it in the best possible condition ... It is disgraceful, too, for a person to grow old in self-neglect, before he knows what he would become by rendering himself well-formed and vigorous in body; but this a man who neglects himself cannot know, for such advantages are not wont to come spontaneously.[2]

By the time of Plato (c. 428 B.C.–c. 348 B.C.), himself a wrestling champion at the Isthmian games, winners were showered with lavish gifts and most of the competitors were professional athletes. Plato distinguished between the physical training of the warrior-athletes who were to guard his ideal Republic and that of the professional athletes. Warriors, said the philosopher, should abstain from intoxicants, should not be allowed to have Corinthian girl friends, should eat no fish and should have only roasted meat when on a campaign. They should avoid "sweet sauces" and other exotic dishes, since "all professional athletes are well aware that a man who is to be in good condition should take nothing of the kind." But, he added, the athletes' habit of body "is but a sleepy sort of thing, and rather perilous to health. Do you not observe that these athletes sleep away their lives, and are liable to most dangerous illnesses if they depart in ever so slight a degree from their customary regimen?" Plato believed that excessive care of the body is inimical to the full development of manly qualities. The man who "takes violent exercise and is a great feeder," he stated, "becomes filled with pride at the high condition of his body, but if he does nothing else he becomes fierce, ignorant and dull, like a wild beast."[3]

As long as the citizen, the warrior and the athlete were all one and the same man, the medical treatment of an athlete differed in no essential way from the general practice of the physician. When competitive sports became so commercialized that they were no longer an integral part of the life of the average citizen, the need arose for physicians with a specialized knowledge of the treatment of athletic injuries. The first team physician in history appears to have been Galen (A.D. 131–201), who tended the gladiators for the ruler of Pergamum, in Asia Minor. Galen had much to say about the training of athletes.[4] He told his readers that exercise produced strength by hardening the organs, increased the respiration and increased the intrinsic warmth, producing better nutrition, metabolism and elimination. Since it facilitated the functions of the digestive system, exercise should be taken before meals. Men training for health alone, Galen advised, should regulate their exercise, massage, bathing, food and sleep by one word: moderation. They should stop exercising before becoming fatigued. But for competition, "it is necessary for athletes, in order that they may prepare themselves for their labors in competitions, to practice immoderately sometimes all day at their objective exercise, which they call training."[4] The athlete required the services of a trainer to teach him the necessary skills and of a physician to advise him what to do to produce a desired effect in the body. After a workout the athlete had a vigorous massage and then a plunge in cold water, which strengthened the body, hardened the skin and improved the digestion. However, in case of fatigue after excessive exercise, a prolonged soaking in warm water was approved by Galen.

Ancient Rome.   In the grimly practical philosophy of the early Romans, the only important objectives of exercise were health and military training. Cato taught his son "gymnastic exercises. Not only did he show him how to throw a dart, to fight in armour, and to ride, but to box also and to endure both heat and cold, and to swim over the most rapid and rough rivers."[5] Augustus Caesar, who was especially fond of boxing, revived the Panhellenic festivals and introduced physical training into the associations of the aristocratic youth being educated for the army or civil service. The Roman crowds, however, preferred watching the gladiatorial games, and even though Augustus revised the rules of harpastron (a variety of football) so as to make the game more brutal,[6] he was unable to arouse their interest in competitive athletics of the Greek variety.

Gladiatorial contests had been introduced into Rome in 105 B.C. in an effort to offset the interest in Greek culture and to promote military training. They proved so popular that gladiator masters, or *lanistae,* a word originally meaning butchers or executioners, were soon buying, selling and renting gladiators on a grand scale. Numbers of schools for the training of gladiators were erected on sites especially chosen for their healthy locations, including some which trained only fighters of animals. These schools, termed *ludi,* had their own kitchens, living and sleeping quarters, prisons, armories, smithies and mortuaries, and were staffed by a large corps of instructors, physicians, actuaries and overseers. The students were fed food believed to build muscle, principally barley and beans, and were given a banquet the night before a contest. Students practiced with wooden swords on straw men, or sought to develop power by hacking at a post with weapons heavier than those actually employed in the arena. Great stress was laid on the importance of massage after exercise to loosen taut muscles.[7]

Medieval Period.   Following the fall of Rome and the ascendance of Christian asceticism, the body was considered worthy only of contempt and humiliation. The church founded universities which emphasized intellectual learning, but which neglected the development of the body. Athletic training during the Dark Ages was used primarily as a means of training fighting men. The *Mirror of Knights*[8] prescribed seven forms of activity: riding, with rapid mounting and dismounting; swimming and diving; shooting with the bow and cross-bow; climbing on ropes, poles and ladders; fencing, wrestling, pushing stones and jumping; dancing and tournaments.

Sixteenth Century. The introduction of gunpowder marked the downfall of the armored knight, but the gentry continued their athletic pursuits. The training of a gentleman of the 16th century has been described by Montaigne in his depiction of his father:

Though he were but a little man, his courage and vigor was great. He was of an upright and well proportioned stature, of a pleasing, cheerfull-looking countenance, of a swarthy hue, nimbly addicted, and exquisitely nimble unto all noble and gentleman-like exercises. I have seen some hollow staves of his filled with lead which he wont to use and exercise his armes withall, the better to enable himselfe to pitch the barre, to throw the sledge, to cast the pole, and to play at fence; with shoes with leaden soles, which he wore to ensure himselfe to leap, to vault, and to run.*

Modern Period. The incessant wars of the 18th century aroused an interest in the role of athletics as a means of increasing the fitness and patriotism of youth. From this movement arose Ling's system of gymnastics in Sweden, and the Turnverein in Germany under the leadership of Jahn. These systems of formal exercise were introduced into the United States, and certain of Ling's calisthenic exercises are used in athletics today as warm-up and conditioning routines. However, the Swedish and German systems in their entirety did not achieve popularity among American students. Both Steiner[9] and Cozens and Stumpf[10] have noted that the American youth has insisted that his physical training be achieved through competitive sports. In them he finds an opportunity to act on his own initiative and to participate as a member of an organized team working toward a mutual goal.

Rowing was the first competitive sport in American colleges, clubs being organized at Yale in 1843 and at Harvard in 1844. An insight into the training routines of the time is given by a description of the program of the Yale crew in 1866:

The crew rose each morning at six and then, in heavy flannels, ran from three to five miles on empty stomachs; in the forenoon they would row from four to six miles and do the same distance in the afternoon, and these rows were not easy paddles, but hard, stiff trials and mostly on time. They ate underdone beef and mutton, with the blood running from it, with a few potatoes or rice now and then, but no other vegetables, and drank weak tea in small quantities.

* From *The Living Thoughts of Montaigne,* presented by André Gide, edited by Alfred O. Mendel, translation by John Florio. Courtesy of David McKay Company, Inc.

Since the taking of water was apt to put back the weight that had been lost through perspiration, the men were given only what they positively could not do without, and the agony of such a course when the men were rowing in the hot sun and perspiring freely can be imagined, and it was further increased by the prohibition of baths; some coaches would not permit their men to bathe for three weeks or more before a race.[11]

Much the same sort of a regimen was followed by English oarsmen of this period. The Oxford crew trained on a diet of underdone beef or mutton, bread, tea and beer, with a little jelly or water cress allowed as a special treat at the evening meal. Vegetables were forbidden, although potatoes, greens and even fruit were allowed the Cambridge crew.[12]

Following the first intercollegiate football game in the United States, played between Princeton and Rutgers on November 6, 1869, interest in this sport quickly became widespread. The introduction of the flying wedge and other dangerous tactics resulted in such an alarming increase in injuries that President Theodore Roosevelt summoned representatives of Yale, Harvard and Princeton to the White House in 1905, urging them to take immediate action to reduce the brutality of the game. On December 9, 1905 Chancellor McCracken, of New York University, called a conference of colleges to determine whether intercollegiate football should be abandoned. As a result of this meeting the game was continued, but some of its injurious features were eliminated.

The athletic trainer at the time was generally a rubber or an ex-pugilist without technical preparation. The appearance of the first edition of Bilik's *The Trainer's Bible* in 1917 was an early step towards the achievement of professional status for the trainer. Ten years later the first detailed studies of the psychological aspects of the training of athletes appeared in Griffith's *Psychology of Athletics,* followed a few years later by his *Psychology of Coaching.* Since then several manuals on the care of athletic injuries have been published.

Scientific Investigation

The introduction of modern methods of scientific investigation into the fields of biology and medicine has resulted in a more accurate understanding of the body's functions and its response to injuries. Among the major studies which have contributed to our understanding of training methods and their results are those of Harvey[13] on the circulation of the blood; Morpurgo[14] and Siebert[15] on strength; Sherrington[16] on the nervous system; Hill[17] and Herxheimer[18] on work efficiency and Cannon[19] on internal homeostasis. Journals published by professional groups interested in human performance carry reports of investigations from which are drawn scientific principles for the training of athletes.

Communication Media

A course in athletic training is ordinarily included in the curriculum of colleges and universities offering a major in physical education. Usually such work is at the upper division level and courses in anatomy, physiology and first aid are prerequisites. In general, the physician who desires to specialize in the care of athletic injuries must rely on experience and independent study. Only a few medical schools, some granting the Doctor of Medicine degree and others granting the Doctor of Osteopathy degree, include this subject in their courses.

Personal interest in this subject among the physicians of the world led to the convening of a medical congress on sports in 1915 and the formation in 1928 of what is now known as the Fédération Internationale Médico-Sportive et Scientifique. This association has the following objectives:

1. To inaugurate scientific research on biology, psychology and sociology in their relation to sports.
2. To promote the study of medical problems encountered in physical exercises and in sports.
3. To organize international congresses to be held simultaneously with the Olympic Games.[20]

At the 1952 Games the International Symposium of the Medicine and Physiology of Sports and Athletics recommended that sports medicine be made a recognized part of the medical curriculum, as it was in the Soviet Union, Czechoslovakia and Norway.[21] This recommendation was not adopted in the United States, but physicians and others interested in sports medicine on their own initiative in 1954 organized the American College of Sports Medicine. This is an affiliate of the Fédération Internationale Médico-Sportive et Scientifique.

Trainers in the United States banded together in 1950 to form the National Athletic Trainers Association for the purpose of raising their professional standards and exchanging information. This organization publishes a quarterly journal and sponsors a yearly athletic training clinic. Other coaching clinics and athletic training clinics are frequently offered in connection with college summer school programs.

Another source of communication among trainers is the news sheets published by suppliers of training room equipment and materials. Their columns are open to trainers and other interested persons for an expression of individual viewpoints and for reports of experiences with original methods.

In spite of the development of professional standards, the ancient postulates of the shaman are still preserved among some trainers. There are individuals, especially among trainers of professional boxers, who keep their methods secret. They may prepare concoctions which they use to hasten the athlete's recovery from injury, or dietary supplements with which they hope to improve his performance or allay fatigue. Some of these secret remedies die with their inventors; others are passed on to their disciples as an extension of the oral tradition of athletic training.

It is from this historical background that those concerned today with the training and protection of athletes and the care of athletic injuries derive their techniques. In the following chapters of this text the details of these subjects are taken up. Together, these represent the state of the art of athletic training as it exists at this writing.

REFERENCES

1. Ryde, David, Effects of Strenuous Exertion on Women. *Nursing Mirror*, pp. 697 *et seq.*, 7 December 1956.
2. Xenophon, *Memorabilia of Socrates*. Translated by J. S. Watson. London: George Bell & Sons, 1877. Book XII:3–8.
3. Plato, *The Republic*. Translated by B. Jowett. New York: The Modern Library, n. d., Book III:403–431.
4. Galen, *De Sanitate Tuenda*. Translated by Robert Montraville Green. Springfield, Ill.: Charles C Thomas, 1951, pp. 53–95.
5. Plutarch, *The Lives of the Noble Grecians and Romans*. Translated by John Dryden. New York: The Modern Library, 1932.
6. Johansen, Otto, The Prevention of Sport Injuries. In Otto Johansen, editor, *Sport and Health*. Oslo: Royal Norwegian Ministry of Education, 1952, p. 181.
7. Friedlander, Ludwig, *Roman Life and Manners Under the Early Empire*. New York: E. P. Dutton & Co., n. d., Vol. II:41–62.
8. Joseph, Ludwig H., Gymnastics from the Middle Ages to the 18th Century. *Ciba Symposia*, 10:1033, March-April, 1949.
9. Steiner, Jesse Frederick, *Americans at Play*. New York: McGraw-Hill Book Company, Inc., 1933.
10. Cozens, Frederick W. and Florence Scovil Stumpf, *Sports in American Life*. Chicago: The University of Chicago Press, 1953.

11. Crowther, Samuel and Arthur Ruhl, *Rowing and Track Athletics*. New York: The Macmillan Company, 1905, p. 227.
12. Drummond, J. C. and A. Wilbraham, *Englishman's Food; History of 5 Centuries of English Diet*. London: Jonathan Cape, Ltd., 1939.
13. Harvey, William, *Excercitatio Anatomica de Motu Cordis et Sanguinis in Animalibus*. Frankfurt am Main, 1628.
14. Morpurgo, B., Ueber Activitäts—Hypertrophie der Willkürlichen Muskeln. *Virchow's Archives, 150:*522, 1897. Cited in Arthur H. Steinhaus, Strength from Morpurgo to Muller—A Half Century of Research. *Journal of the Association for Physical and Mental Rehabilitation, 9:*147–150, September-October, 1955.
15. Siebert, W. W., Untersuchungen über Hypertrophie des Skellet-muskels. *Zeitschrift für klinische Medizin, 109:*350–359, 1928. In Steinhaus, *op. cit.*
16. Sherrington, Charles, *The Integrative Action of the Nervous System*. New York: Charles Scribner's Sons, 1906.
17. Hill, A. V., *Muscular Movement in Man*. New York: McGraw-Hill Book Company, 1927.
18. Herxheimer, H., cited in Arthur H. Steinhaus, Chronic Effects of Exercise. *Physiological Reviews, XIII:*103–147, January, 1933.
19. Cannon, Walter B., *The Wisdom of the Body*. Revised Edition. New York: W. W. Norton & Company, Inc., 1939.
20. La Cava, Giuseppe, The International Federation for Sports Medicine. *Journal of the American Medical Association, 162:*1109–1111, November 17, 1956.
21. Karvonen, J. M., Editor, *Sport Medicine*. Helsinki: Finnish Association of Sports Medicine, 1953, p. 6.

CHAPTER II

Kinesiological
Factors in Athletics

Athletic performance is in large part a dynamic expression of the design of the human body. Variations in body configuration are related to the efficiency of its response to the demand placed upon it by various physical activities. By applying this principle the coach can more accurately guide the aspirant in the selection of sports activities best suited to the candidate's special physical characteristics.

Constitutional Morphology

The belief that an individual's morphology is related to his capacity for athletic performance appeared early in written history. The ancient Greek coaches classified their Olympic prospects as bear-athletes, lion-athletes and eagle-athletes. Hippocrates (460–370 B.C.) recognized two body types: habitus apoplecticus (short, thick) and habitus phthisicus (long, thin), a basic distinction which has persisted to the present day. The first step in improving the accuracy of classification was taken in 1654, when Johannis Sigismundi Elsholzius established a method of taking body measurements and coined the word anthropometria to describe it. It was not until 1871 that Quetelet, a Belgian astronomer, placed the new science on a firm statistical basis.[1] Forty-one different classifications of constitutional types have been offered in a convenient summary compiled by Krogman.[2]

Most of the authors used three groupings, which were generally variations of the expressions round, muscular and slender. Retaining these conventional classifications, Sheldon and his collaborators[3, 4] developed a detailed method of classifying morphological characteristics and correlated them with athletic performance. Their method, which they termed somatotyping, was based upon the relative predominance of the particular embryonic layer from which the various body tissues are derived: endoderm, mesoderm and ectoderm. The characteristics of each type may be summarized as follows:

Endomorphy—Roundness and softness of body, small bones, large head, short neck, smooth contours, central concentration of mass, short, tapering limbs, comparatively small, weak extremities, soft, smooth skin, hypoplastic genitalia.

Mesomorphy—Large, heavy bones, massive musculature, neck usually fairly long, broad shoulders, thoracic volume predominates over abdominal volume, relatively slender waist, broad hips, coarse, thick skin, genitalia nearly always well developed.

Ectomorphy—Linear, fragile, delicate body, thin bones, slight muscles, small head, long, slender neck, round shoulders, relatively long thorax, weak upper arms and thighs, thin and dry skin, genitalia usually hypertrophic.

Jones[5] reported that mesomorphy had little or no relation to weight and that taller individuals tend to have a lesser mesomorphic component. Thus the combination in one individual of extreme height and the rugged characteristics of the mesomorph, which would constitute an ideal build for many sports, is seldom found.

The physical performance of extreme somatotypes in motor and strength tests was studied by Sills and Everett.[6] They found that:

1. Mesomorphs are stronger than endomorphs and ectomorphs.
2. Endomorphs are stronger than ectomorphs.
3. Ectomorphs are superior to endomorphs in speed, agility and endurance.
4. Mesomorphs are superior to both endomorphs and ectomorphs in agility, speed and endurance.
5. The excess weight is a handicap to endomorphs and the insufficient strength is a handicap to ectomorphs in the performance of physical tests.

Willgoose and Rogers[7] administered the Physical Fitness Index Test to 153 male college students. An average score of 100 points has been established on national norms in this test. They reported

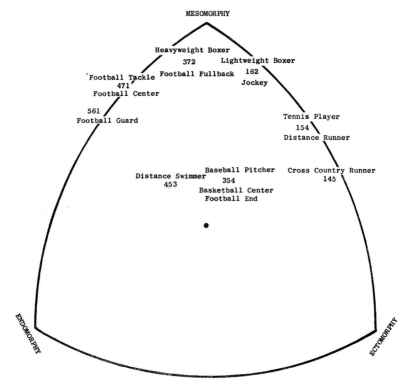

Figure 2. Somatotype distribution of various athletic specialties, showing predominance of mesomorphy. (Adapted from Sheldon, *Atlas of Men.*)

that extreme endomorphs scored 68.4 points, extreme mesomorphs scored 112.8 points and extreme ectomorphs scored 102 points.

The endomorph comes into his own in one sport—long-distance swimming. English Channel swimmers have been found to be decidedly obese, or of stocky build with fat concealing the muscular pattern. The low thermal conductivity of fat and the decreased rate of heat loss appear to be the chief factors enabling endomorphs to maintain body temperature in cold water for a long time.[8] The increased buoyancy of fat as compared with muscle is also an advantage in distance-swimming. It has been suggested that a third advantage may be their enormous fuel reserve in the form of stored fat, but it does not appear that the energy requirements of distance swimming are severe enough to utilize excess stores of fat.[9]

Obviously, all individuals are not extremes of any somatotype, but rather each individual possesses some degree of each of the three components. For convenience in describing the degree to which each component exists in an individual, Sheldon has assigned a numerical value on a scale of 1 (minimum) to 7 (maximum) to each of the three components. An individual who was comparatively low in endomorphy, about average in mesomorphy and somewhat above average in ectomorphy would be described as a 245. On the basis of this scoring system Sheldon and his

Figure 3. William T. Tilden II, somatotype classification 154, lean and powerful. (United States Lawn Tennis Association.)

Figure 4. Joe Louis, somatotype classification 372, bulky, with catlike speed.
(*The Ring.*)

collaborators[4] have given somatotype descriptions of individuals
successful in different categories of athletic performance. The dia-
gram in Figure 2 shows the location of certain typical athletic
physiques on Sheldon's triangular chart. Two examples of different athletic physiques, somatotyped by Sheldon,[4] are shown in
Figures 3 and 4.

As an example of the use of Figure 2, its application to wrestling
may be considered. Boardman[10] and others have described the
typical Olympic wrestler as having a short neck and powerful
shoulders, wide trunk, massive muscles and great muscular strength.

This description might apply to the 361 or 471 somatotype. In a study of a group of Big Ten college wrestlers, Kroll[11] found that they tended toward the agility type, with a somatotype rating of 354. Since the style of wrestling in Europe and the Near East stresses strength rather than agility, it is possible that Boardman's description actually applies to the foreign wrestlers.

Champion weight lifters have been studied by Tappen.[12] He found that they were grouped well toward the top of the scale in mesomorphy, toward the bottom in ectomorphy and were ungrouped in the endomorphy scale. Typical somatotypes for these champions were 261, 361 and 471. A compact body structure, probably associated with greater muscle mass in the arms and shoulders, seemed to favor performance in the press lift. Both the press and the snatch were unfavorably affected when the arms were relatively long, but while skeletal proportions may have had some influence on performance, muscular strength was much more important.

Relation of Stature to Performance

In general, lifters with heavy body weight can lift greater loads than can lifters with lighter body weight, but the lighter man is stronger in proportion to his body weight. The relationship which exists between the weight-lifting ability of a champion lifter and his body weight is expressed by the Lietzke[13] formula, utilizing the world record total lifts in the three Olympic lifts in a given weight class (W_T) and the body weight in that class (B_w) as follows:

$$\log W_T = 1.458 + 0.6748 \log B_w.$$

Applying this formula, when log W_T in pounds is plotted against log B_w in pounds, shown in Figure 5, the lighter weight-lifting champions are seen to be as strong or stronger relative to their body weight than are the heavier champion weight lifters.

According to Amar,[14] individuals of small stature are not only relatively stronger than are tall ones, but are also quicker, because they have a lesser body mass to be moved. This superior strength and quickness in relation to body size explains why tumblers, gymnasts and divers are usually short. Regardless of the strength-per-unit-of-body-weight advantage of the lighter individual, the larger person customarily possesses greater total strength. It has been estimated that the combined influence of the body build,

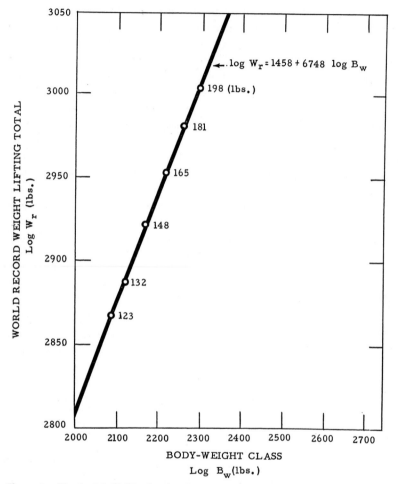

Figure 5. Plot by M. H. Lietzke showing the uniform relationship between body weight and weight lifting performance. (Redrawn from *Science.*)

height and weight factors comprise up to 75 per cent of all the factors determining strength.[5] Table 1 depicts the relation between body height, body weight and performance. This table, together with Figure 2, may be used to assist individuals in the selection of sports appropriate to their physique. Further studies are needed to show the effects of other body build factors, such as shoulder width, ratio of length of forearm to upper arm, and ratio of trunk length to leg length, upon performance in weight-lifting.

The tall man with the long legs has the advantage in high jumping, which is largely a matter of propelling the center of gravity of the body upward. To begin with, the tall man's center of gravity is higher. The lean man has an advantage, since every excess pound is a burden for the muscles to lift over the bar. Krakower[15] found that the most significant peculiarity of high jumpers was the extreme length of their legs, with relatively short upper bodies. While they tended to be above average in height,

Table 1. Relation between Body Height, Weight, and Performance

BODY HEIGHT	BODY WEIGHT	SPORT	
		MEN	WOMEN
Tall	Heavy	Heavyweight boxing Football end Football tackle Heavyweight wrestling	Field hockey goalie Soccer goalie Lacrosse
Tall	Medium	Discus thrower, javelin thrower Basketball center Baseball pitcher	Modern dance Softball pitcher Volleyball
Tall	Light	High jumper, hurdler Tennis Middle distance runner Fencing Cross country runner	Tennis Basketball Softball first base
Medium	Light	Distance runner Badminton Baseball second baseman Lightweight boxer	Fencing Badminton Softball infielder
Short	Light	Soccer forward Tumbling Figure skater Jockey	Tap dancing Tumbling Soccer forward
Short	Medium	Gymnastic apparatus Handball Springboard diver Water polo guard	Diving Skiing Figure skater
Short	Heavy	Baseball catcher Ice hockey defense Weight lifting	Softball catcher Backfield-soccer Backfield-hockey
Medium	Heavy	Shot putter Football fullback Football guard, tackle or center	Speedball Archery Bowling
Medium	Medium	Distance swimming Golf Bowling	Swimming Field hockey forward Golf Synchronized swimmers

their short upper bodies made their total height less than might have been expected. This build is advantageous to a jumper, since the trunk, which is dead weight in high jumping, is lighter. The athlete who is "split high," however, is poorly designed for heavy work, and the high center of gravity is a disadvantage in maintaining balance in physical contact sports. Many tall basketball players do not like to leave the floor in rough play because a comparatively light pressure against their legs while in the air will cause them to crash to the floor.[16] For the same reason excessive height is a disadvantage in judo. Long-legged men often find these levers awkward to manipulate in sports such as soccer, and their high center of gravity makes abrupt changes of direction more difficult.

The crural index (ratio of the length of the lower leg to that of the thigh) may be related to human performance in jumping and running. Davenport[17] found that this index is higher in nearly all jumping animals than in running forms. As a species of animal, man falls into the slower runner group, characterized by a comparatively low crural index. In theory a relatively high crural index should render an individual more fit for climbing and jumping, while a relatively low one should better fit him for running. A longer lower leg may develop a greater velocity at the distal end, contributing to the momentum of the leg in carrying the body over the high jump bar. It may be a disadvantage in running or hurdling unless sufficient muscular strength is available to overcome this added resistance. The long-legged athlete may need extra strengthening in his training program.

The length of the calcaneus may also be important in athletics. The longer this heel bone, the greater its mechanical advantage in enabling the jumper to utilize the power of the gastrocnemius-soleus group to propel himself upward. The efficiency of the calcaneus as a lever depends upon its ability to transmit the force of the calf muscle contraction to the "resistance" offered at the site of the contact of the foot with the ground.

In running and jumping the arch of the foot is subjected to severe strains. If it sags, the muscle force exerted at the heel will be imperfectly transmitted to the metatarsals. The integrity of the arch is maintained principally by the plantar calcaneonavicular ligaments. Several muscles (tibialis anterior, peroneus longus and flexor hallucis longus) assist in holding the bones of the foot together to form a firm structure.[18] Loewendahl[19] has pointed out that while the calf muscles initiate the rise of the heel, the toe flexors (particularly the flexor digitorum longus) give the propelling force or final phase of the take-off.

The tall baseball pitcher or tennis player has a natural advantage in the greater range of motion afforded by the longer length of his limbs. This enables him to obtain greater acceleration of the ball and affords him greater scope in his placement of the ball. A long olecranon process, like a long calcaneus, should provide an additional advantage for the man who has adequate arm extensor strength to utilize it. The taller football end or baseball first baseman presents a better target for the thrower and can catch the ball sooner or reach farther for it. In basketball the height of an exceptionally tall player is such an advantage in controlling the play at the basket on both offense and defense that he can completely dominate the game.

A long arm should be an aid to the javelin thrower or the discus thrower, since greater velocity can be developed at the end of this longer lever. The boxer or fencer with a longer arm may be able to score on an opponent at a distance where he cannot be reached in return. Big hands may be an aid to the boxer in furnishing a heavier weapon with which to strike his opponent, or to the baseball player or football end in catching the ball. Large hands and feet may be effective paddles for the swimmer if he has the strength to operate them.

Even the conformation of the head and face have implications for athletics. A thin skull may present a definite hazard to boxers.[20] A prominent nose or protruding teeth are apt to be broken in physical contact sports. Protuberant eyes may furnish better peripheral vision for the basketball player, but invite eye injury in the boxer. The boxer's best protection for his eyes is a pair of prominent orbital margins. Boxing is particularly dangerous for the myope, since his eyes are not only apt to be more protuberant, but are more readily blinded.[21] It has been estimated that about 5 per cent of the detachments of the retina are due to athletic injuries. Persons with a tendency to retinal detachment may be allowed to swim, but not to dive.[22]

Comparatively few successful fighters possess long jaws. The most effective blows to the jaw are those which come from the side and below, so as to hit the opponent about one-half inch forward of the mental foramen. Oblique blows to the lower jaw cause a forceful torsion of the head, and shear strains due to rotation of the head are the essential cause of both concussion of the brain and the usual cerebral contusions.[23] The leverage exerted by a long jaw increases the effectiveness of such blows.

Although athletes are frequently described as "barrel chested," Weisman[24] has shown that this description is not accurate, at least for track and field competitors. These individuals tend to have a flat, broad chest, and may also possess a broad, transverse heart which, in Weisman's opinion, permits better function than a long narrow heart in a deep, narrow chest.

Feminine Body Build

The athletic performance of women is affected by their morphological characteristics. Various studies indicate that man is about 43 per cent muscle, women about 36 per cent muscle. In proportion to weight and size, the muscles of the female are weaker than those of the male. The pelvis of the female is much broader after adolescence, which gives a marked obliquity to the femur. This mechanical disadvantage interferes with the running ability of girls and makes it more difficult for them to maintain their balance on precarious footing. Women's arms and legs are proportionally shorter than men's. The shorter legs lower the center of gravity and make them more stable, but are a disadvantage in jumping. The inward inclination of the upper arm accounts for women's difficulty in throwing a ball and in handling equipment requiring a rotary motion. The alleged differences between the width of shoulder of men and of women, when reduced to a percentage of height, were found to be so small that they could not be used as a differentiator between the sexes.[25, 26]

The panniculus adiposus, or subcutaneous fat layer, gives women their rounded contours and encases them in a blanket of fat which enables them to resist both cold and heat noticeably better than men do. Body fat is actually a secondary sex characteristic, since on the average it accounts for about 18 per cent of the body weight of men and 28 per cent of that of women. This has a detrimental effect on most forms of female athletic performance, since it represents a greater percentage of dead weight to be moved, but is an advantage in distance-swimming.

Selection by morphological means is an instrument in the

coaches' armamentarium in the development of successful athletes. Although other factors, such as motivation and diligence in training, may override the morphological constituents of success, the athlete's chance for success is enhanced if he engages in sports well suited to his special physical characteristics.

REFERENCES

1. Tucker, William A. and William A. Lessa, Man: A Constitutional Investigation. *Quarterly Review of Biology, 15*:265–289, September, 1940.
2. Krogman, Wilbur Marion, The Historical Aspect of the Study of Human Constitutional Types. *Ciba Symposia, 3*:1058–1065, December, 1941.
3. Sheldon, W. H., S. S. Stevens and W. B. Tucker, *The Varieties of Human Physique.* New York: Harper & Brothers, 1940.
4. Sheldon, William H., C. Wesley Dupertius and Eugene McDermott, *Atlas of Man.* New York: Harper & Brothers, 1954.
5. Jones, Harold E., The Relationship of Strength to Physique. *American Journal of Physical Anthropology, 5*:29–40, March, 1947.
6. Sills, Frank D. and Peter W. Everett, The Relationship of Extreme Somatotypes to Performance in Motor and Strength Tests. *Research Quarterly, 24*:223–228, May, 1953.
7. Willgoose, Carl E. and Millard L. Rogers, Relationship of Somatotype to Physical Fitness. *Journal of Educational Research, 42*:704–712, May, 1949.
8. Pugh, L. G. C. and O. G. Edholm, The Physiology of Channel Swimmers. *Lancet,* No. 6893:761–768, October 8, 1955.
9. Abrahams, Adolphe, The Physiology of Channel Swimmers. *Lancet,* No. 6896: 924–925, October 29, 1955.
10. Boardman, Robert, Worlds' Champions Run to Types. *Journal of Health and Physical Education,* IV:32 *et seq.,* May, 1933.
11. Kroll, Walter, An Anthropometrical Study of Some Big Ten Varsity Wrestlers. *Research Quarterly, 25*:307–312, October, 1954.
12. Tappen, N. M., An Anthropometric and Constitutional Study of Championship Weight Lifters. *American Journal of Physical Anthropology, 8*:49–64, March, 1950.
13. Lietzke, M. H., Relation Between Weight-Lifting Totals and Body Build. *Science, 124*:486–487, 14 September 1956.
14. Amar, Jules, *The Human Motor.* New York: E. P. Dutton & Co., 1920.
15. Krakower, Hyman, Skeletal Symmetry and High Jumping. *Research Quarterly, 12*:218–227, May, 1941.
16. Morehouse, Laurence E. and John M. Cooper, *Kinesiology.* St. Louis: The C. V. Mosby Company, 1950.
17. Davenport, C. B., The Crural Index. *American Journal of Physical Anthropology, 17*:333–353, January-March, 1933.
18. Cobb, Montague W., Race and Runners. *Journal of Health and Physical Education, 7*:3 *et seq.,* January, 1936.
19. Loewendahl, Evelyn, Muscle Development in Athletic Training, *Journal of the Association for Physical and Mental Rehabilitation, 5*:23–24, September-October, 1951.
20. Chenoweth, L. B., Medical Supervision of Boxing. *Ohio State Medical Journal, 47*:913–914, October, 1951.
21. Doggart, James Hamilton, The Impact of Boxing Upon the Visual Apparatus. *Archives of Ophthalmology, 54*:161–169, August, 1955.

22. Foreign Letters. *Journal of the American Medical Association, 164*:594, June 1, 1957.
23. Holbourn, A. H. S., Mechanics of Head Injuries. *Lancet,* No. 6268:438–441, October, 1943.
24. Weisman, S. A., Track Stars Are Not Barrel Chested. *Journal-Lancet, 73*:280–282, July, 1953.
25. Carpenter, Aileen, Strength, Power and 'Femininity' as Factors Influencing the Athletic Performance of College Women. *Research Quarterly,* IX:120–127, May, 1938.
26. Tuttle, W. Gerard, Women Who Work for Victory. *Mechanical Engineering, 65*:657–660, September, 1943.

CHAPTER III

Physiological Factors in Athletics

Athletics is one of the ways in which a person finds the best that is in him. The favorable responses he obtains from a period of intense athletic conditioning are immediately and easily detectable, and thus satisfying. The individual who has experienced the vigor and euphoria due to superb functioning of his entire organism preserves in his being a pattern upon which he can draw with benefit all of his life.

The process of conditioning for athletics is a deliberate one. Through repeated exposures graded in intensity and complexity the athlete changes himself into a more resilient and effective person. The organism responds in two different ways to the conditioning process: by an improvement in the organization of the neurophysiological mechanisms, and by adaptive alterations in body tissues.[1] The ways in which the human organism responds to the demands made upon it denote the ways in which athletic training schedules are best planned.

NEUROPHYSIOLOGICAL MECHANISMS

Endurance

Endurance is the ability to continue work. This is limited by two factors: the willingness to work on in spite of the pain of fatigue, and the capacity of the homeostatic mechanism to make rapid and extensive adjustments within the functioning organism.

The process of learning to endure the pain of fatigue is necessarily an uncomfortable one. The athlete exposes himself almost daily to the dull aches of muscular effort and the burning anguish of laborious breathing. After the first week of training the persistent athlete will note with satisfaction that he can run with relative ease past the post which earlier marked his point of exhaustion. At this point he is still not without muscle and lung discomfort, but he accepts these as a necessary part of the performance and he has learned that they will do him no harm. They now hurt less because he has an increased tolerance, arising from a gradually lessened sensitivity to the acid metabolites of muscular work and the irritating dryness of excessive ventilation.

As he runs further without slackening his pace the pain and discomfort mount until he soon must again collapse. This point represents his new level or tolerance—his new limit of endurance.

Aside from the lowering of sensitivity thresholds, certain homeostatic adjustments are taking place in the athlete's body as it becomes experienced to increased metabolic demands. The blood circulates more freely, owing to more effective adjustments by the vasomotor system which now goes into action even before the activity is commenced and shifts the blood to the working muscles in just the right amounts as the work is continued. Pulmonary ventilation now keeps pace with the requirements for gaseous exchange rather than over-responding to the excitement of exercise, producing giddiness due to chemical imbalance resulting from hyperventilation. The runner no longer fights for air with a continually expanded chest, but permits a full excursion of his thoraco-diaphragmatic bellows to provide an efficient ventilation of his lungs. The athlete's sweat is almost entirely free from eye-stinging salt, since the glands have found a way to put out the water needed for cooling while conserving the salts needed to maintain the delicate fluid balance of the body.

These two factors, sensitivity and homeostatic adjustment, have combined to enable the energy production to enlarge, rising to

20 times the resting level almost immediately upon call for all-out muscular work. This ability to work under forced draft is facilitated by an increased "willingness" of the body to take on an oxygen debt which need not be repaid until after the work is finished.

Second Wind

The phenomenon termed "second wind" is a sensation which signals the attainment of homeostatic adjustments during hard muscular steady state exercise. Early in the work, before second wind occurs, there is a piling up of lactic and other metabolic acids, a lag in the production of sweat and peripheral dilatation, and a lag in the vasomotor shifting of blood from splanchnic pools to the working muscles. As a result, the work is performed with difficulty and pain, the body becomes overheated and the athlete feels sluggish.

At the onset of second wind, which may have nothing whatsoever to do with respiration, the athlete experiences a sensation of sudden relief because of the homeostatic adjustments in which energy production is facilitated and is balanced by the mechanisms of heat dissipation. A new level of homeostasis has been reached which is functioning adequately to support the intensity of the work under way.

Strength

The increased strength is due to a large extent from the experience received in handling the loads undertaken.[2] Inability to lift a supermaximal load is due, to a large part, to the lack of "knowledge" by the reflective neuromuscular coordinating system as to how best to bring the muscular fibers into action.

In approaching an unfamiliar task the athlete tends to overmobilize his muscular forces, exerting more effort than required. During a few repetitions the neuromuscular coordinating system learns exactly how much effort is needed. The weight is lifted using almost the precise degree of contractions necessary, and the work among co-contracting and stabilizing muscles is distributed more effectively. As weights are added and further experience is provided by repetitions of the lifts, better mechanical leverage positions are found and remembered. The use of momentum is discovered and incorporated with the mechanical advantages, neural impulses are sent to the working muscles so as to bring a sufficient number of fibers into action at precisely the right time, while impulses into the antagonistic muscles are reduced to lessen resistance—all acting to improve efficiency and to make the best use of available power.[3, 4]

Effect of Fatigue on the Learning Process

If the athlete tries to continue practicing finely skilled movements after he becomes fatigued, he begins to substitute gross motions for fine ones and generalized efforts for specific ones. Wrong movements tend to supervene, and the athlete's progress is set back. Thus the athlete practices fine skills only while he is fresh. When he becomes fatigued he shifts to tasks employing gross movements designed principally to develop endurance.

Progression from Volition to Reflex Control

At first every detail of a new skill requires the athlete's full attention. His eyes track the movements of the ball and bat, or whatever may be involved. Close attention is paid to the physical-sensory proprioceptive impulses as they guide the body parts through the intended pattern. The novice thinks of his stance, his knees, his head, his elbow, his hand or various other segments of his body as the movement is made. This is a necessary step in putting the parts of the movement together and employing proper mechanical principles. As soon as possible, however, the athlete's attention is shifted from small details to larger ones, and finally to the whole action, without a thought given to any single part. After an outstanding performance the highly skilled athlete has absolutely no recollection of the exact manner in which he performed the feat—and this is as it should be.

The coach who is persistent in calling attention to the details of an athlete's movement throughout the season is over-coaching. Ideally, changes of style and attention to mechanics are accomplished during the off-season and, at the latest, during pre-season practice. Any attention to such details during the competitive season is made at the expense of the athlete's performance. Of course, in the poorly skilled athlete who has many seasons of competition ahead, and in the athlete who has developed a devastating fault in his technique, the weakness is corrected whenever convenient, preferably in practice sessions early in the week, but never just before or during the event.

It is an unfair tactic to "help" an opponent during competition by inviting his attention to the way he is using a body part. The result is well illustrated by the fable of the "centipede who was happy quite, until a frog in fun said, 'Pray which leg comes after which?' which set his mind in such a pitch he lay distracted in the ditch, figuring how to run." The athlete calls this "paralysis by analysis."

Specificity

The athlete who trains for one event is making little or no improvement in his performance in other events. At the end of a season of basketball a player can run up and down the floor all evening without extreme fatigue. In the swimming pool, however, this same athlete will find that the endurance he gained in basketball has somehow been left on the basketball court, and that he can swim only as well, and as far, as he could before the basketball season started.

Each athletic event makes specific demands in terms of its pattern of load, rate, repetition and duration. The neurophysiological adjustments to these demands are also specific. When a new task with a different demand in intensity of load, rate, repetition or duration is undertaken an entirely new pattern of neurophysiological adjustments must be acquired. These adjustments are so precise that a slight change in the weight of a club or ball will affect the trained athlete's performance. A heavy shot or discus used as a special training device will train the athlete to use that particular implement. But, when the athlete transfers to the lighter, regulation shot or discus, he also tends to transfer the timing and coordination for the heavier implement which is improper for the lighter. Thus he starts again essentially from the beginning adjusting to the lighter implement.

Although special exercises are valuable to strengthen weak muscles or to improve endurance, performance of the event is the best way to train for the event.

ADAPTIVE ALTERATIONS

Chronic Effects of Athletic Training

In addition to the improvements of the organization of the neurophysiological mechanisms described above, training makes imprints upon the organism which are marked enough to differentiate athletes from non-athletes.[1] There is a power-giving hypertrophy of muscles, heart as well as of the skeleton. The heart beats in a slower rhythm, delivering a greater volume at each stroke. Previously dormant alveolar capsules are opened to provide a greater surface for the passage of gases between the lungs and the oxygen-hungry blood. Through the turbulent flow induced by exercise the blood cleanses itself of its aged and fragile corpuscles which are replaced by young and vigorous ones. Increased chemical buffers in the blood can handle larger amounts of the waste acids of metabolism. The working muscles are threaded with new capillaries which provide improved irrigation and drainage.

Nothing but vigorous exercise will bring about these changes. The apparent indefatigability of the champion distance-runner or swimmer is achieved only at the expense of thousands of hours of heart-pounding exertion. These are not the gifts of any age, sex, or race—they are the hard-earned rewards of repeated exhaustive effort.

Warming Up

The process which elicits the acute physiological changes that prepare the organism for strenuous physical performance is known as "warming up." Warming up improves performance and prevents injury in vigorous activities by two essential means.

First, a rehearsal of the skill before competition commences, fixes in the athlete's neuromuscular coordinating system the exact nature of the impending task. It also heightens his kinesthetic senses. Execution of shots in billiards, taking a few serves in tennis, or shooting a few baskets brings into focus the precise movements which will be employed in the game, thus enhancing performance when the game begins.

Second, the rise in body temperature facilitates the biochemical reactions supplying energy for muscular contractions. Elevated body temperature also shortens the periods of muscular relaxations and aids in reducing stiffness. As a result of these two processes there is an improvement in accuracy, strength and speed of movement, and an increase in tissue elasticity which lessens the liability to injury.

The value of warming up exercises to improve performance in endurance events, which have low elements of skill, speed or strength, is questionable.

To gain the greatest benefit from the warming up procedures, they should imitate as closely as possible the movements which are to be used in the event. Warming up with a heavier implement, or using two bats or clubs, will impair coordination. If such overweight objects are used for the purpose of raising body tem-

Figure 6.   General warm-up exercises. A1, Trunk Circle. A2, Trunk Circle. B, Spine and Leg Extension. C, Sit-up. D, Push-up. E, Bridge.

Figure 6 (Continued). F, Side Leg Raise. G, Billig Stretch, H1, Side Straddle Jump. H2, Side Straddle Jump. I, Running in Place.

perature, they should be discarded well before the event is to commence, and the warm up should continue with an instrument which is to be employed in the event.

The duration of the warm-up period varies with the event. In ballet, the dancers spend two hours before the performance, commencing with very light movements and gradually increasing the intensity and range of motions until the moment before their appearance. This, they feel, reduces the risk of a pulled muscle which would destroy the perfection of their movements. Marathon runners simply report to the starting area and await the starting gun. There may be individual variations in the need for a warm up, and the coach provides for this by scheduling arrival at the field of play at least half an hour in advance of the time the event is to commence.

Massage is widely used in the preparation of athletes for competition, but scientific studies do not verify its hypothetical advantages. Application of ice packs to the abdominal wall in the belief that it will elicit an adrenalin reaction or reflexes which move the blood from the abdominal cavity to the working muscles is also without sufficient evidence to warrant its use in athletics.[6]

Planning Athletic Training Schedules

Practice Schedule. The first part of the workout is devoted to several minutes of warming up exercises, consisting of light running or stride-jumping exercises to elevate body temperature, followed by exercises which mimic the movements of the event, but which start with light motions and gradually work up to the intensity of the actual event.

The practice period is spent mainly in the performance of the event, or in the performance of drills which simulate the elements of the event. Wherever possible, practice periods follow the same time schedule as does the game, divided into periods such as quarters, and the athletes are worked hard during each quarter and given rest for a period equivalent to that allowed by the rules of the game. If fruit or other nourishment is given at game halftime, it is also provided at practice half-time. A pattern such as this requires considerable planning by the coach, but it assures that the athletes will be ready for game demands.

The end of the practice period is followed by special exercises to increase strength, flexibility and endurance. In many events, such as baseball, the game itself does not provide sufficient activity to develop the physical requirements demanded by special occasions arising during a game. In others, such as swimming, the environmental medium does not furnish sufficient resistance to develop the organism. Swimmers supplement their water work with weights during the season, otherwise they will find their preseason strength gains gradually dimishing as the weeks go by.

Special instructions in technique, training procedures and so forth which require the athletes to be inactive for a period of time are given before the practice period starts.

Learning Order. Because of the specificity of training, the tempo of the event is established first.[3] The motions of the event are first performed at game tempo without regard for accuracy or endurance. Once the tempo of the performance has been established, the next objective is to improve the accuracy or other skill elements of the event. Improvements in skill will aid endurance, but special emphasis will eventually be placed upon the development of endurance. If lack of strength makes it impossible to achieve the tempo of the event, practice of the event is deferred until sufficient strength has been developed. Special strength programs and endurance exercises are designed to simulate the event as closely as possible.

Pace. The most effective means of distribution of effort in an event in which the athlete can regulate his rate of work is a steady pace. Accelerations are costly and far exceed the "saving" when the athlete slackens his speed during a race. The plan "to run fast while I am fresh, so I can get far enough ahead to take it easy when I get tired" is pure folly. In the effort to take the lead the athlete's muscles manufacture toxins of fatigue which impair his performance throughout the race. The anaerobic debt contracted under this plan is exceedingly costly and makes devastating demands on the oxygen consumption. At a steady pace this same quantity of oxygen could be used more effectively to maintain homeostasis at a high steady state level. From the metabolic point of view, each lap of the race, excluding the start and the finish, is best completed at exactly the same rate.

In a runner employing a full range of motion to gain a long stride, a minor modification in pace may be allowed for a slightly greater stride-length earlier than later in the race, when physiological contracture develops. However, a slightly shorter stride throughout the race would probably yield him a better performance.

Interval Training. In order to employ the principles of specificity, tempo and pace in an endurance training program, a system known as interval training has been developed. A convenient distance which can be traversed at the desired speed, and which is well within the athlete's endurance capacity, is selected. In training for running a mile, for example, the athlete runs 440 yards in 60 seconds. An interval, say 5 minutes, is then allowed, during which the athlete slows his run to a restful jog or walk. At the end of this interval he runs another 440 yards at the 60 second pace, followed by another 5 minute rest interval, and then another 440 yards, continuing this program for a predetermined number of runs.

Using this system of endurance training, the athlete has the alternative of grading the intensity by varying any one of the four elements while holding the other three constant. As mentioned before, it is not advisable to alter the speed. If the distance is increased, the athlete will have a tendency to develop a state of exhaustion too early in the practice period, so that the total work output for the day will be curtailed. The same result will occur if the rest intervals are shortened. The better plan would appear to be to increase the number of repetitions while holding speed, distance and rest interval constant. In this manner progressively more work is accomplished, which will assure the achievement of the desired physical conditioning.

If the athlete's practice period is limited to two or three hours a day, the system will have to be modified. This is because the athlete will soon be able to continue the program beyond this period and his endurance will fall off, not improve, if his total daily output of work is not steadily increased. His acquisition of skill enables him to perform with less effort; with lessened effort physiological demands decrease and condition deteriorates. With restrictive limitations in practice time, the athlete can hold his speed, distance and repetitions constant and gradually decrease the rest interval. This interval-shortening method will provide a gradual increase in distance, and thus total work load, but the rate of increasing total work load, and therefore training effects, will not be as great as when practice time is unrestricted. He can judge by his state of fatigue each day the extent to which he will reduce his rest interval the following day.

Maximal Training Capacity. The question now logically arises, "How much time should an endurance athlete devote to practice?" The answer is simply, "All of the time he can make available." The capability of the trained human organism for physical work is limited only by the need for sleep, meals, rest periods and measures to prevent staleness. The endurance athlete who has the entire day, every day available for nothing but athletic training has a definite advantage over the athlete with similar capacities who must use part of his time and energy each day for other activities, such as school or work.

The maximal daily work load is governed by work efficiency and recuperative ability. The objective in work efficiency is to achieve the greatest total amount of daily work without developing fatigue great enough to carry over to the next day. This is accomplished by distributing the work and by providing suitable rest periods, which prevents work-reducing exhaustion. Interval training is a good method of achieving efficiency.

Recuperative Ability. Recuperation is a process which takes place between each muscular contraction, between each stride, between each bout of work, during each period of rest and during sleep. The athlete who can make best use of each of these periods can best maintain a higher level of work without fatigue. Recuperative ability is also enhanced by the improved functioning of the physiological processes which occur during training.

The athlete cannot, however, store up rest. Longer hours of sleep, beyond nine hours, will not make the athlete stronger—they will decondition him and make him weaker. Afternoon naps and a lazy and completely relaxed posture during most of the day will also have a deconditioning effect. Rest is useful only following work; rest without work is debilitating.

Rest following work is the period during which the organism strengthens itself. Recovery following work is enhanced by conditions which will improve circulation and facilitate chemical reactions within the body. Warmth and mild movements will provide these conditions in athletics. The worst procedure the perspiring athlete can follow between events is to stand quietly and become cold.

Seasonal Objectives

When all of the above considerations are put together in the form of a season's training schedule, they form a pattern within which the coach and trainer can provide for maximal development of the athlete. In general, the objectives of each phase of a competitive season are the following.

Pre-Season. At least six weeks are needed to develop the elements of athletic fitness for competition: strength, flexibility and endurance. The work related to the development of these elements is laid out to provide a systematic progression in intensity. This is the period when artificial aids such as heavy implements, kickboards and belts are used to overcome specific weaknesses. Such devices often develop bad skill habits, so they are used with care. These special devices are laid aside when the competitive season commences.

During the pre-season practice periods the tempo of the event is established. The elements of the event are practiced through drills and miniature competitive situations. Gradually these drills and miniature competitions are put together and, finally, full scale rehearsal of the competitive event, complete with officials, is performed by intersquad teams. During this time the trainer and his assistants have an opportunity to "shake down" their organization, and to instruct the athletes in the use of ankle wraps and other protective devices.

Early Season. Competition during this period is with non-conference opponents. It is scheduled with a view to integrate the newcomers into the varsity team, to develop smoothness and precision. Attention is paid to fundamental patterns of performance. Emphasis is now shifted from the skill elements to the whole movement, from the individual performer to the team performance. During this time the coach and trainer are alert to factors affecting the development of team spirit, morale, reactions to gains and losses and interpersonal relationships. This is the period of frequent injury because of the drive to win a place on the first team and because of the strangeness of the playing field and the competitive environment. The trainer and his assistants are on the alert to care for each minor injury and pulled muscles and to fight against infections. Protective strapping, padding or harnessing is employed for all sprains, no matter how minor. This protects the athlete from allowing a minor injury to develop into a major one. Efficiency and teamwork among the physician, the trainer and the training room assistants are developed.

League Competition. Emphasis is now shifted to strategy and to developing the squad into a smoothly functioning precision unit. The coach realizes that further improvements in skill and condition are unlikely. The squad he is now working with is the best he is going to have for the remainder of the season, and his job is to make it function at its best. Staleness is an ever-present bugbear. The trainer and his assistants have established routines and their work load in applying rehabilitation procedures is heavier. The team physician is concerned with returning injured players to competition.

Championships. This is the "dessert" of the athletic season. The team is using what it has found to work best. Over-coaching must be guarded against. If the team is tired, or has been riddled by injuries, morale may hang on a word or a look. In this situation the coach must be the most stable person in the club. The dilemma of playing an injured athlete is acute, for he faces a lifetime of regret if he is left out of the game, and he also faces the risk of a lifetime of regret for sacrificing his future well-being for the championship. The trainer may experience the feeling that the whole team is held together by his adhesive tape.

Post-Season. This is longest season of all and the one during which certain objectives are best accomplished. This is the season to work on analysis of form and changes of style. Motion pictures of the athletes in competition are now reviewed for mechanical faults. Decisions to change techniques of performance are made and carried out. The poorly coordinated athlete is given special rhythm exercises, such as rope jumping using a heavy rope. Faulty conditioned reflexes, such as flinching or closing of the eyes while batting, are methodically corrected. Techniques to prevent injury, such as methods of falling or receiving blows, are taught to athletes singly or in small groups. Attempts to change style, or to develop skills for a new position or a new event, are made now, for they can be discontinued before it is too late. If the athlete needs to gain weight, or to lose weight, a gradual program of weight control is instituted.

Detraining or deconditioning does not cause sudden deterioration. Strength, endurance and flexibility persist for months after cessation of athletic competition, unless the athlete becomes totally sedentary. The only danger is that the athlete becomes overweight as he maintains his habits of food intake and lessens his physical activity. Normally, though, the athlete will engage in sports of one kind or another the year around. The athlete, having achieved and enjoyed the state of superb well-being arising from his athletic training, will tend to continue the habits of healthful living gained from such a regimen.

REFERENCES

1. Morehouse, Laurence E. and Augustus T. Miller, *Physiology of Exercise.* Second Edition. St. Louis: The C. V. Mosby Company, 1953.
2. Rasch, Philip J. and Laurence E. Morehouse, The Effect of Static and Dynamic

Exercises on Muscular Strength and Hypertrophy. *Journal of Applied Physiology, 11:*29–34, July, 1957.

3. Morehouse, Laurence E. and John M. Cooper, *Kinesiology.* St. Louis: The C. V. Mosby Co., 1950.

4. Hunsicker, Paul and George Greey, Studies in Human Strength. *Research Quarterly, 28:*109–122, May, 1957.

5. Karpovich, Peter V. and Creighton J. Hale, Effect of Warming-up upon Physical Performance. *Journal of the American Medical Association, 162:* 1117–1119, November 17, 1956.

6. Happ, William P., Jr., W. W. Tuttle and Marjorie Wilson, The Physiological Effects of Abdominal Cold Packs. *Research Quarterly, 20:*153–169, May, 1949.

CHAPTER IV

Behavioral Factors in Athletics

Before movement can take place there must be a change of muscular tension on both sides of the joint to be moved. The effectiveness with which this muscular teamwork can be accomplished is one of the factors which determine limits of speed, endurance, power, agility and accuracy in all athletic performance. In static or slow resistive activities, such as executing a handstand or in supporting a heavy barbell, the muscles on both sides of the joint are acting strongly to fix the body joints in the desired position. When rapid motion takes place, as in running or throwing, the muscles which close the body joints are shortening and those on the opposite side are lengthening to permit movement. There is still tension on both sides, but on the lengthening side it is considerably reduced.[1]

Any excessive tension in the lengthening muscles acts as a brake and thereby slows and weakens the action.[2] Such antagonistic tension increases the energy cost of muscular work, resulting in early fatigue. The outstanding characteristic of the expert athlete is his ease of movement, even during maximal effort. The novice is characterized by his tenseness, waste motion and excess effort.

That rare person, the "natural athlete," seems to be endowed with the ability to undertake any sports activity, whether he is experienced in it or not, with ease. This ease is an ability to perform with minimal antagonistic tension. It is present in some athletes more than in others,[3] but can be improved in all.

Winning Attitude

The state of mind of the athlete as he faces his event determines the degree of excess tension he will carry into the event. The athlete free from excess tension as he awaits his performance is typically self-confident. He has what is commonly known as "a winning attitude." He sees himself as master of the athletic situation confronting him. To many athletes being a champion is a matter of psychological necessity.[4] Fed by previous successes and having completely rationalized previous failures, he feels himself a Triton among the minnows.

Feelings of Insecurity

Anything less than an attitude of confidence is apt to lead to excess tension in the athlete. The one who visualizes the event to be performed as exceedingly difficult or with little hope of success is nurturing within himself the seeds of tension. Nagged by disbelief in his ability, the event takes on additional obstacles. Added to the demands of the event are the fear of censure by his friends and apprehension of loss of status on his team. He sees himself as incapable and about to face personal disgrace. Continued frustration breeds tension and develops pressures which the athlete cannot alleviate.[5] There is evidence that weight trainers take up body building primarily to compensate feelings of inadequacy and inferiority,[6, 7, 8] and many athletes remain basically insecure even after years of professional experience.[9]

The Pep Talk

The coach, trainer and team mates play an important role in building the proper state of mind of an athlete before competition. The athlete, facing a trial of his utmost capacity, is sensitive to a word, a look or a touch. The self-confident athlete sometimes needs only to be left alone.

The apprehensive athlete, piling on tension by the minute, needs support. The process of developing self-confidence in such an individual is an integral part of the conditioning process. The trainer or the coach may represent the authority-figure to the athlete and become his anchor point of emotional security. The relationship of these two persons with the athlete is a crucial factor in his development.[10]

Undue pressure or coercion magnifies the athlete's tension by exaggerating his imaginary picture of the impending event. Quietly reassuring him of his capability, or reminding him of previous successful performances in former games or in practice is often helpful in bolstering the player's morale before the event. The coach helps to reduce excessive tension by enabling the athlete to make a better interpretation of the situation. This can often be accomplished by placing the event in proper perspective in the continuum of life activities. A young athlete's mother helped relieve tension when she told him, "On your way home from the game, pick up a loaf of bread."

Each team member brings with him to the dressing room his own set of attitudes: aggressive, frightened, lackadaisical. The coach who seeks to inspire his team by threats, ridicule and harassment probably hinders his team's performance more than he helps it. An approach directly centered on game strategy, delivered with confidence and reassurance and without affectation, is the one most helpful in developing a positive mental state. A short, quiet, sincere prayer is often used effectively.

Voluntary Relaxation

An athlete may be trained to employ various techniques of relaxation whenever he recognizes excessive tension. The following procedure represents a method of voluntary relaxation. After three or four repetitions, the athlete will have mastered the fundamental techniques and will be able to recognize and release excess tension. These instructions are in the words of the coach or trainer. They are to be read in a matter of fact tone, distinctly and not too fast, with a brief pause at the end of each sentence.

RELAXATION INSTRUCTIONS

Sit comfortably in your chair. Let your weight sink into the seat of your chair. Don't hold yourself on the chair. Feel heavy in your chair.

Put both feet flat against the floor, and let the weight of your legs down through your feet and into the floor. Don't hold your feet and legs off the floor. Give them down to the floor.

Let your knees fall slightly apart if they want to. Don't hold them together. Let them go. You are letting the chair and the floor have your weight. Don't hold any of it back. Give the chair and the floor as much weight as you can. Feel heavy.

Place you hands, palms down, on your thighs. Let the fingers spread out and become loose; let the thumbs fall away from the fingers. Shift your arms so that your elbows are comfortable. Now let your wrists sink heavily into your thighs.

Lower your shoulders so they are comfortable. Don't hold your shoulders up as though saying "I don't know"; let them fall; don't draw them back, let them down the sides. Don't hold your shoulders forward, hugging yourself, let them out and down.

Balance your head easily above the shoulders, not forward so that the muscles in the back of the neck hold on to it, not backward or to either side, but well balanced and held without effort. Not pulled in like a turtle or stretched up like a rooster, but resting easy in a well-balanced position.

Pay attention to your breathing. Notice the stream of breath as it enters the nostrils on each inhalation, and as it leaves the nostrils on each exhalation. Allow it to become as gentle and smooth as possible. Now take a deep sigh.

Place your hands on your abdomen and notice how they rise and fall as you breathe in and out. Your abdomen moves your hands outward as you take in a breath, and your abdomen and your hands fall inward as you breathe out. Breathe in, move the hands out; breathe out, let the hands move inward. Slowly breathe in, hands out; breathe out, hands in. Now take another deep sigh.

Close your eyes. Turn your eyeballs downward as if you were looking at a black spot on the floor between your feet.

Let the head fall backward slightly. Imagine that the muscles of your eye are hammocks, and in these hammocks your eyeballs are resting. Now let this hammock loose and let your eyeballs sink deeply toward the back of your head as far as they will go. Think of looking into blackness; the blackest black background you can imagine. Imagine looking at a curtain of black velvet. The deepest black curtain of black velvet.

Now imagine that you do not have a joint in your body and just feel limp like a rag. Feel heavy, like a sack of grain, and feel that you are sinking down into your chair. You just have to rest, and not do a thing. Just give yourself up and make no more effort to follow instructions or anything else. You are going to rest a bit. Just let yourself go, and rest quietly without trying to do anything at all. Just rest.

Following a period of voluntary relaxation, the athlete is aroused gradually by a series of stretching movements. He is told:

Push the right heel forward; stretch, and relax. Left heel. Shrug the shoulders; lift them high, let them fall, and relax. Yawn. Come slowly to a standing position. Stretch arms upward. Reach for the ceiling with the right hand. Left hand. Arms out to the side; and stretch. Yawn. Stretch. A big sigh.

Pre-Game Tension

As an event approaches, the athlete often notices a feeling of weakness in his midsection. He may complain of "butterflies in his stomach." His viscera are churning with nervous excitement;

he feels nauseated and may vomit; his heart pounds; he may feel a throbbing in his throat; he may experience pain in his lower back. The experienced athlete recognizes these sensations not as an inner weakness but as an inner surplus. The coach and trainer know that these signs indicate a preparedness for violent activity. In fact, the athlete who expresses a feeling of euphoria before an event is probably in a poor state of readiness.

The explanation for this probably lies in the function of the adrenomedullary activity, augmented by the stimulating effect of the competitive situation. The effect of adrenaline (epinephrine) secretion is to accelerate heart action, causing the blood pressure to soar, driving the blood through the muscles. The glycogenolytic system is triggered off, increasing blood sugar.[11] All of these responses (given the term "adrenalburger" by many athletes) are helpful in preparing the athlete for activity.

Cheering

Athletic performance is enhanced by the presence of spectators. At an annual relay meet, when the shot put circle was brought from a remote area to a position in front of the grandstand, the records were markedly improved. The increase in sensory stimuli when spectators are in sight, with the band and cheering section in action, serves to strengthen the responses of the athlete.[12] The athlete himself can further heighten his responses by intense concentration on the task. The additional nervous impulses diffuse into the working muscles, strengthening their contractions.[13]

Cheering is most effective in endurance events when the athlete is beginning to tire. If cheering is commenced at the beginning of an event, the inexperienced athlete may have a tendency to lose his sense of pace and overextend himself. When the athlete begins to tire cheering, in addition to strengthening his responses, tends to prolong his endurance by raising his threshold of sensitivity to fatigue.

Distractions

Skillful performances requiring a high degree of accuracy and steadiness, such as foul throwing in basketball, are best achieved in quiet surroundings with no distractions. A slight wave of the opponent's hand, a stamp of the foot, or a sudden shout from a spectator can produce sensory irradiations sufficient to reduce coordination. This mechanism is at the reflex level of human behavior and even many seasons of athletic experience cannot erase the distracting effects of extraneous stimuli. Efforts to train athletes to ignore these stimuli by introducing distractions during practice sessions generally end in negative results.

Excess Effort

One of the greatest adjustments the novice athlete must make to competition is to overcome the natural tendency to try too hard—to hurry, strain, press and try to run the whole race, or play the whole game at once. As the athlete forces himself to give everything he has to the performance, his mental demands exceed his physical capacities. The result may be described as generalized, rather than specific, effort. Overall tension and unnecessary muscular contractions act as brakes, reducing speed and dissipating energy. The body performs better when the athlete lets it go than when he tries to drive it. When the athlete is running as fast as he can, he should not feel as though he ought to be running faster.

Collapse

The athlete who strains to achieve a performance beyond his capacity, whether the event be one of skill or endurance, is plunging headlong into collapse. In the confusion of excess effort, muscles contract aimlessly and the underlying reflexes which make for smooth performance are overridden. The riotous muscles send out showers of afferent impulses which return through the circular paths of the nervous system to drive the muscles further into purposeless contraction.

Additional efforts to force his faltering body toward the now unattainable goal produce a torrent of afferent impulses which inundate the higher centers of the central nervous system. Disintegration of the higher centers of control ensues. Mental confusion and neuromuscular confusion end in collapse. It is now too late for sheer will power to straighten out coordinations and get the living machine functioning smoothly again.

To prevent collapse, the factors contributing to it are recognized and overcome before they begin their disintegrating chain of events, for once they begin they are almost impossible to reverse. The decision to diminish the pace, to slacken the effort in the face of challenging rivals and cheering spectators is a most difficult one.

But the athlete realizes that he must now try to gain second place instead of first, or to finish the event rather than to collapse in the middle of it.

The athlete controls his performance in a race as a jockey does his horse. The jockey uses the reins during the first part of the race and saves his whip for the closing moments at the finish. It is a good plan for the athlete to run the first part of his race with his head and the last part with his heart.

Overfatigue

The athlete who has not realistically appraised his ability in terms of his competition may tend to make up with effort what he lacks in ability. His movements are made with continuous tension rather than an easy alternation of force and recovery. He drives through his practice session, piling one drill on top of another, instead of alternating work and rest. He goes to bed at night fearing that he has not worked hard enough that day and that he must work harder tomorrow, and his futile straining is projected into his dreams where his opponents pass him by. Thus he exhausts muscular energy physically, instead of replenishing it, even when he sleeps.

Lacking the restorative power of relaxation, rest and sleep, the athlete finds himself in a constant state of weariness which is not improved by inactivity or hours in bed. He suffers from overfatigue, a condition which is difficult to correct, for it requires a complete reorganization of the daily habits of living. He relearns the coordination of concentration and relaxation, perhaps with the aid of rhythmic music or perhaps by rehearsing some simple dance movements. He reestablishes a pattern of alternating work with rest, by making a clear distinction between the two periods, and with the full understanding that rest is as important as work in the development of athletic condition.[14]

To recuperate, he achieves a realistic body image. Utilization of techniques of relaxation, voluntary letting go of muscle tension, abdominal breathing, steam baths and massage aid him in the restoration of his sense of well-being. The former glow and sparkle return and he feels a sense of calm buoyed by inner strength.

Staleness

It is a general observation that "winners never become stale." The coach takes this principle into account in scheduling opponents to assure a balance of victory and defeat. However, when defeat comes unexpectedly or too often, an epidemic of staleness strikes the squad.

Staleness is a dullness and a feeling of resentment toward the entire routine of athletic competition—the trouble of reporting and dressing for practice, the discomfort of injuries, the challenge of the game or the event, the exhortations of the coach, the idiosyncrasies of team mates, and the distastefulness of effort and fatigue. The psychosomatic response to these attitudes is early and marked. Some athletes lose appetite and lose weight, others indulge in compulsive overeating and become obese. Loss of sleep and a sense of insecurity lead to tension and irritability. The whole functioning of the body is upset; indigestion, eyestrain, sick headaches, backaches, sinusitis and various allergy reactions are early signs. Later, if staleness persists, spastic colon and peptic ulcers appear.

Prevention of staleness is best accomplished, as mentioned before, by a balanced schedule of winning and losing. There are several means by which the coach combats staleness: planning team practice sessions which are action-packed and not too long; injecting variety into practice sessions to keep the season interesting; occasional unannounced layoffs or special events, or a team trip to a winter resort or the beach for a holiday weekend. Ingenuity in devising anti-staleness measures pays great dividends in releasing strain and pressure. The coach and trainer devote constant attention to the development of the behavioral qualities which produce a spirited, hard-working team.

REFERENCES

1. Levine, Milton G. and Herman Kabat, Cocontraction and Reciprocal Innervation in Voluntary Movement in Man. *Science, 116:*115–118, August 1, 1952.
2. Davis, R. C., Electromyographic Factors in Aircraft Control. The Relation of Muscular Tension to Movement. Report No. 55–122. Air University, School of Aviation Medicine, Randolph Air Force Base, December, 1956.
3. Slater-Hammel, Arthur T., An Action Current Study of Contraction-Movement Relationships in the Tennis Stroke. *Research Quarterly, 20:*424–431, December, 1949.
4. Johnson, Warren R., Daniel C. Hutton and Granville B. Johnson, Jr., Personality Traits of Some Champion Athletes as Measured by Two Projective Tests: Rorschach and H-T-P. *Research Quarterly, 25:*484–485, December, 1954.
5. Huxley, Aldous, The History of Tension, in Otto V. St. Whitelock, editor, Meprobamate and Other Agents Used in Mental Disturbances. *Annals of the New York Academy of Sciences, 67:*675–684, May 9. 1957.
6. Henry, Franklin M., Personality Differences in Athletes, Physical Education and Aviation Students. *Psychological Bulletin, 38:*745, October, 1941.
7. Thune, John B., Personality of Weightlifters. *Research Quarterly, 20:*296–306, October, 1949.

8. Harlow, Robert G., Masculine Inadequacy and Compensatory Development of Physique. *Journal of Personality, 19:*312–323, March, 1951.

9. Rasch, Philip J., John F. Fahey and Robert Magrill, The Role of the Athletic Commission Physician. *Journal of the American Osteopathic Association, 56:*657–662, July, 1957.

10. Weinberg, S. Kirson and Henry Arond, The Occupational Culture of the Boxer. *American Journal of Sociology,* LVII:460–469, March, 1952.

11. Bush, I. E., Species Differences in Adrenocortical Secretion. *Journal of Endocrinology, 9:*95–100, January, 1953.

12. Morehouse, Laurence E. and Augustus T. Miller, *Physiology of Exercise.* Second Edition. St. Louis: The C. V. Mosby Company, 1953, p. 231.

13. Karpovich, Peter V., Physiological and Psychological Dynamogenic Factors in Exercise. *Arbeitsphysiologie, 9:*626, 1937.

14. Knowlton, G. Clinton and Robert L. Bennett, Overwork. *Archives of Physical Medicine and Rehabilitation, 38:*18–20, January, 1957.

CHAPTER V

Genetic and Endocrine Factors in Athletics

Internal factors affecting the athlete's performance usually express themselves in his behavior and the alert trainer utilizes these signs in planning the athlete's workout regimen and in the referral of problems to the team physician.

Genetic Factors

The limit of athletic performance in an individual, to some degree, is set by heredity. The cells, which are the motor and communication systems that constitute the power and the control of the human body, each contain some 44,000 pairs of genes, which are the agents for the transmission of hereditary characteristics. The athlete's genetic endowment is modified by several extrinsic factors, such as climate, disease, injury and dietary and social habits.

Perhaps no individual possesses a "perfect" complement of genes. It is probable that all individuals have deviations or deficiencies in some degree. Some genetic variations may result in physical characteristics which are assets in athletic performance. Other deviations or deficiencies may result in weaknesses which limit physical function.

Genetic factors within the cells produce variations in physical characteristics, such as the long legs of the jumper, the large feet of the swimmer and the slow heart rate of the runner. They were propagated through the athlete's immediate and distant ancestry. Occasionally, physical deviations are caused by infections, malnutrition or other influences during pregnancy.

Although most athletes are likely genetically well endowed, their efforts to achieve maximal physical performance may often be finally limited by certain genetic deficiencies. If an athlete fails to respond favorably to a program of strength or endurance training, or if he fatigues easily or recovers slowly, a medical examination may be indicated. Such examination may uncover certain types of anemia or deficiencies in muscle chemistry. Some deficiencies can be readily determined by blood and urine analyses and can be corrected by dietary supplements of chemical substances which the body is not adequately manufacturing.

Endocrine Factors in the Male Athlete

The growth of the young athlete is controlled for the most part by a secretion from the anterior lobe of the pituitary gland called somatotropic hormone (STH). STH promotes the formation of proteins from amino acids and the multiplication of cartilage cells in the epiphyses, leading to increases in the dimensions of the bones and the accumulation of protein in the body. An overabundance of STH during adult life produces a marked enlargement of the feet, hands and face. This syndrome is termed acromegaly and is the explanation for the freakish appearance of certain professional wrestlers.[1] If pituitary malfunction arises before ossification is complete, an overgrowth of the skeleton results. This is known as gigantism and may produce individuals seven feet, or more, in height.

The adequacy of the anterior pituitary secretion is evidenced in clinical tests by the concentration of amino acids in the blood and urine. A low level is the sign of a positive nitrogen balance, which is indicative of the fact that the amino acids are being properly synthesized into body proteins. High amino acid levels in blood and urine indicate a negative nitrogen balance, which is detrimental to

growth. If this condition is not medically corrected before the individual makes further demands upon his protein metabolism in vigorous athletic competition, growth will be impaired.

Growth in the male athlete is promoted by the testicular secretion, testosterone. Testosterone is an androgenic hormone which increases retention of nitrogen in the tissues, promoting positive nitrogen balance. Growth then occurs in the muscles, bones and other tissues, particularly in the genital organs. During pubescence, when testosterone production is rapidly increasing, there is a spurt of growth in height and weight. Meanwhile, this hormone is also acting to cause epiphyseal calcification, which eventually terminates the process of bone growth.

A high school athlete who has a highly active testosterone secretion, as evidenced by enlarged genital organs, will probably be taller, heavier and stronger than his team mates. These physical characteristics give him advantages which enable him to become an outstanding athlete while in high school. However, if the same androgenic hormone which caused his early growth also acts to terminate his growth at an early age, his height, weight and strength advantage will be only temporary. In college he will see some of his slower growing team mates gradually equal and eventually surpass him. This phenomenon may be one reason for the failure of some outstanding high school athletes to continue to be equally successful in college athletics. It may be one explanation of the observation that an athlete has "burned out."

When the androgenic secretion is inadequate during the growth period, epiphyseal closing is delayed and the youth continues to grow beyond the usual adolescent period. He becomes tall, with long arms and legs, a broad, flaring pelvis and narrow shoulders—a poor physique for athletic performance.

The adrenal cortex secretions also affect growth. Excessive adrenocortical secretions before puberty stimulate growth. As in the case of the androgenic secretion, excessive adrenal cortical secretion promotes premature epiphyseal closure, with ultimate dwarfing of the stature. Some of the adrenocortical secretions are catabolic and cause increased nitrogen, calcium and phosphorus excretion, resulting in inhibition of the growth process. Periodic determinations of the levels of these substances in the urine of young athletes can be used to insure that the demands of competition will not impair growth.

Endocrine Factors in the Female Athlete

Menstruation. Disturbances of endocrine secretions in women may have a profound effect upon their athletic performance. There is some evidence that the exceptional physical and mental stresses connected with athletic competition may produce changes in the normal menstrual cycle, but that these are usually so slight and of such short duration that they place no limitation on healthy, well-trained women.[2] Harnik[3] claims that women will not be harmed even by strenuous sports during menstruation and that all normal activities should be continued during this time. It has been noted that menstruation does not interrupt the performance of ballerinas and acrobats. According to the authors of the Amateur Athletic Union report,[4] 85 per cent of women can compete and perform up to their usual standard during the menstrual period; the remainder may have increased pain or a profuse flow.

Karpovich[5] reported that early dynamometric tests had indicated that women's muscular strength decreased a few days before menstruation began and continued at a lower level throughout the menstrual period, but that other investigators had found that 55 per cent of the women participating in track and field athletics suffered no decrease in efficiency during their menstrual periods. The data collected by Jokl[6] are in reasonably close agreement with the latter findings.

Whether a woman athlete should compete during menstruation seems to be largely a matter of individual preference. Not only anatomical and physiological, but also sociological and esthetic considerations are involved. On the basis of experience in caring for women athletes, Ryde[7] recommended that they be urged to compete on important occasions. He also observed that vaginal tampons were convenient to wear during exertion.

If any of the following changes are noted to occur periodically in women athletes, referral to the team physician for medical attention to endocrine function is indicated:

1. Slumping of posture; relaxed longitudinal arches of the feet.
2. Joint sensitivity, or either restricted or abnormally increased range of joint motion.
3. Fingernail peeling or breaking off of soft fingernails.
4. Muscles become soft, boggy, doughy and weak.
5. Wet axilla and palms and flushing of the ears.
6. Premenstrual dull heaviness in pelvis and lower back, swollen and sensitive breasts, headache, nausea and vomiting, tension "like a too tightly wound

clock," or "dull crabbiness," depression and fall of energy, or premenstrual tension-type spurt of energy.
7. Light or heavy menstrual flow.
8. Emotional instability and temper tantrums.
9. Hypersensitivity to palpation pressure, easy bruising, aches and pains always in one place or another.
10. Acne.[8]

Pregnancy and Athletics. Participation in athletics is neither advantageous nor disadvantageous to fertility. While the present studies are too limited to permit a definite statement, it has been suggested that the better abdominal development of female athletes may shorten the course of labor.[9] As a safety precaution, pregnant athletes are usually barred from competition. However, a platform diver placed third in the 1952 Olympic Games while three and a half months pregnant. Another pregnant athlete was on the skiing team. Both subsequent births were uneventful. Numerous other examples of women winning championships while pregnant have been recorded.[4, 10] Ryde[10] recommended that a pregnant woman should give up competition in the second and third trimesters, and the authors of the Amateur Athletic Union study urged caution in horseback riding, high-jumping and skating while pregnant because a fall might result in malposition of the fetus.

Developmental Hormones

Thyroid. While the pituitary and androgenic secretions promote growth, the thyroid secretion acts to produce the differentiation required for development. The activity of the thyroid is controlled by the anterior lobe of the pituitary body, whose output is in turn regulated by the concentration of thyroid hormone in the blood. Hypothyroidism in the adult results in a lowered basal metabolism, apathy and lack of vigor.

The parathyroids lie on or are imbedded in the thyroid gland. The primary action of parathormone is to regulate the excretion of inorganic phosphate in the urine. Because of the reciprocal relationship between phosphate and calcium, this controls the calcium balance of the body. This balance is normally positive during growth. When it is negative the bones become brittle and fracture easily. Calcium may be transferred from the skeleton to the soft tissue. Hypocalcemia results in occasional muscular spasms, accompanied by a loss of appetite, diarrhea, dullness, drowsiness and general muscular flaccidity.

Insulin. The pancreatic secretion, insulin, affects growth and development only to the extent that it alters carbohydrate metabolism. An oversecretion of insulin results in an excessive consumption and deposition of blood sugar, causing an abnormally low sugar concentration, known as hypoglycemia. Hypoglycemia stimulates the medulla of the adrenal glands, producing adrenaline. Adrenaline releases sugar from storage and increases the sugar concentration of the blood. Thus, adrenaline lessens the hypoglycemic response to the oversecretion of insulin.

An undersecretion of insulin results in diabetes. The presence of this ailment is indicated by such symptoms as thirst, increased appetite, loss of strength and weight and increased urination. It can be controlled by suitable injections, and sufferers from this disease have successfully participated in vigorous athletic competition. At least three participants in Davis Cup play and one of the greatest swimmers in the 1956 Olympic Games were diabetics.[11, 12]

Estrogens. The ovarian hormones are mainly concerned with the development of the female sexual characteristics. During puberty the rising estrogenic level, particularly estradiol, brings about development of the breasts, pelvis and subcutaneous fat. Feminine contours are developed at the sacrifice of strength and endurance. A female deficient in ovarian secretions may develop masculine characteristics, which afford an advantage in athletic competition.

Emotional Factors in Maturation

Emotional upsets can obstruct growth and development by disturbing the internal secretions or by affecting nutrition. Emotional stresses arising from participation in a competitive athletic program can cause a depression of the appetite to the extent that well-prepared, nutritious meals will be rejected. If such episodes are frequent or prolonged, a condition of malnutrition permanently affecting growth and development can result. Prolonged emotional upsets can affect the internal secretions to the extent that their functions in supporting growth and development may be impaired. Thus, despite the benefits of good physical environment and adequate nutrition, satisfactory progress in physical growth and development will not result in the presence of serious and continued emotional disturbances.

The disorders described above are serious problems and demand highly skilled professional treatment. The responsible coach or trainer who is alert to growth and developmental changes in his daily contact with his young charges has a unique opportunity to observe their progress. If he has reason to believe that growth and development are not proceeding normally, he can report his observations to the team physician.

GROWTH SCHEDULES

A careful record of growth is an important aid in assessing the health status of the young athlete. Ordinarily, twice yearly notations of height and weight are sufficient to plot growth satisfactorily. If the gains appear unsatisfactory, a monthly or weekly record should be kept. During a season of athletic competition, a daily record of body weight is a highly useful and convenient form of detecting early signs of physical deterioration.

Growth changes are of some use as guides in judging adequacy of growth. They must be used with caution, since they do not account for wide individual and racial differences. In boys over 16 years of age and girls over 13 there is an extreme spread in individual differences. A more detailed assessment of growth may be kept by using a chart such as the Wetzel Grid[13] or the "Growth Spectrum"[14] which presents a graphic estimate of body build, development, nutritional status, age advancement and maturation. Nomograms for the calculation of "normal" weights of children from $5\frac{1}{2}$ to $17\frac{1}{2}$ years of age have been presented by Massler and Suher.[15] As with any other diagnostic instrument, the effectiveness of these devices depends upon their use in combination with other carefully made observations.

Graphic records of height and weight gains have a motivational value for boys and girls whose maturation rate is retarded or who are overweight or underweight. Daily entries on a graph show the effects of improved nutrition, rest and other hygienic procedures on height and weight. Some young athletes, although highly skilled, may lack the physical capacity to support both growth and participation in a highly organized competitive athletic program. In these children improvements in hygienic regimens fall short of increasing physical capacity to the point required to meet the demands of both growth and sports activities. In such cases the necessity for temporary suspension of participation in competitive athletics may be indicated.

Additional Problems of Growth Failure in Young Athletes

In addition to the reasons discussed above, the following factors may also influence growth:

1. Genetic or constitutional factors, such as in the normal small-statured persons.

2. Congenital skeletal defects, such as disordered formation of cartilage or bone. Some of the champion weight-lifters in the lightest body weight class have been achondroplastic dwarfs.

3. Acquired skeletal disease, such as tuberculosis or rickets.

4. Irregularities of cardiovascular or of kidney function.

5. Deficiencies associated with chronic infections and other diseases affecting metabolism.

6. Chronic chest cavity disability with peripheral tissue impairment signs, including clubbing of fingers and "watch crystal" finger nails.

REFERENCES

1. Turner, C. Donnell, *General Endocrinology*, Second Edition. Philadelphia: W. B. Saunders Company, 1955.
2. Ingman, Ove, Menstruation in Finnish Top Class Sportswomen. In M. J. Karvonen, Editor, *Sport Medicine*. Helsinki: Finnish Association of Sports Medicine, 1933, pp. 169–172.
3. Harnik, M., Sport and Menstruation. In *First Asian Physical Education Health and Recreation Congress*. Manila: Bureau of Printing, 1955, pp. 30–33.
4. *A. A. U. Study of Effect of Athletic Competition on Girls and Women*. New York: Amateur Athletic Union, n. d.
5. Karpovich, Peter V., *Physiology of Muscular Activity*, Fourth Edition. Philadelphia: W. B. Saunders Company, 1953.
6. Jokl, Ernst, Some Clinical Data on Women's Athletics. *Journal of the Association for Physical and Mental Rehabilitation, 10*:48–49, March-April, 1956.
7. Ryde, David, Effects of Strenuous Exertion on Women. *Nursing Mirror*, 7 December 1956, pp. 697 *et seq.*
8. Billig, Harvey E., Jr., Personal communication.
9. Niemineva, Kalevi, On the Course of Delivery of Finnish Baseball (Pesapallo) Players and Swimmers. In *Sport Medicine, op. cit.*, pp. 169–172.
10. Ryde, David, The Effects of Strenuous Exertion on Women. *The Practitioner, 177*:73–77, July, 1956.
11. L'Etang, H. J. C., Physical Disabilities in Sportsmen. *Journal of the Association for Physical and Mental Rehabilitation, 10*:50–52, March-April, 1956.
12. Cureton, Thomas K., Science Aids Australian Swimmers. *Athletic Journal*, XXXVIII:40–44, March, 1957.
13. Wetzel, N. C., Physical Fitness in Terms of Physique, Development and Basal Metabolism. *Journal of the American Medical Association, 116*:1187–1195, March 22, 1941.
14. Naimark, George M., the "Growth Spectrum": A Simplified Chart for Assessment of Growth. *Journal of Pediatrics, 50*:586–590, May, 1957.
15. Massler, Maury and Theodore Suher, Calculation of "Normal" Weight in Children. *Child Development, 22*:75–94, June, 1951.

CHAPTER VI

Age and Sex
Factors in Athletics

Factors in Maturation

Age and maturational factors relating to the development of athletic skills and training are shown in Table 2.

Age 8 and Under. Before the age of 9 most boys and girls are not mature enough for athletic competition. The school child in the third grade and below has a short interest span. He tires easily, but recuperates quickly. Large muscles are better developed than small ones, and the heart is growing rapidly. Handedness is established. The physiological age of girls is about a year ahead of that of boys. These young children enjoy simple, large-muscle activity of many kinds. Strong dramatic and rhythmical interests are dominant in the age group from kindergarten through third grade. Their concern is with themselves and not with the group. Although the young child needs adult encouragement and support, he also needs freedom to use and develop his own powers with a minimum of interference and pressure. This is not the age for organized athletic competition.

Ages 9–11. During the ages of 9, 10 and 11 there is usually a period of rapid growth and increase in power. Girls forge further ahead. The use of small muscles improves and eye-hand coordination

Table 2. Factors in Maturation of Athletes

FACTORS	AGE 6–8 / SCHOOL GRADES I, II, III	9–11 / IV, V, VI	12–14 / VII, VIII, IX	15–17 / X, XI, XII	18+ / COLLEGE
Growth and Glandular	Slow and steady. Girls a year ahead.	Plateau followed by rapid growth in height. Girls forge further ahead.	Rapid weight gain. Sexual maturity in girls two years ahead of boys.	Sometimes subject to glandular imbalance and uneven growth of different parts of body.	Bone growth completed.
Neuromuscular	Large muscles better developed. Handedness established.	Improved use of small muscles. Good eye-hand coordination.	Rapid muscular growth.	Improved muscular co-ordination.	
Cardiovascular and Respiratory	Heart growing rapidly.	Heart subject to strain. Lungs and circulatory system almost mature.		Heart growing rapidly.	
Behavioral	Self-assertive, aggressive, boastful, uncooperative. Need adult encouragement, warmth and patience.	Like team games. Marked interest in difference between boys and girls.	Sometimes awkward and lazy. Loyalty to team stronger in boys than in girls.	Occasional emotional instability. Preoccupied with acceptance by social group.	
Athletic	Opportunity for activity of many kinds, especially large muscle. Freedom to use and develop own powers with minimum of interference and pressure.	Rough and tumble play. Training in skills, but without pressure. Swimming.	Touch football, softball, gymnastics, speedball, contests between individuals within school.	Tackle football, basketball, baseball, soccer, volleyball, interschool competition of a varsity pattern.	Championship schedules.

is good. The lungs and circulatory system are almost mature, but the heart is subject to strain. In an effort to imitate the performance of star athletes and idols of an older age, there is a danger of over-exertion.

Toward the end of this period, about the sixth grade in school, the differences in interest between boys and girls become marked and the period of boy-girl participation with enjoyment disappears. Desires for individual and dual sports are sharpened during the fourth grade, and the urge for team sports appears generally about the fifth grade. This period is one of rough-and-tumble play.

Nearing the end of this prepuberal period (grades five and six) the children are ready to be introduced to a wide variety of experiences in those sports which do not involve heavy body contact. Through a sampling of many sports they establish a groundwork in play fundamentals. Skill training, without pressure, can take place. Great variations in individual growth make for unfair competition if contestants are matched simply on the basis of age, and the slower growing children mark themselves as failures in the group whose approval they seek. The body image which a person recognizes as his own may become firmly established at this time. Success or failure in physical activities during this period may result in permanent fixations,* inhibitions, maladjustments and lifetime negative attitudes towards exercise and sport.

Ages 12–14. Grades seven, eight and nine comprise the period for self-testing events. Youths in these grades are 12 to 14 years of age. Weight gain and muscular growth are rapid. Although ossification of bones is well advanced, the bones and ligaments at 14 years of age are not yet strong enough to withstand heavy loads, such as are imposed in gymnastic pyramids, or hard contact sports, such as tackle football. Youngsters in these grades are sometimes awkward, restless and lazy. Improved physiological responses can be developed through physical training, and counseling, and guidance may assist the youth in making psychological adjustments to his rapidly changing physical self.

This is an age when loyalties shift easily and swiftly, when teams are chosen on the spot and the new allegiances are made for teams named after an animal, color or an imaginative title of their own invention. When short-schedule leagues in sports such as basketball,

---

* It was Freud's view that fixation in childhood is the principal cause of neurotic breakdown in later life.

flag football, soft ball, swimming, tennis, volleyball, table tennis and soccer are provided, each new form of competition offers the participants new opportunities for leadership. The interests of the majority of elementary and junior high school children are best served by an athletic program consisting of instruction and voluntary informal recreation.[1]

Many champion athletes have started serious training in their chosen event before the age of fourteen, to the exclusion of other forms of recreation. The advantages of this earlier background to success in athletics is not to be denied. Whether or not such an early specialization makes a significant contribution to championship performance in later years is open to question.

Hale's[2] study of the maturation levels of champion Little League Baseball players revealed that physiologically they were as much as 2.5 years in advance of their chronological ages. He concluded that the accepted normal maturation levels of modern American children should be reexamined and that age limitations upon athletic competition should be re-evaluated. These findings are supported by certain other studies of school children which indicate that many American children who are otherwise healthy are incapable of meeting school standards of instruction and classroom behavior because of delayed maturational levels.[3] Perhaps these studies simply describe the wide individual differences which may exist within one school grade.

The ninth grade in school, when pupils are approximately 14 years old, is a level at which it is particularly difficult to make definite characterizations applicable to all boys or girls. Some are well advanced into maturity and others have not yet reached puberty. In deciding the readiness of youths for certain athletic competitions, maturational levels of the prospective participants should be taken into consideration. These are usually determined by pubic hair indices or by wrist x-rays. Both procedures are in the province of the team physician.

Age 15 and Above.   At age 15 and above, when pupils reach the tenth grade, they are generally ready for competitive sports. To the vast array of sports opportunities can now be added the opportunity for the most skilled to participate on varsity teams. Many slow-growing potential athletes in grades ten to twelve who are not yet of varsity caliber will, through intramural and recreational sports, develop competencies which will serve them well later in varsity competition when their growth catches up to that of their contemporaries.

Decline in Fitness After 30. The capacity for intense effort in both men and women slowly decreases after 30 years of age. First to decline is speed and fine neuromuscular responses. In part this may be due to the decrease of conduction velocities in nerves,[4] and in part it may be due to changes associated with ageing in the central mechanisms of the brain concerned with the organization of incoming data and outgoing action.[5] Impairment of oxygen uptake also associated with age makes work requiring continuous movement difficult. Many elderly persons can perform heavy muscular work if rapid movements are not required.[6] If training is maintained, there is very little decline in physical fitness in later years.[7] Capacity for light work remains at a high level past 60 years of age.

Beyond 30 years of age, however, the amount of training necessary to maintain a high level of athletic performance is progressively increased. Also, the level of condition falls faster during periods of cessation of training in the older athletes. Consequently, older athletes must plan to spend more time and effort in training if they wish to compete successfully with younger opponents.

By referring to Table 3 it can be seen that the age of maximal proficiency in sports ranges from 23 to 34 years and varies for different events. Younger athletes excel at violent and vigorous contact sports and excellence of performance in non-contact sports can be continued to an older age. Boys and girls of 13 and 14 frequently qualify for Olympic teams in non-contact sports. In some of the 1952 Olympic women's swimming events the average age of the contestants was less than 20 years. In general, top level performances are attained by women at an earlier age than by men in the corresponding events. Perhaps the earlier maturation of women accounts for their attainment of athletic prowess at an earlier age.

Table 3. Years of Maximal Proficiency in Sports[9]

Sport	Age
Major league batting championships	26–29
Major league pitching championships	26–31
Major league stolen base championships	25–29
Professional boxers	25–26
Tennis champions	25–29
Professional ice hockey players	24–28
Professional football players	23–27
Bowling champions	30–34
Golf champions	25–29

Dangers of Strenuous Athletics in Older Adults

Strenuous athletics can be performed safely and successfully by 40 and 50 year old persons only if training has been maintained since youth, and if disease or advanced tissue degeneration has not weakened the organism. The dangers in athletic competition for the older athletes lie principally in undertaking spasmodic bouts of strenuous exercise in otherwise sedentary periods of life.

The Ex-Athlete

After high school or college the athlete usually becomes engulfed in the process of earning a living, advancement in his position and raising a family. Opportunities for him to engage in athletics become more and more limited, and he becomes increasingly sedentary as the years go by. Twenty-five years later the ex-athlete typically emerges from his engrossment—he has established his financial and occupational status and his children are no longer dependent upon him. With his new freedom he seeks nostalgically to recover old pleasures. He recalls his former athletic prowess and, in moments of elation, attempts to repeat some of his performances. The result is certain to be painful, likely to be injurious and may possibly be fatal.

Deteriorating Effects of Sedentary Life

Physical inactivity has a softening effect and the stresses and strains of overfatigue and disease weaken the organism. Some of the debilitating effects of prolonged physical inactivity are weakening of bones by depletion of calcium,[10] a deterioration of muscle tissue and tone as a result of negative protein balance (which occurs during inactivity in spite of a full diet), a loss in the total protein substance, especially myosin, a retarded circulation and a retention of carbon dioxide in the tissues which increases body acidity, promotes retention of water, reduces alkali reserve and the rate of oxidative reactions.[11]

Reconditioning of the Aged Athlete

A resumption of physical activity fitted to individual capacity will retard and possibly reverse the above changes if deterioration is not too advanced. The reconditioning procedure must commence at a very low intensity of activity and must progress very gradually in order to avoid strain and other injury. It is unwise to engage in sports competition for the purpose of reconditioning. In the excitement of a game situation the ex-athlete is likely to forget his infirmities and will follow old patterns of response to rivalry at the expense of his physical welfare. The gradual return of the ex-athlete to activity will bring about adjustments in body weight, mobilization of body joints, strengthening of skeletal and heart musculature as well as an increase in endurance resulting from improved vasomotor tone and biochemical condition. These objectives are best achieved through a well ordered program combining frequent and regulated exercises with other hygienic regimens. After a level of condition supporting vigorous activity has been regained, participation in appropriate sports can be safely resumed. However, in order to maintain a desirable level of condition it will be necessary to supplement sports participation with additional specific exercises.

GIRLS AND WOMEN IN ATHLETICS

Limits of Female Capacity

The physical performance of girls up to about 13 years of age is equal to that of boys. At 5 years of age the development of girls is about a year ahead of that of boys and at 10 years the development has advanced to about two years ahead of boys. The superiority in height and weight of girls over boys gives them a slight advantage in running and body contact activities. In muscular strength, agility and endurance, however, there is no significant difference. At puberty, development of ability for strenuous exercise stops or even declines in girls, while it continues to advance in boys. The difference in athletic ability between boys and girls widens sharply after 13 or 14 years of age. At maturity women have only about one-half the strength and endurance for vigorous activities that men have. At the championship level the athletic performance of men is superior to that of women. Below this performance level, however, there is considerable overlapping and the best women are superior to the average male athletes.

There are several physiological factors which limit the capacity of women for endurance activities of a strenuous nature. The heart rate of women is more rapid at rest than that of men. This differential is attributable to the fact that women's hearts are smaller and, consequently, the capacity of the heart to deliver blood is less per beat than that of men. This characteristic cardiac inefficiency becomes more marked when exercise is commenced. At the onset of exercise the heart rate in women increases more rapidly and their hearts beat faster during exercise than do those of men. After exercise the heart rate of women is slower to recover to normal. The severity of exercise which can be tolerated by women is limited by oxygen carrying capacity. Women have fewer red blood corpuscles and thus a smaller hemoglobin supply. Women also have an inferior lung capacity, a smaller maximal pulmonary ventilation, and a lower maximal oxygen intake. In general, the endurance performance of the best women is comparable to that of the poorer male athletes.

Muscular Strength of Women. The speed of contraction is less in women than in men. This may possibly be a limitation in the nervous system. Muscular development in women can be achieved through weight training.

Dexterity of Women. At all ages the capacity of women for skilled work which is not strenuous is equal to or superior to that of men.

REFERENCES

1. *Desirable Athletic Competition for Children.* Washington, D.C.: American Association for Health, Physical Education and Recreation, 1952.
2. Hale, Creighton, Unpublished study, 1956.
3. Morehouse, Laurence E., American Living—a Threat to Fitness. *Journal of Health-Physical Education-Recreation, 27:20-et seq.,* September, 1956.
4. Norris, Arthur H., Nathan W. Shock and Marvin J. Yiengst, Age Differences in Ventilatory and Gas Exchange Responses to Graded Exercise in Males. *Journal of Gerontology, 10:145–155,* Spring, 1955.
5. Welford, A. T., *et al., Skill and Age.* London: Oxford University Press, 1950.
6. Durnin, J. V. G. A. and V. Mikulicic, The Influence of Graded Exercises on the Oxygen Consumption, Pulmonary Ventilation and Heart Rate of Young and Elderly Men. *Quarterly Journal of Experimental Physiology and Cognate Medical Sciences, 41:442–452,* October, 1956.
7. Simonson, Ernst, Changes of Physical Fitness and Cardiovascular Functions with Age. *Geriatrics, 12:28–39,* January, 1957.
8. Jokl, Ernst, *et al., Sports in the Cultural Pattern of the World.* Helsinki: Institute of Occupational Health, 1956.
9. Lehman, Harvey C., Chronological Age vs. Proficiency in Physical Skills. *American Journal of Psychology,* LXIV:161–187, April, 1951.
10. Allison, Nathaniel and Barney Brooks, Bone Atrophy: A Clinical Study of the Changes in Bone which Result from Non-Use. *Archives of Surgery, 5:499–526,* November, 1922.
11. Dock, William, The Evil Sequelae of Complete Bed Rest. *Journal of the American Medical Association, 125:1083–1085,* August 19, 1944.

CHAPTER VII

Nutrition in Athletics

The performance of an athlete in events which test his physical functions to the utmost is largely dependent upon a ready supply of the nutrient materials required by his working tissues. Slight nutritional deficiencies which he could tolerate well while doing light work can markedly impair his maximal athletic performance. Thus, diet is an important feature of a daily training regimen.

Elements of Adequate Nutrition

Keys[1] and Van Itallie *et al.*[2] have described four ways in which diet may influence performance:

1. It may supply energy-yielding nutrients.
2. It may facilitate the energy-yielding reactions.
3. It may counteract physico-chemical changes identified with fatigue.
4. It may reduce excess fat in the body.

To receive these benefits the athlete must be provided with a well-balanced diet containing a variety of attractive, nourishing food every day in the week. There are no super foods which can be eaten on the day of the game to make up for unsatisfactory nutritional habits during the practice periods. The substances which are utilized to support the effort in brief periods of strenuous exercise have been provided to the working tissues over a long period of time and are not supplied wholly by the pre-game meal.[3]

Racial and religious dietary practices and individual idiosyncrasies are determinants in the athlete's selection of food. Thus it is impossible to indicate a single standard diet suitable to all athletes.

The body acts as a homeostatic mechanism to maintain a constant internal environment during the demands of competition. As the food passes through the alimentary tract the body is able to select the nutritive components it needs for operation and repair. In some instances when certain elements are lacking in the diet a protective mechanism is triggered off which apparently exerts an influence in the choice of food to meet these needs. The organism has the power to manufacture some of the required nutrient substances from materials in the body if these substances are not provided in the diet.

The daily energy requirements of most athletes in hard training are not as great as are those of lumberjacks and other workmen engaged in arduous labor. Football players and other heavyweight athletes eat more because of their greater size. At most training tables the biggest problem is to prevent the athletes from eating so much that they make undesirable weight gains.[4] Studies of 28 athletes at the 1948 Olympic Games showed that their caloric intakes ranged from 2,113 to 4,739 calories daily, with an average of 3,350 daily—about the quantity required by a medium-sized man engaged in light work. In individuals of the same size, the caloric intake was about the same regardless of the events in which they specialized.[5] The general rule for all athletes is that the food intake must maintain the athlete at the optimal body weight for maximal performance, and must furnish the calories, amino acids, vitamins and minerals necessary for growth, development and function.

Carbohydrates. The major part of the caloric requirement for body growth and function is furnished by carbohydrates, with proteins and fats playing a secondary role. There has been much discussion of the relative effects of carbohydrates, proteins and fats on muscular efficiency. Gemmill[6] concluded that work efficiency was practically the same on all diets. However, the high carbohydrate diet yielded a 5 per cent greater efficiency than the high protein or high fat diet.

Carbohydrate is stored first in the form of glycogen in the liver and muscle, where it represents a readily available source of energy. Christiansen, Krogh and Lindhard[7] suggested that before long continued strenuous work the diet must provide ample energy, mainly in the form of carbohydrate, to fill up these stores. When the absolute maximum of work is to be obtained, about two days lay-off from heavy work is required to secure a complete filling up of these stores.

During prolonged physical activity a decrease in the glycogen stores is accompanied by an increase in the symptoms of fatigue. When sugar is fed these symptoms disappear. One of the early studies of Marathon runners[8] showed that following the race the most striking change in the important constituents of blood was the marked fall of blood sugar (hypoglycemia).* The blood sugar level was closely allied to the condition of the runner at the finish of the race, and it was observed that the state of the exhausted runner was similar to that seen in progressive insulin shock. The investigators suggested that the competitors should take sweets during the race.

Feeding large amounts of sugar to an athlete in the hope of providing quick energy or high efficiency may have an opposite effect to the one desired. In individuals hypersensitive to dietary sugars, a slight rise in the blood sugar stimulates the pancreatic beta cells in the islets of Langerhans to overproduce insulin. The heavy flow of insulin accelerates the oxidation of sugar, increases the deposition of sugar in the liver and muscles and depresses gluconeogenesis in the liver. As a result there is an over-response and the blood sugar falls below normal, causing the individual to suffer from a mild state of hypoglycemia. If further carbohydrate is ingested, the insulin is utilized and a temporary hyperglycemia is produced. This secondary hyperglycemia is followed again by hypoglycemia.

The victim of hypoglycemia may exhibit such symptoms as a craving for sweets, nervousness, headache, inattention, anxiety, irritability and tension. These reactions may seriously affect an athlete's coordination and endurance. The hyperinsulin reaction to produce hypoglycemia following an overdose of sugar, or hunger, as when the pre-game meal has been too light or eaten too long before

* Hypoglycemia is only one factor contributing to the condition of collapse in an athlete and it is difficult to isolate any one of a variety of functional stresses imposed simultaneously. For a discussion of some of the mechanisms involved in hypoglycemia see Douglas Hubble, Some Principles of Homeostasis. *Lancet,* II: 301–305, August 17, 1957.

Table 4.   Low and High Carbohydrate Foods

LOW CARBOHYDRATE HIGH PROTEIN FOODS

VEGETABLES
Avocados
Cabbage
Celery
Cucumber
Endive
Lettuce
Olives
Radish
Tomatoes
Tomato Juice
Watercress
Artichoke
Asparagus
Beans, string, soy
Beet Greens
Beets
Broccoli
Brussels Sprouts
Cauliflower
Eggplant
Kale (Collard)
Leeks
Mushrooms
Okra
Rhubarb (no sugar)
Sauerkraut
Spinach
Squash
Swiss chard
Carrot
Onions
Rutabagas
Turnips

FRUITS
Papaya
Grapefruit or Juice (no
   sugar)
Lemons
Muskmelon, Cantaloupe
   or Honeydew
Strawberries
Watermelon

DAIRY PRODUCTS
Butter
Buttermilk
All cheese
Cream: Average or thick
Milk: Whole, skim

MEATS
Bacon
Beef Roast
Beef Steak
Beef
Chicken
Ham
Heart
Lamb
Liver
Lean Meat
Pork Chops
Sweet Breads
Turkey
Veal Cutlets
Veal Roast
Fowl

FISH
Bass
Codfish
Halibut, fresh
Oysters, raw
Salmon, canned
Sardines, canned
Trout: Brook or Lake
Tuna
Herring

NUT MEATS
Brazil
Butternuts

MISCELLANEOUS FOODS
Broth
Cod Liver Oil
Cooking Fat
Custard, without sugar*
Eggs
Gelatin, no sugar
Ham
Lard
Mineral or Salad Oil
Soy Bean Flour
Cottonseed Flour
Cottonseed Bread
Cottonseed Crackers
Coffee and Tea

* Use Sucaryl for sweetening.

competition, may adversely affect team morale by making the athletes irritable and uncooperative. Athletes hypersensitive to dietary sugars may benefit by a low carbohydrate diet. A list of low and high carbohydrate foods is shown in Table 4.

Fat.   Fat molecules are very large. Before they can be absorbed from the intestinal tract fat must be split into its two components: glycerol and fatty acids. Glycerol can be readily oxidized to yield energy for muscular work. Fatty acid is oxidized to form a coenzyme, at which point the process of fatty acid oxidation becomes indistinguishable from that of carbohydrate. Fats and carbohydrates are thus largely interchangeable as body fuel. There is some evidence

Table 4. (*Continued*)

HIGH CARBOHYDRATE FOODS

VEGETABLES
Artichokes, Jerusalem
Lima Beans
Parsnips
Peas, green
Beans, kidney or lima
Chili Sauce
Corn
Potatoes
Succotash
Potato Chips

FRUITS
Blackberries
Cranberries
Gooseberries
Oranges or Orange Juice
Peaches
Pears
Pineapples
Apples
Apricots
Blueberries
Cherries

Currants
Grapes or Grape Juice
Huckleberries
Raspberries
Bananas
Plums
Prunes

DAIRY PRODUCTS
Malted Milk and Milk shakes

CEREALS, BREAKFAST FOODS
Cream of Wheat
Cornflakes
Oats
Puffed Rice
Rice
Shredded Wheat Biscuits

NUT MEATS
Almonds
Chestnuts
Coconuts
Filberts
Hickory

Peanuts
Peanut Butter
Pecans
Pistachios
Walnuts: Black, English

MISCELLANEOUS FOODS
Alcoholic Beverages
Carbonated Drinks
Chocolate
Cocoa
Ginger Ale
Honey
Ice Cream
Macaroni
Spaghetti
Sugar, any form
Chewing Gum

BREADS, CAKES, PASTRIES
Bread
Crackers
Cake
Cookies
Pie
Pudding

From Billig, H. E., Jr.: *Journal of the American Medical Association, 146:*1179–1183, July 28, 1951.

that the consumption of fat tends to be high in those engaged in hard work under severe environmental conditions. Calories derived from fat were observed to form about 45 per cent of the total food intake of Finnish professional wrestlers.[9] Most of the fat in a well-nourished individual is stored as reserve fuel, and the fatty tissue also serves as a mechanical protection against bruises and cold. Studies made upon rats suggest that growth, reproduction and physical capacity are improved by the inclusion of fat in the diet, but the effects varied considerably with the source of the fat employed. The significance of these studies for the feeding of the athlete is not yet established.

Foods high in fat "stay by" an athlete longer. There is delayed digestion because fat is less quickly attacked by the enzymes. With digestion retarded, the high fat meal passes through the stomach more slowly. As long as there is food in the stomach, hunger contractions are inhibited.

Athletic training increases the extent to which the athlete may derive energy from fat metabolism.[10] However, the fat portion of the athlete's diet should not be more than double that of carbohydrate. If dietary carbohydrate is inadequate, some of the fatty acids are not oxidized and a toxic acidosis results.[10] Such acidosis depletes the reserve of acid-neutralizing bicarbonates in the blood thus lowering the body's defenses to the fatigue-producing acid metabolites which are the products of hard muscular work.

The slow passage of fat-laden food through the digestive tract permits decomposition. Some of the products of food decomposition are highly irritating to the tender membranes lining the stomach and intestines and may cause diarrhea. Other highly irritating products are formed when the glycerol component of cooking fat becomes overheated.[11]

Protein.   Protein molecules, like those of fat, are large and complex. In the digestive process these are broken down into simple units termed amino acids. At least twenty-one different amino acids are known. Ten of these are the so-called "nutritionally essential" amino acids required for normal growth. It is in the form of amino acids that protein is absorbed from the intestinal tract and utilized by the tissues. These are the principal source of nitrogen, a chemical element indispensable to the body's structure and function. After the tissue-building needs of the body are met by dietary protein, the excess amino acids are broken down into nitrogenous and non-nitrogenous parts. Within four hours after ingestion the nitrogenous excess of dietary proteins is excreted in the urine[12] and for this reason inclusion of protein in all three daily meals is necessary for the growing athlete.

The two primary adjustments in food intake which are combined to produce optimal development of lean body mass in the athlete are the nitrogen and calories.[13] Nitrogen is necessary for the building and repair of body tissues and calories are needed in amounts necessary to support the total energy demands for basal and work metabolism. Dietary sources of nitrogen and calories—proteins, fats and carbohydrates—taken in excess of body needs are stored as fat.

In conditions in which there is an accelerated demand for proteins, such as heavy muscular work and when an increase in muscular mass is taking place during growth or hypertrophy, there may be a drain upon blood proteins—hemoglobin and albumin—producing anemia.[14, 15] When these conditions exist, a diet containing extra proteins serves to decrease the degree of anemia and to promote recovery.

There are also drawbacks to too much protein in the diet, because high protein foods are generally deficient in alkaline-producing substances. A meal of high protein foods should be balanced with alkaline-containing fruits and vegetables.

Proteins may be obtained from both animal and vegetable sources. The nutritional superiority traditionally attributed to proteins from animal sources may be due to the vitamins and minerals which they contain.[16] Athletes, however, seem to attach importance to the inclusion of liberal amounts of animal protein foods in their diet, and it has been suggested that this may be related to certain combinations of amino acids which are present in animal meats but which are not found in proteins of vegetable origin.[17]

Essential amino acids must be available in the tissues at the same time and in proper proportions for effective tissue synthesis. As an example, if bread is eaten alone as a source of protein, about half of its amino acids are wasted because of the lack of lysine, one of the essential amino acids. However, if bread and milk are eaten simultaneously, or if the bread is enriched with milk proteins, the lysine from the milk makes up for its lack in the bread. However, the milk proteins would fail to supplement those of the bread if the bread were eaten for breakfast and the milk were taken at supper.

Dietary proteins furnish not only important organic constituents of muscle, but also of glandular tissues and blood plasma. In addition they may enhance the development of resistance to infections, the healing of wounds and the functioning of the liver. Thus the major role of protein in the body is in the construction and preservation of the integrity of body tissues.

Vitamins. Vitamins are organic compounds other than protein, carbohydrate or fat and are essential for some specific body function. They do not furnish energy or build tissue, but may serve as catalysts essential for transformation of energy, for the working of certain enzyme systems or for the regulation of the metabolism of certain tissues. Bourne[18] asserted that since vitamins are utilized in large quantities to support the metabolic demands of strenuous athletic activities, the athlete may not be able to obtain sufficient vitamins in his diet and that such a vitamin shortage would be a limiting factor in the athlete's performance. This condition may be especially liable to occur in boxers, wrestlers or jockeys who are on a low caloric

Table 5. Essential Vitamins[16, 19, 20]

VITAMIN	RECOMMENDED DAILY ALLOWANCE	SOURCES	DEFICIENCY SIGNS
Vitamin A (Carotene)	5000 I. U.	Fish liver oils, milk fat, green leafy vegetables and yellow vegetables and fruits, such as sweet potatoes and peaches	Subnormal dark adaptation, cessation of bone growth in young, infections of the eye, respiratory organs, genito-urinary tract and mouth. Atrophy of the epithelium, dryness of the skin and hair, cutaneous eruptions on the extremities and body, substitution of stratified keratinized cells for normal epithelial tissue
Thiamine (Vitamin B$_1$)	1.8 mg.	Cereals, lean pork, egg yolk, legumes, milk, lean beef, potatoes, cabbage	Diarrhea, tenderness of calf muscles, impairment of position sense, tension, irritation, general weakness, insomnia, lassitude, fatigue, irritability, aches and pains, constipation, loss of appetite, loss of weight, changes in the texture of the skin, anorexia
Riboflavin (Vitamin B$_2$)	1.8 mg.	Milk, liver, kidney, heart, pork, egg yolk, cereal grains, legumes	Redness of the tongue, conjunctivitis, lesions in the corner of the mouth, greasy accumulations around the nose, eyes, and in some cases ears, scrotal dermatitis, nervous disturbances
Vitamin B$_{12}$	Unknown	Liver, kidney, meat	Fiery-red lesions of the mucous membranes, functional deficiency, growth deficiency
Ascorbic Acid (Vitamin C)	75 mg.	Citrus fruits, berries, melons, tomatoes, green peppers, raw cabbage, salad greens, fresh leafy green vegetables, potatoes	Hemorrhage, structural changes in gums and teeth, changes in growing ends of bones which may cause confusion with rickets, defective calcification and displacement of bones, pain in joints, anemia, damage to heart and sex organs, degeneration of muscle structure, listlessness, irritability, lesions around the teeth

(Ergosterol, D₂) (Dehydrocholesterol, D₃)		fish liver oils, sunlight	known as rickets, beading at the junction of the ribs, bowed legs, enlarged joints
Vitamin E (Tocopherols)	Unknown	Wheat germ oil, lettuce, field pea seedlings, whole cereals, egg yolk, cottonseed oil, rice germ oil	Functional changes in reproduction, and in muscle and liver metabolism in animals. Significance for humans not determined
Vitamins K₁ K₂	Unknown	Carrot tops, outer leaves of cabbage, spinach, kale, cauliflower, pork, alfalfa, bacterial synthesis in the intestinal tract	Lowering of blood prothrombin concentration, prolongation of blood clotting time, hemorrhage
Niacin	18 mg.	Milk, liver, lean meats, fish, eggs, tomatoes, green peas, kale, mustard greens, turnip greens, collards, wheat germ	Gastrointestinal disturbances, diarrhea, difficulty in ingesting solid foods, mental disturbances, depression, redness, burning and infection of tongue, lips, gums, palate and mucous membranes, dermatitis
Pyridoxine (Vitamin B₆)	Unknown	Rice, wheat, corn, liver, egg yolk, milk, lettuce, salmon, tomatoes, spinach, peas, green beans	Dermatitis, usually about the eyes, in the eyebrows and at the angles of mouth, conjunctivitis
Pantothenic Acid	Unknown	Dried yeast, liver, eggs, broccoli, cauliflower, lean beef, skim milk, potatoes, molasses	Undetermined. May include postural hypotension, rapid heart rate, constipation and muscle weakness
Folacin (Vitamin M) (Folic Acid) (Pteroylglutamic Acid)	Unknown	Liver, kidney, fresh green vegetables, lean beef, veal, wheat cereals	Diarrhea, anemia, loss of appetite, increase in basal oxygen consumption, decreased utilization of carbohydrate, decreased nitrogen retention, epithelial changes
Biotin (Vitamin H)	Unknown	Liver, kidney, heart, chicken, milk, salmon, yellow corn, spinach, peas, bacterial synthesis in intestinal tract	Exfoliate dermatitis, pronounced pallor, mental depression, general lassitude
Methyl Group Choline Betaine Methionine	Unknown	Pork liver, beef liver, egg yolk, defatted wheat germ, liver sausage, peanuts	Accumulation of fat in the liver, growth failure, renal hemorrhagic degeneration
Flavones (Vitamin P, Citrin) (Rutin)	Unknown	Citrus fruit	Capillary fragility, hemorrhagic conditions

diet while making weight, thus engendering a need for supplementing the athlete's diet with extra vitamins.

Vitamin deficiencies in an athlete often manifest themselves by such symptoms as weakness, fatigue, constipation, loss of appetite, headache, disturbed sleep, excessive irritability, depression, inability to concentrate, unpleasant sensations in the fingers and toes, burning tongue and gas. These disturbances are easily aggravated by athletic performance, particularly if it is of a highly competitive nature. When such symptoms occur a check of the athlete's diet may reveal that he is not getting a sufficient supply of vitamins. To facilitate this check, a summary of sources of vitamins and signs of vitamin deficiency is presented in Table 5.

Antivitamins. Substances called antivitamins counteract the vitamins so that deficiency disorders may appear even when there is an ample intake of vitamins. As examples, an unidentified factor in corn suspends the action of niacin, and a substance called avidin found in raw egg-white counteracts the function of biotin.[20] Other vitamins have their effective antivitamins but these are not usually found in foods.

Vitamin Destruction.   Vitamins are all soluble either in fats, oils or in water. The B-complex vitamins and vitamin C are water-soluble and can be washed out of food by improper cooking in water. Thiamin is lost in the refining of sugar and in the milling of flour and rice. The fat-soluble vitamins are destroyed by pasteurization, boiling or any form of treatment that results in oxygenation. To some extent such vitamins are now being restored to processed foods, such as flour, margarine and milk. Ingestion of mineral oil in large amounts prevents the absorption of oil-soluble vitamins A, D, E, and K.

Massive doses of vitamins in excess of the quantities required by the body serve no useful purpose and may even be harmful. It has been shown that extra amounts of vitamins A, B, C, D, E and K do not result in improved muscular performance.[1, 17] Toxic symptoms have been reported from the ingestion of excessive quantities of vitamins A, D, Folacin and the methyl group.

The indiscriminate consumption of vitamins is generally condemned by nutritionists and physicians.[21] According to Tuttle,[22] vitamins fall into the same category as drugs. They are useful principally in treating deficiencies. Once that deficiency has been met, additional quantities are of no benefit.

Mineral Needs. The body requires seven principal mineral elements—calcium, magnesium, sodium, potassium, phosphorus, sulfur and chlorine, and six so-called "trace" elements—iron, copper, iodine, manganese, cobalt and zinc. It is as yet uncertain whether fluorine, aluminum and boron are essential nutritional items, and the dietary requirements of most of the minerals have not yet been determined. Excessive quantities of some of these minerals may be as detrimental as insufficient quantities. A list of some of these elements, daily requirements, sources and deficiency or excess signs is presented in Table 6.

As is the case with the vitamins and antivitamins, there are substances which prevent the proper utilization of various minerals. Spinach, beet greens and chard have been found to contain large amounts of oxalic acid which interferes with the utilization of calcium. On the other hand, orange juice may increase calcium retention. Excess magnesium may inhibit the calcification process. A high intake of potassium increases the excretion of sodium salts, whereas experimental magnesium deficiency was observed to result in an abnormal accumulation of calcium in the soft tissues. Excessive use of laxatives has been cited as a cause of potassium depletion.[23]

Alkalies. The metabolic acids formed in the cells are neutralized by the alkaline buffers in the blood. It would seem to be a reasonable assumption that an increase in the alkali reserve would be a definite advantage to an athlete. Denning[24] and Dill[25] and their coworkers advanced some evidence that a runner in an alkaline state does perform better. However, it has been shown that the alkaline reserves were within normal limits in a group of outstanding distance-runners,[26] and that strenuous athletic training apparently does not result in any change in the alkaline reserve.[27] Keys[1] concluded that such changes in the alkaline reserve as might result from dietary alterations have little effect on ability to perform work.

Phospholipids and Steroids. Fatty acids are combined with phosphoric acids and other substances to form phospholipids. These are present in all body fluids and are essential ingredients of cellular structure. Deposits of these fatty substances on blood vessel linings impair circulation and thus limit the function of the tissues fed by these vessels. If this condition is prolonged, it leads to early degeneration. Diet alone does not seem to prevent the deposit of fatty substances. When athletic training is resumed, following a long period

Table 6. Principal Mineral Elements

MINERAL	RECOMMENDED DAILY ALLOWANCE	SOURCES	EFFECTS OF IMBALANCES
Calcium	0.8 g.	Milk, cheese, broccoli, cabbage, collards, kale, leeks, lettuce, rutabaga, turnip tops	Deficiency: Improper calcification of bones and teeth, abnormal heart action, muscle pains, weakness, tremor, spasms, reduced nerve responsiveness. Excess: "Calcium rigor"
Phosphorus	1.32 g.	Cheese, oatmeal, wheat, beef, eggs	Deficiency: Reduction in growth, malformed teeth, low vigor and endurance. Excess: Impeded absorption of iron
Iron	12 mg.	Eggs, molasses, liver, beef, dried fruits	Deficiency: Anemia, flattened and lusterless finger nails, wrinkling and dryness of the skin, difficulty in swallowing, fissures at the corners of the mouth. Excess: Structural changes in the organs, gastritis, hemorrhage
Sodium	5 g. More if sweating excessively	Table salt	Deficiency: muscle cramps, edema, oliguria Excess: Restlessness, tension, high blood pressure, fast pulse
Potassium	Unknown	Vegetables, meat	Deficiency: Carbohydrate metabolism disturbed, vomiting, diarrhea, impaired kidney function, electrocardiographic changes Excess: Extreme relaxation, called "potassium inhibition," potassium intoxication, electrocardiographic changes
Chlorine	Obtained with sodium	Table salt	Deficiency: Muscle cramps, indigestion, stomach upsets
Iodine	0.15–0.30 mg.	Iodized table salt	Deficiency: goiter

of inactivity, the level of exertion should be low to avoid strain on the weakened tissues.

Steroids are lipoid substances such as cholesterol, vitamin D, the sex hormones and the life-maintaining adrenal gland hormones. Although the steroids and phospholipids have little value as fuel, they are important for tissue function and repair. The role of diet in the formation and metabolism of steroids and phospholipids is not yet understood.

Planning the Athlete's Diet

A variety of food at every meal is necessary for good nutrition. The athlete's daily diet should include protein food (meat, cheese, fish or eggs), milk, vegetables, fruit and whole grain breads and cereals. A study of the food preferences of athletes at the 1952 Olympic Games showed that beef, lamb and chicken were in demand; little fish was eaten; foods fried in fat were avoided; the consumption of milk, butter, raw vegetables and fruit was heavy; wheat and graham bread were very popular; canned raw foods were avoided; milk, ice water, fruit juices and mild Pilsner beer were the favored beverages; ice cream was the most popular dessert; honey, maltose and glucose were widely used.[28]

The reaction of the body to different types of foods is determined to some extent by the order in which they are eaten during a meal. Meat and meat extractives call forth a generous flow of gastric juice. Fatty foods and foods covered with fatty gravies, sauces and oily dressing stay longer in the stomach and give a feeling of satiety which persists for a long period. A meal composed mainly of carbohydrates has an opposite effect and passes quickly from the stomach so that one feels hungry shortly afterward. A satisfying meal would thus start with a soup containing meat extractives, followed by meat, potatoes and other vegetables. Buttered bread and salad with an oil dressing would accompany the main course. A sweet dessert would bring final satiety to the meal.

Food Appeal. The athlete works hard and foregoes many pleasures. In an otherwise Spartan regimen, the athlete's needs for the nicer things of life can to some extent be satisfied by making his meals appealing to his senses. The colors, forms and decorative arrangements of foods in the salad bowl and on the dinner plate can be made attractive to the eye. The aroma and flavor of delicious hot soups and broiled meats excite the sense of smell. The crispness of fresh fruits and of salads, the lightness of hot biscuits and the flakiness of pastries are pleasing to the palate. Sauces and condiments heighten the appeal of the bland foods. The sound of pouring liquids and sizzling of platters appeal to the hearing. When the dining room is attractive and comfortable, and the meal can be enjoyed at leisure with congenial companions, then the function of digestion and other physiological processes involved in nutrition proceed at their best. The notion that fighting men should be fed like savage beasts is false. The importance to health and morale of a pleasant atmosphere in the dining area has been recognized by the United States Armed Services and is receiving increasing attention in the interior design of ships and camps.

Cooking. In general, the minimum of cooking consistent with sterilization, softening and enhancement of flavor is desirable. Starch is the exception, for it is indigestible when raw. The raw starch in cereals, rice and potatoes is held within cells which are broken open by hot water or steam. When the cells break open the starch absorbs water, swells and becomes porous, so that it becomes accessible to digestive juices. The use of steam and pressure rather than boiling water for cooking vegetables and fruits lessens the loss of vitamins.

Roughage. Some indigestible material, such as the cellulose portion of fruits and vegetables and the hulls of cereals such as bran, serves an important purpose in assisting in the process of elimination. These cellulose materials pass through the intestinal tract either unchanged or swollen with water. Other indigestible food components, such as seeds, also pass through the gastrointestinal tract practically unchanged.

FLUIDS. The body requires a constant supply of water. Water constitutes about two-thirds of the body weight and is utilized in all body processes. It regulates body temperature and in athletics it is not uncommon to sweat off a gallon of water during practice on a hot afternoon.[29] This loss is partly offset by a decrease in the excretion of water in the urine and the net deficiency is readily made up by the drinking of beverages during and following the activity.

When large amounts of water are lost by sweating, there is also a loss of body salts. The salt loss in activity is especially marked in untrained athletes. If the salt deficit is not made up in the diet, retention of water in the body is diminished and dehydration occurs. Dehydration lowers athletic efficiency by reducing the blood volume and causing muscle weakness and cramps. When the athlete performs in hot environments, water and salt should be replaced hourly.

The major sources of water are plain drinking water and other fluids in the diet, and the water that is contained in solid foods. Fruits and some vegetables are as much as 90 per cent water. Bread, which seems dry, is about 30 per cent water. Some body water comes from the oxidation in the blood of carbohydrates, fats and proteins.

Drinking large amounts of water or of other beverages before or during a meal tends to delay digestion. Fluids dilute stomach acids and convert foods to a semiliquid state which hastens the passage of food from the stomach. Cold beverages may inhibit the function of the gastric glands.

Distribution of Meals. Breakfast is an important meal for athletes as it supplies much of the fuel which will be consumed throughout the day. Omission of breakfast adversely affects work output, reaction time and muscle tremor.[30] For this reason the breakfast meal of the athlete should contain at least one-third of the daily caloric intake.

Since team practice is usually held in the afternoon, the athlete's lunch should not be large. It should, of course, be well balanced in essential foods to support the extreme catabolic stresses of athletic performance and should contain about one-fourth of the daily caloric intake.

The evening meal should contain foods abundant in proteins, vitamins, and minerals to replace those lost during practice. A bedtime snack may be eaten if the athlete is not overweight. Since energy needs are low during sleep, foods eaten at night are likely to be stored in the body as fat. Sample daily menus are shown in Table 7.

The Pre-Game Meal. The stomach should be comparatively empty at game time. When the digestive tract contains food, energy is required to digest, absorb and utilize it. If the tract is relatively empty, this energy can be used for competitive purposes. Digestion is impeded by violent exercise, especially if it is accompanied by the excitement of competition.[31] The blood

Table 7. Sample Daily Menus for Athletes

BREAKFAST	LUNCHEON	DINNER
I. One-half grapefruit	Vegetable soup	Soup with meat stock
Oatmeal	Lamb chops	Baked fish
Crisp bacon	Baked potatoes	Mashed potatoes
Eggs	Tomatoes	Baked yellow squash
Sweet rolls	Bread	Cottage cheese and peach salad
Milk or cocoa	Milk or tea	Bread
	Pudding	Beverage
		Ice cream and cake
II. Baked apple	Chicken noodle soup	Soup with meat stock
Corn flakes	Creamed tuna	Roast beef
Crisp bacon	Scalloped potatoes	Baked potatoes
Eggs	Bread	Lima beans
Toast	Milk or tea	Celery and apple salad
Marmalade	Fruit	Bread
Milk or cocoa		Custard
III. Orange juice	Tomato soup	Soup with meat stock
Cooked wheat cereal	Beef stew	Roast chicken
Crisp bacon	Lettuce salad	Candied sweet potatoes
Eggs	Bread	Peas
Sweet rolls	Milk or tea	Sliced tomato salad
Milk or cocoa	Cake	Bread
		Pudding
IV. Tomato juice	Celery soup	Soup with meat stock
Rice flakes	Macaroni and cheese	Steak
Crisp bacon	Carrot strips	Browned potatoes
Eggs	Bread	Asparagus
Toast	Milk or tea	Lettuce salad
Jam or jelly	Custard	Bread
Milk or cocoa		Fruit

is shunted from the digestive organs to the working muscles. This hinders the metabolism of the food by reducing the supply of oxygen. There is an inhibition of the secretion of acid in the stomach and of the muscular contractions of that organ. A stomach distended by a full meal may limit action of the heart and may limit the excursion of the diaphragm enough to affect the depth of breathing. A full stomach may mechanically limit agility and the range of forward bending.

Ideally the athlete eats three to four hours before competition, since it has been shown that an ordinary mixed meal leaves the stomach in about that time,[32] and excessive food intakes should be avoided. He is apt to suffer if he eats nothing for seven or more hours before competition. When the stomach is empty, or nearly so, the athlete may undergo pains from spasms of hunger contractions. These occur in cycles and psychological tension mounts with each repetition. During the agony of a hunger spasm the aggressive spirit essential for the athletic event may turn into self-concern. In prolonged work without food there may occur a depletion of glucose in the tissues and in the blood. In this condition the athlete suffers from incoordination, weakness and early exhaustion.

Considering the above factors, the pre-game meal consists of nutritious foods which leave the stomach fairly rapidly, such as soups, fruit juices, cereals, bread, lean meat, puddings and candies. Perhaps the most common pre-game menu consists of bouillon, beef, a vegetable, bread and fruit. The athlete does not include in his pre-game meal any item which he has found by experience to be gas-forming or distressing in any other way. Foods which certain individuals have found to be gas-forming include navy beans, green bell peppers, cooked cabbage, cucumbers, radishes, cantaloupe and apples. Uncommon foods and those which are unfamiliar to the athlete are not introduced just before athletic competition. Since the athlete's appetite for a pre-game meal may be upset by the emotional tensions associated with competition, quiet and comfortable surroundings are chosen for the meal. The food is savory in order to stimulate the flow of gastric juices.

During days of practice the schedule of meals and exercise simulates game conditions as closely as possible, so that the body becomes conditioned to the metabolic processes involved and the stress of the game is not complicated by stress of digestion. Types and quantities of foods on game days do not differ widely from practice days.

Pre-game meals may vary slightly, depending upon the time of day of the game. For an evening game the breakfast is generous in protein and might include bacon or ham and eggs, cereal, toast, fruit and milk. The noon meal is composed of foods such as eggs, milk, lean meat or fish and bread, which leave the stomach fairly quickly. A light snack about three hours before game time consists of bouillon, poached egg on toast, fruit juice and pudding. For an afternnon contest scheduled to begin at 2 o'clock, only one meal is eaten beforehand. This pre-game meal, eaten at 10 o'clock, consists of easily digested but satisfying foods, such as bouillon, broiled steak, peas, toast, tea and fruit.

Half-Time Feeding. A glass of cool water at half-time is refreshing and serves to replace some of the fluid lost during activity. However, intake of large quantities of water results in some interference with the movement of the diaphragm as a result of increased intra-abdominal pressure. A disinclination for exertion may arise from this distention, and heat cramps may occur due to failure to replace the salt washed out when a large quantity of water is drunk after copious sweating. In some athletes drinking of cold water may produce nausea.[33] Since there is an immediate over-compensating diuretic effect, it is best not to drink large quantities of fluid during the stress of the game. Sucking a cool orange between events quenches thirst, supplies some glucose and other nutrients and helps the contestant to relax.

Pre-Game Schedule

Preparation of an athlete for competition may take weeks and months, but all of these efforts can be nullified just before game time if he is improperly nourished or fatigued. Protection against such adverse conditions is assured by keeping the squad together 24 hours before the event. A sample schedule is shown below.

```
Friday
      4:00  Bus to hotel.
      5:00  Relaxation.
      6:00  Dinner.
      7:00  Leisurely walk.
      8:00  Movie.
     10:00  Bed
```

Saturday
- 8:00 Breakfast (optional).
- 9:00 Meeting of specialists with coaches.
- 10:30 Pre-game meal.
- 11:00 Relaxation.
- 11:30 Team meeting.
- 12:00 Bus to stadium.
- 12:30 Tape, dress and relax. (Oranges optional.)
- 1:15 Field warm up.
- 1:45 Return to dressing room for final instructions.
- 2:00 Game.

REFERENCES

1. Keys, Ancel, Physical Performance in Relation to Diet. *Federation Proceedings, 2:*164–187, September, 1943.
2. Van Itallie, Theodore B., Leonardo Sinisterra and Frederick J. Stare, Nutrition and Athletic Performance. *Journal of the American Medical Association, 162:*1120–1126, November 17, 1956.
3. Haldi, John and Winfrey Wynn, The Effect of Low and High Carbohydrate Meals on the Blood Sugar Level and on Work Performance in Strenuous Exercise of Short Duration. *American Journal of Physiology, 145:*402–410, January, 1946.
4. Upjohn, Harold J., *et al.,* Nutrition of Athletes. *Journal of the American Medical Association, 151:*818–819, March 7, 1953.
5. Berry, W. T. C., *et al.,* The Diet Haemoglobin Values and Blood Pressure of Olympic Athletes. *British Medical Journal,* No. 4508:300–304, February 19, 1949.
6. Gemmill, Chalmers L., The Fuel for Muscular Exercise. *Physiological Reviews, 22:*32–53, January, 1942.
7. Christensen, E. Hohwu, A. Krogh and J. Lindhard, Investigations on Heavy Muscular Work. *Quarterly Bulletin of the Health Organization of the League of Nations,* III:388–417, 1934.
8. Levine, Samuel A., Burgess Gordon and Clifford L. Derick, Some Changes in the Chemical Constituents of the Blood Following a Marathon Race. *Journal of the American Medical Association, 82:*1778–1779, May 31, 1924.
9. Cathcart, E. P., The Physiological Approach to Fitness. *British Medical Journal,* No. 4048:273–276, August 6, 1938.
10. Grollman, Sidney and Norman E. Phillips, Possible Relationship of Ketone Bodies to the Alactacid Debt. *American Journal of Physiology, 177:*73–76, April, 1954.
11. Proudfit, Fairfax T. and Corinne H. Robinson, *Nutrition and Diet Therapy.* Eleventh Edition. New York: The Macmillan Company, 1955.
12. Evans, Charles Lovett, *Principles of Human Physiology.* Twelfth Edition. Philadelphia: Lea and Febiger, 1956.
13. Allison, James B., Evaluation of Dietary Proteins. *Nutrition Reviews, 14:*130–131, May, 1956.
14. Yamaji-Renpei, Studies on Proteinmetabolism in Muscular Exercise, I. Nitrogenmetabolism in Training of Hard Muscular Exercise. *Journal of the Physiological Society of Japan, 13:*476–482, October, 1951.
15. ———, Studies on Proteinmetabolism in Muscular Exercise, II. Changes of Blood Properties in Training of Hard Muscular Exercise. *Ibid.,* pp. 483–489.
16. Sherman, Henry C. and Caroline Sherman Lanford, *Essentials of Nutrition.* Fourth Edition. New York: The Macmillan Company, 1957, p. 109.

17. Editorial, Food for the Athlete. *Lancet,* No. 6517:152–153, July 24, 1948.
18. Bourne, G. H., Nutrition of Athletes. *British Journal of Nutrition,* 2:261–263, 1948.
19. Clark, Guy W., *A Vitamin Digest.* Springfield: Charles C Thomas, Publisher, 1953.
20. *Present Knowledge in Nutrition.* Second Edition. New York: The Nutrition Foundation, Inc., 1956.
21. Editorial, Vitamins and Iron for Athletes. *Journal of the American Medical Association, 159:*735, October 15, 1955.
22. Tuttle, W. W., Problems in the Trainer's Program. *Athletic Journal,* XXIV: 44–45, October, 1943.
23. Schwartz, William B. and Arnold S. Relman, Metabolic and Renal Studies in Chronic Potassium Depletion Resulting from Overuse of Laxatives. *Journal of Clinical Investigation,* XXXII:258–271, March, 1953.
24. Denning, H., J. H. Talbott, H. T. Edwards, and D. B. Dill, Effect of Acidosis and Alkalosis upon Capacity for Work. *Journal of Clinical Investigation, 9:*601–603, February, 1931.
25. Dill, D. B., H. T. Edwards and J. H. Talbott, Alkalosis and the Capacity for Work. *Journal of Biological Chemistry, 97:*lviii, July, 1932.
26. Robinson, S., H. T. Edwards and D. B. Dill, New Records in Human Power. *Science, 85:*409–410, April 23, 1937.
27. Robinson, S., and P. M. Harmon, The Lactic Acid Mechanism and Certain Properties of the Blood in Relation to Training. *American Journal of Physiology, 132:*757–769, April 1, 1941.
28. Jokl, Ernst, *et al., Sports in the Cultural Pattern of the World.* Helsinki: Institute of Occupational Health, 1956.
29. Morehouse, Laurence E. and Augustus T. Miller, Jr., *Physiology of Exercise.* Second Edition. St. Louis: The C. V. Mosby Company, 1953.
30. Tuttle, W. W., *et al.,* Effect of Omitting Breakfast on the Physiological Response of Men. *Journal of the American Dietetic Association, 26:*332–335, May, 1950.
31. Wilson, A. M., Stress, Food and Exercise. *Todays' Health, 31:*41, February, 1953.
32. Hutchinson, R. C. and W. A. Krahl, The Effect of Food Intake on Performance. *Borden's Review of Nutrition Research,* May-June, 1954.
33. Little, C. C., H. Strayhorn and A. T. Miller, Jr., Effect of Water Ingestion on Capacity for Exercise. *Research Quarterly, 20:*398–401, December, 1949.

CHAPTER VIII

Weight Control Programs in Athletics

In the last chapter it was shown that dietary foodstuffs are utilized to build or repair tissue or to provide energy, and that excesses are stored in the body as fat. Thus obesity is the result of a prolonged overabundance of dietary foodstuffs. In a caloric deficient diet, the fat stores are depleted first, before the muscle, nerve and other body tissues are sacrificed to provide energy.

As discussed previously, fat is of benefit to certain athletes in cushioning blows in body contact activities, in developing momentum, as in football, and in improving buoyancy and insulation in cold water swimming. In sports in which the athlete is required to move his body mass with speed and agility, or over a wide range of motion, fat represents a brake and a dead weight. It does not serve as a lubricant. The extra networks of capillary circulation established to serve fatty tissue are a drain upon the blood supply, impairing the endurance of athletes.

Thus, the fat component of body weight is often a limiting factor in athletic performance, and the athlete often must include weight control as a part of his training regimen. Perhaps the ones who give the most attention to weight control are boxers, wrestlers and jockeys, who must either keep their body weight within specified limits or be declared ineligible for competition in a particular weight class. Weight reduction in athletes is accomplished by two processes. The first is a long-range program of weight control in which the athlete subsists for several weeks on a slightly caloric-deficient diet, which results in a gradual weight loss of up to two pounds a week. The second is a program of rapid weight reduction by partial starvation and dehydration known as "making weight" in which the athlete temporarily lowers his body weight several pounds the last two or three days before a match.

In this chapter the factors in planning weight control programs will be considered first. Then detailed programs of weight gaining, weight reduction, and procedures for making weight will be presented. The use of the daily weight chart in revealing individual and team responses to the athletic training regimen and to competition will also be noted.

Factors in Weight Control

There are five factors which may contribute to overweight or underweight in athletes:

1. Inherent, genetically determined differences in food utilization and deposition of fat.[1]

2. Differences in heat loss relative to body mass, with heat conservation most efficient in individuals with lowest mass/surface area ratio. Athletes with a body build characterized as stout will expend fewer calories than their leaner team mates of equivalent body mass because of less surface area exposed.

3. Different activity rates, including resting activity and involuntary motion.

4. Distribution of meals.

5. Emotions.

The first two, genetic factor and body build, the athlete cannot control. His weight control program is influenced to some degree by his control of activity, meals and emotions. In spite of this complexity of factors, the all-inclusive principle of weight control may be simply stated: If one eats a single bean more than he needs he will gain weight; a bean less, and he will lose.

Relation of Exercise to Weight Control. Athletes are commonly thought to be hyperactive individuals, but they are no different now from what they were in the days of Plato. Many good athletes are in the habit of sleeping 12 hours out of each 24, and are reposed and inactive during their waking hours except for the few minutes of action during workouts or competition. The languid athlete, while eating less than his more energetic team mate, may become overweight. His approach to weight control might be to do with an hour less of sleep and stepping up his physical activity during the day. Food intake is not automatically increased by exercise. One study found that differences in the average body weights of those doing light work, medium work and heavy work were not statistically significant.[2]

Inactivity can be more important than overeating as a contributor to obesity. Normal-weight high school girls were found by Johnson and her co-investigators[3] to be active and to consume an average of 2706 calories daily, while their obese school mates tended to be sedentary and consumed an average of only 1965 calories daily. It was the difference in physical activity, not in the diet, which made the difference in weight. At a dance, for example, the normal weight girls spent twice as much time in actual dancing as did the obese girls.

When it is considered that the burning of a pound of body fat requires from 3500 to 4230 calories, it appears that athletic activity alone makes very little contribution to weight control. Table 8 shows the energy cost of various activities and, for comparative purposes, also shows a dietary equivalent.

Although exercise burns up relatively few calories (it would take 7 hours of mountain climbing—with an empty stomach—to consume one pound of body fat) the daily difference in physical activity between active and sedentary habits can easily amount to 500 calories. In one week this mild extra activity would consume a pound of fat.

Table 8. Caloric Equivalents of Work and Food

(154 pound man working one hour)

ACTIVITY	CALORIES[4]	FOOD EQUIVALENT[5]
Sitting	100	1 banana
Riding a bicycle 5.5 m.p.h.	190	3 slices of white bread
Rowing for pleasure	300	⅓ cup of fruit jelly
Walking up 8.6% grade at 2.4 m.p.h.	430	1 cup of ice cream
Swimming side stroke at 1 m.p.h.	550	¾ cup of shelled peanuts
Walking up 36% grade at 1 m.p.h. carrying a 43 pound load	680	2 pork chops
Rowing 12 m.p.h.	1500	1 cup of mayonnaise

Athletes desiring to *gain* weight need to reverse the above procedure—to reduce their daily physical activity. In order not to jeopardize sports performance, the reduction in activity should be made outside of the team practice period. This energy-saving adjustment may be accomplished by increasing the period of sleep one-half hour, arranging daily commitments so that they can be met without hurry, and by training in relaxation and release of tension to conserve energy.

Meal Distribution

More weight is lost on the same number of calories if the food intake is divided into three meals than if eaten for the most part in one large meal. Food eaten in a short period of time produces a high respiratory quotient and rapid conversion of carbohydrates to fat. The specific dynamic action of foodstuffs elevates the metabolism, but carbohydate transformed into fat cannot contribute to this oxidative mechanism.[6] The extra heat of food in one large meal lasts only a quarter of a day, whereas if the same quantity of foodstuff is divided into three meals the metabolism is kept elevated for sixteen to eighteen hours of the twenty-four. The heat from the specific dynamic action of foods is not great enough to become a limiting factor in athletic performances in hot weather.[7] Therefore, there is no need for the athlete to reduce his protein intake during summer competition.

Contributions of Breakfast. Aside from the advantage to weight control of the specific dynamic action of foods eaten at breakfast, a full breakfast has other values. Overweight athletes who adhere to a strict diet all day often succumb to hunger and eat a massive meal in the evening. This tendency, which is more predominant in endomorphs,[8] may be related to the function of the hypothalamus, which is the center of hunger and surfeit. A person's hypothalamus may determine his constitutional tendency to be lean or obese.[9]

The athlete who is trying to lose weight may not be hungry at breakfast time. If he skips breakfast, thinking that he can thereby cut down his daily caloric intake, he runs the risk of setting off a chain of events which will plague his control of food intake all day long. After mid-morning his blood sugar level falls to hypoglycemic proportions. As a result, he feels empty, irritable and unsteady. He craves food, especially sweets. Candy bars or sweet rolls satisfy this craving only temporarily. If he is hypersensitive to dietary sugar, his insulin overproduction depresses his blood sugar level so that at lunch time he is ravenous, especially desiring more sweets.

If he satisfies his "sweet tooth" at lunch with a jelly sandwich, a soft drink and a chocolate bar, his blood sugar again climbs and falls in roller-coaster fashion. A thick malt at mid-afternoon repeats the cycle. The hungry athlete consumes such snacks with virtuous justification because of his sacrifice of breakfast. At dinnertime he feels that he has not had a satisfying meal all day so he gorges himself. This again shocks his insulin mechanism to the extent that he requires a sweet for a bedtime snack, which he justifies on the basis that this is really a part of his next morning's breakfast.

A breakfast well balanced in carbohydrates, fats and proteins prevents these episodes. The athlete on a weight reduction program needs a full breakfast to support his day's activities and to stabilize his carbohydrate metabolism. Food eaten at breakfast is absorbed by the body during the most active daytime hours and is less likely to be stored as fat.[10]

Breakfast in the athlete's reducing diet might consist of:

        Fruit—citrus or tomato juice
        Cereal—cooked or dry with milk and sugar
        Egg—poached or boiled
        Bacon—one crisp strip
        Toast—one slice, buttered
        Milk, tea or coffee

Emotional Factors

Eating may become an athlete's way of reacting to feelings of insecurity. The necessity for relief from the psychic stresses of training and competition may drive him to seek the physical gratification of a full belly. If it appears that the athlete's increasing weight is possibly related to emotional or personality disturbances, this situation should be discussed with the team physician.

Hot Baths and Massage

Hot baths and massage are ineffective methods for reduction of body fat. It would be necessary for an athlete to take 370 hot baths, and on each occasion the body temperature would have to be raised 2° F. for one hour, to lose one pound of adipose tissue.[11] As a comparison, a slightly greater increase in the metabolic rate could result from the simple act of chewing gum.

It is impossible to cause reduction of fat in a given area of the body by massage. In one laboratory experiment, in which vigorous massage was given in an attempt to reduce the amount of fat present in animal tissues, it was found that the fat content was unchanged even though the massage was sufficiently heavy to produce multiple hemorrhages.[12] Mechanical vibrators are equally ineffective in fat reduction.[13]

Weight Control Chart

A convenient method of correcting body weight employs a daily weight chart shown in Figure 7. The principle of the chart is to show that only a slight caloric deficit is necessary in order to lose weight, or a slight caloric excess to gain weight. (The one bean principle.)

Using this method, the athlete records his pre-breakfast weight on his own chart each morning (Fig. 8). The position of the weight mark on the chart in relation to the slope gradient indicates the dietary modifications to be made that day. The objective is to control food intake and physical activity each day so that the weight mark the following morning will be on the slope gradient. In this way, the body adjusts itself to the slight caloric deficit or excess. Following such procedure, within a week the athlete can predict with accuracy the effects of a mid-afternoon candy bar or a bed-time snack upon his next morning's weight, and act accordingly.

Using the weight chart it is not necessary to count calories. The weight scales show how well the food intake has met the requirements of the day's activities. Slight fluctuations due to daily changes in climatic conditions, such as temperature and humidity, can be disregarded. The body adjusts to its water needs through thirst and no attempt to alter water intake need be made during a weight control program.

Constructing the Weight Chart. Using graph paper with one-quarter inch squares on the chart in Figure 8, fill in dates across the top, as shown in Figure 7.

Weight Reduction. Record pre-breakfast weight (nude) about eight spaces down from the top of the left edge of the chart. Mark off one pound for each two squares. From the starting weight, count seven squares (days) to the right, and count down from one to four squares, depending upon the desired rate of weight loss, and make a mark. Do not plan to lose more than two pounds each week. Connect lines between the starting weight and the one week mark and extend the slope gradient across the chart to the desired weight. More than one sheet may be needed if many pounds are to be lost. At the desired weight, draw a horizontal "leveling off" line and extend it for at least two weeks, during which time the new habit of weight control will be acquired.

The weight chart may be used by the overweight young growing athlete to help him maintain his weight at a nearly constant figure while he grows taller, with the objective of utilizing some of the body fat as a portion of his daily nutrition. His slope gradient might be horizontal or nearly so. In the growing athlete the requirements for specific nutrients are higher than in the adult athlete, and the young athlete cannot afford a drastic reduction of food intake, because of his needs for growth and development.[1]

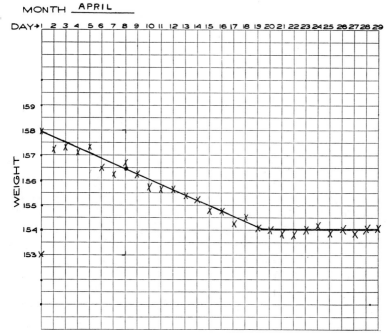

Figure 7. Sample weight control chart.

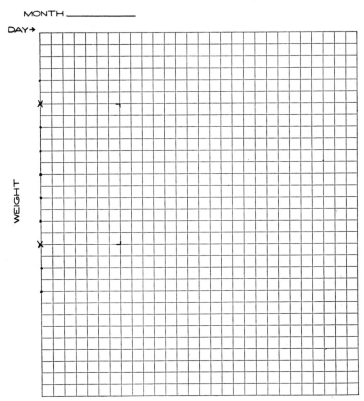

Figure 8.   Athletes' weight control chart.

In view of the danger of affecting growth and development, the weight reduction program of the growing athlete should be prescribed and carefully supervised by the team physician.

Weight Gaining.   Record pre-breakfast weight about eight spaces up from the bottom of the left edge of the chart. Fill in the pounds along the left edge of the chart, one pound for each two squares. Construct the slope gradient by counting across seven squares (days) and up one square for each one-half pound to be gained. Do not plan to gain more than one pound each week. Connect the starting weight and the one week mark and extend the line upward until the desired weight is reached. Use more than one sheet if necessary. At the desired weight, extend the line horizontally for at least two weeks to help establish the caloric balance at the new body weight.

Using the Weight Chart. Each morning before breakfast record the nude weight on the chart. Throughout the day adjust the food intake and activity in an endeavor to bring the weight to the slope gradient the next morning. Adjustments are made by following these rules:

If Over the Slope Gradient
   a. Eat a large breakfast.
   b. Eat a moderate lunch.
   c. Eat a light dinner.
   d. Eat nothing before bedtime.
   e. Eat no between-meal snacks.
   f. Eat no candy, gravy, mayonnaise, or soft drinks.
   g. Increase physical activity.

If Under the Slope Gradient
   a. Eat midafternoon and bedtime snacks.
   b. Eat sweets, gravy and mayonnaise.
   c. Increase rest periods; sleep longer and take a midday nap, if possible.
   d. Decrease physical activity.

Making Weight. Athletic events in which there are body weight classifications place a premium on the athlete competing at the minimum weight at which he can maintain strength and endurance. In events such as boxing and wrestling, the larger athlete within the weight classification has the advantage of height, reach, leverage and, usually, strength. To make use of these advantages, body fat is gradually reduced to a minimum through a weight control program such as the one above. In addition, body weight is periodically reduced still further before weighing-in prior to each competitive bout by the "making weight" process. This is not to be confused with a weight control program, for it is only a temporary expedition and is accomplished by partial starvation and quick reduction of body fluid.

Depending upon the amount of weight loss desired, two or three days before the contest the athlete commences a fast which permits only scanty amounts of food and water. About eight hours before weighing-in, if the weight is not down to the desired level, the athlete may take off a few more pounds—up to five per cent of his body weight[14, 15]—by jogging in rubberized sweat clothing or by sitting in a heat cabinet for short periods until the desired weight is reached. Taylor *et al.*[16] have reported that strength measurements and the maximal oxygen intake per kilogram of body weight show no decrease up to a loss of 10 per cent of the body weight.

When the athlete is well conditioned to the heat of exercise he tends to retain his body salts during sweating, and large amounts of water—up to eight pounds in two hours in a 175 pound athlete—can be lost through perspiration without altering body functions or capacities for performance. If the athlete is poorly conditioned, the salts must be replaced or he may suffer from heat cramps and muscular weakness after excessive perspiration. One salt tablet for each three pounds of weight lost can be taken while the athlete is replacing his water loss after weighing-in. During a making-weight fast the amount of fecal elimination is of course reduced. The athlete may not realize this, complain of constipation and mistakenly resort to the use of cathartics.

If weighing-in is four hours or more before the event the athlete may drink two to four glasses of water immediately and may have more fluids with his pre-game meal. If weighing-in immediately precedes the event, water intake is restricted to two glasses to insure complete absorption. If the fluid is taken in the form of fruit juice, some nutrition is provided.

The water lost in making weight will be replaced within two or three days by fluid intake guided by thirst. Salty foods or salt tablets taken with fluids aid in restoring the normal chemical conditions within the body. Although periodic programs of making weight, followed by recovery periods of a week or ten days, can be conducted without harming body functions, a complete water-fast prolonged beyond one day upsets the internal chemical balance, causing a deterioration of function and possible permanent damage. Thus, the team physician should supervise all making-weight programs and his instructions should be followed carefully by the athlete.

Significance of Uncontrolled Weight Fluctuations

The graphic record of daily weight shows at a glance an athlete's caloric balance. In a growing athlete a cessation of weight gain may indicate that a growth spurt is utilizing energy to such an extent that nutritional intake is inadequate to support both growth and activity. During periods of rapid growth, workout loads may be made less strenuous to bring the total energy expenditure within the athlete's nutritional capacity.

In the more mature athlete a marked gain or loss of weight over a period of three or four days is an indication that he may be suffering from emotional upsets or other causes (possibly economic) which affect his nutrition or rest.

Staleness may often be detected in its early stages on the daily weight chart. Some of its symptoms are a lack of appetite and insomnia, and these result in rapid and immediate weight loss. At times staleness may become epidemic in a whole squad, particularly if it is experiencing a losing season. The total weight of an entire team of 20 athletes may fall off 100 pounds within one week. This slump is a definite sign that a layoff or other change of routine is indicated.

REFERENCES

1. Peckos, Penelope S., Caloric Intake in Relation to Physique in Children. *Science, 117:*631–633, June 5, 1953.
2. Mayer, Jean, Purnima Roy and Kamakhya Prased Mitra, Relation Between Caloric Intake, Body Weight, and Physical Work; Studies in an Industrial Male Population in West Bengal. *American Journal of Clinical Nutrition, 4:*169–179, March-April, 1956.
3. Johnson, Mary Louise, Bertha S. Burke and Jean Mayer, Relative Importance of Inactivity and Overeating in the Energy Balance of Obese High School Girls. *American Journal of Clinical Nutrition, 4:*37–44, January-February, 1956.
4. Morehouse, Laurence E. and Augustus T. Miller, *Physiology of Exercise.* Second Edition. St. Louis: The C. V. Mosby Company, 1953, pp. 238–239.
5. Bogert, L. Jean, *Nutrition and Physical Fitness.* Sixth Edition. Philadelphia: W. B. Saunders Company, 1954, pp. 614–623.
6. Tepperman, Jay, John R. Brobeck and C. N. H. Long, The Effects of Hypothalamic Hyperphagia and of Alterations in Feeding Habits on the Metabolism of the Albino Rat. *Yale Journal of Biology & Medicine, 15:*855–874, July, 1943.
7. Pitts, G. C., F. C. Consolazio and R. E. Johnson, Dietary Protein and Physical Fitness in Temperate and Hot Environments. *Journal of Nutrition, 27:*497–508, June 10, 1944.
8. Mitchell, H. H., Overnutrition and Obesity. *American Journal of Clinical Nutrition, 1:*66–76, September-October, 1952.
9. Dorfman, Wilfred, The Challenge of Obesity. *New York State Journal of Medicine, 56:*1642–1645, May 15, 1956.
10. Portis, Sidney A., *Breakfast in the Modern Reducing Diet.* Chicago: Cereal Institute, Inc., n. d., p. 5.
11. Martin, G. M., Use of Bath, Massage and Exercise in the Reduction of Weight. *Your Weight and How to Control It.* Garden City: Doubleday and Co., 1949, p. 199.
12. Rosenthal, C., Physiology of Massage. *Handbook of Physical Therapy.* Chicago: American Medical Association, 1939, p. 78.

13. Hernlund, Vernon and Arthur H. Steinhaus, Do Mechanical Vibrators Take Off or Redistribute Fat? *Journal of the Association for Physical and Mental Rehabilitation, 11:*96, May-June, 1957.
14. Tuttle, W. W., The Effect of Weight Loss by Dehydration and the Withholding of Food on the Physiologic Responses of Wrestlers. *Research Quarterly, 14:*158–166, May, 1943.
15. Droscher, Nathan, The Effects of Rapid Weight Loss Upon the Performance of Wrestlers and Boxers and Upon the Physical Proficiency of College Students. *Research Quarterly, 15:*317–324, December, 1944.
16. Taylor, H. L., *et al.*, Performance Capacity and Effects of Caloric Restriction With Hard Physical Work on Young Men. *Journal of Applied Physiology, 10:*421–429, May, 1957.

CHAPTER IX

Drugs in Athletics

The attempt to supercharge the athlete's diet with vitamins, minerals, and other dietary supplements is only one aspect of "doping," that is, of employing chemical agents to improve performance. Historically speaking, such attempts are not new. The berserker rages recorded in the Norse sagas of 1200–1400 A.D. are believed to have resulted from ingestion of the mushroom *Amanita muscaria,* which contains a drug called bufotenine.[1] Under its influence the warriors were said to have howled like wolves, bit chunks from their shields and to have ruthlessly hewed down all who crossed their path, friend or foe. The fury lasted about a day, followed by one or more days of dullness of mind and feebleness of body.

Three aspects are involved in administering drugs to athletes: (1) The ethical problem of how far it is consistent with good sportsmanship to use stimulants to improve performance; (2) the legal aspects of the protection of the athlete who lacks the safeguards with which vigilant Racing Commissions and the Association of Official Racing Chemists protect racing animals,[2] and (3) the medical aspects of the possibly harmful physiological and psychological effects of these substances. Although a detailed consideration of the ethical and legal aspects of this practice is beyond the scope of this text, it is the considered opinion of the

97

authors that the use of drugs to influence athletic performance is unsportsmanlike and degrading. In military combat or in medical support of life processes, the use of drugs is justified. In athletic competition, where man is testing himself, the use of drugs to extend physical capacity is indefensible.

Drugs Affecting the Autonomic Nervous System

Ephedrine. Ephedrine is an alkaloid obtained from various plants. Administration of the drug results in an elevation of the blood pressure, acceleration of the heart rate, constriction of the peripheral blood vessels, increase in the cardiac output, dilation of the bronchioles and stimulation of the respiratory center. In asthmatics this provides relief of respiratory distress, increases the vital capacity, inspiratory capacity and expiratory reserve volume and decreases functional residual capacity, all without altering total lung volume. The drug has been widely used by professional boxers in the hope of improving their respiratory functions, but the work of Whitfield *et al.*[3] indicates that it has little effect on persons not suffering from asthma or emphysema. Overdoses of ephedrine result in insomnia, nervousness, tremor and restlessness.

Nicotine. The use of tobacco by athletes is almost universally banned by American trainers. It is, however, difficult to justify this ban on the basis of what is known of the pharmacological effects of smoking. A careful study of the long-range effects of smoking on physical performance has not yet been made. Smoking immediately before tests of endurance, speed, skill, strength, power and accuracy does not appear to affect significantly performance or recovery in either smokers or non-smokers. Muscular tension and tremor and both simple and complex reaction time are likewise not significantly affected by smoking.[4-11] The smoking of one cigarette caused a slight increase in the heart rate and blood pressure for 30 to 60 minutes in one group of subjects but had no statistically significant effect on oxygen metabolism.[10] In one study of 1,200 consecutive patients, there was no statistically significant difference in the height of smokers and non-smokers. The average weight of the smokers was significantly less.[11] Excessive smoking may interfere with proper nutrition. As a result smokers often gain weight when they give up the habit.

On the basis of present knowledge it cannot be demonstrated that smoking has any serious effect on the physical performance of the average athlete. The variability of results within the tests reported in the literature suggests that there is a wide variation in individual sensitivity to smoking. Obviously the tobacco-sensitive athlete should not smoke. Properly this should be an individual matter based upon experience. This requires a degree of maturity which is not often present in high school and college students and the trainer may find it easier to protect his tobacco-sensitive athletes by enforcing a general no smoking rule.

Drugs Affecting the Central Nervous System

Alcohol. Alcohol is a depressant of the central nervous system. It is universally agreed that in large amounts it is detrimental to athletic performance but there is no such general agreement regarding its use in small or moderate quantities. One survey[12] found that most American coaches, trainers, physicians and physical educators condemned the use of alcohol by athletes but noted that few gave scientific reasons for their answers. European athletes are generally accustomed to drinking wine and beer and these are not banned from the training table. Their coaches may recommend the use of alcohol to dispel feelings of fatigue during and following periods of athletic competition.[13] Karpovich[14] examined the experimental evidence regarding the effects of small amounts of alcohol and found that the differences of opinion regarding its influence could not be reconciled. He concluded that further studies were necessary to determine whether the use of moderate quantities of alcohol were deleterious to those accustomed to them. Since relatively large quantities of alcohol are definitely harmful to skilled performance, and since the drug is habit-forming, its use by athletes cannot be recommended.

Amphetamine. This drug (Benzedrine, Dexedrine) is a powerful stimulant to the central nervous system. It has been claimed that when administered orally this drug increases the power for voluntary muscular work and suppresses the appearance of fatigue.[15] It is now generally agreed that these effects are purely subjective. Administration of Benzedrine stimulates the respiratory center and increases cardiac work and output. It causes a diminution in appetite and at one time was widely used indiscriminately to induce loss of body weight.[16] In toxic doses it may cause restlessness, dizziness, increased reflexes, tremor, insomnia, tenseness, irritability, confusion, aggressiveness, increased libido, hallucinations, delirium, anxiety, panic states, suicidal or homicidal tendencies, fatigue and depression.[17] Its use by normal persons for masking fatigue caused by physical operation has been condemned by pharmacologists and physicians.[18]

Caffeine. This agent is a purine derivative found in coffee, tea, cocoa, maté, kola nuts, guarana and various other plants. It creates an artificial sense of well-being and allows the user to work for long periods. It stimulates the heart and central nervous system, increases work output, allays fatigue[19] and shortens reaction time, although delicate muscular coordination and accurate timing may be adversely affected.

Coffee, tea and cola drinks probably owe their popularity to the mildly stimulating effect of their caffeine content. The average cup of coffee contains between 100 and 150 mg. of caffeine. Individual susceptibility to its effects varies markedly; those with a high degree of nervous system irritability may become restless and unable to sleep. The amount of caffeine in drinks of this type is too small to have any effect on athletic performance. Denying their use to athletes who are accustomed to them may prove more disturbing than the stimulation received from them. In some athletes who are not habituated to coffee drinking, a single cup may produce hyperirritability and gastro-intestinal upset.

Cocaine. An increased capacity for muscular work may result from the use of cocaine due to the masking of the sense of fatigue. It is said to have been widely used in the early six-day bicycle races in the United States.[20] The feeling of well-being it induces is followed by a period of depression. The drug is habit forming and highly toxic.

Desoxyephedrine. This drug (Methamphetamine, Pervitin, Methedrine) is chemically similar to amphetamine and ephedrine. It was used by the German armed forces during World War II for its stimulating properties and as a result has received considerable attention. Literature on the action of this drug has been reviewed by Ivy and Goetzl[21] and by Haley.[22] Desoxyephedrine produces cardiac and central nervous system stimulation. Blood flow through the muscles is increased, peripheral vasoconstriction is induced and fatigue is depressed. It does not hasten recovery from fatigue and its use to mask the effects of fatigue may lead the user to attempt dangerous amounts of overwork. Large doses result in hyperglycemia, increased metabolic rate and cardiovascular disturbances. Addiction may occur, resulting in chronic intoxication and a loss in body weight.

Nikethamide. A pyridine derivative, known also as Coramine, has been used by European athletes to offset the appearance of vasomotor circulatory disturbances due to violent physical effort.[20] The drug reflexly stimulates respiration by its effect on the chemoreceptors of the carotid body. Its effect on the circulation is not striking. Experimental studies with dogs have shown that large doses result in an increase in coronary blood flow and cardiac output, but this is offset by a decreased mechanical efficiency of the myocardium.[23] In toxic amounts the drug causes convulsions from excitation of the higher motor centers and death may result from respiratory paralysis.

Pentylenetetrazol. Sold under such trade names as Metrazol in the United States and Cardiazol in Europe, it stimulates the central nervous system and the cardiovascular system and affects the neuromuscular junction. It has been widely used by athletes in Europe.[20] Haldi and Wynn[24] found that administration of 100 mg. of Metrazol, 5 mg. Benzedrine, or 250 mg. caffeine alkaloid approximately one hour before swimming had no effect on speed in swimming the 100 yard sprint.

Drugs Affecting the Circulatory System

Cytochrome C. Cytochrome A, B, and C are constituents of hemoglobin. They are widely distributed in plant and animal tissues where they play an important role in the oxidation process. An Italian physiologist has recently reported that injection of cytochrome C intravenously has a marked effect in reducing muscle fatigue and in increasing endurance.[25] Research data on this substance is too scanty at present to justify a definite conclusion.

Digitalis. The principal source of digitalis is the dried leaf of the foxglove plant. It possesses the unique ability to increase the force of cardiac contraction. The increased force of systole results in a reduction in the heart rate. Although it is extremely valuable in the treatment of congestive heart failure and has been used in some instances by European athletes,[20] its use is accompanied by toxic effects and there is no justification for its employment by normal individuals.

Nitroglycerin. Racing cyclists have reported that they suffer less from shortness of breath after a violent sprint if they have first taken a 0.5 mg. tablet of nitroglycerin.[20] The basic action of this drug is to relax smooth muscle, notably the coronary blood vessels. Myocardial ischemia due to pathological changes may thereby be relieved and the heart enabled to work more efficiently. However, even therapeutic doses may be accompanied by such unpleasant side effects as nausea, vomiting, weakness, restlessness, pallor, cold sweat, syncope, incontinence and collapse.[17] Excessive doses convert hemoglobin to methemoglobin and cyanosis and functional anemia result.[26]

Oxygen. Since one of the main limiting factors in physical exertion is the amount of oxygen which can be taken up by the organism, physiologists have been interested in the possibility of using pure oxygen rather than ordinary mixed air as a means of improving athletic performance and hastening recovery from fatigue. Karpovich[27] found that there was an improvement in the speed of sprint swimming when oxygen was inhaled prior to the start of a race. He attributed this to the increased ability to hold the breath. The use of oxygen in athletics became a matter of heated controversy at the 1936 Olympics, when the victories of the Japanese swimmers were attributed to the fact that they inhaled oxygen just before the start of the races.

Miller *et al.*[28] have studied the effect of administration of oxygen to subjects working on a treadmill. They found that its use before exercise did not affect the heart rate, blood pressure, blood lactate or endurance of the subjects. When oxygen was given during exercise there was a decrease in maximal blood lactate concentration, but it was doubtful whether this was great enough to be of physiological significance. Recovery was not aided by the administration of oxygen after exercise.

Hormones

Adrenal Cortical Hormone. Studies of adrenal cortical response during competitive crew racing[29] led to the conclusion that physical and emotional stress elicits adrenal stimulation. This response may represent a necessary link in the process by which homeostasis is maintained during such stress. During violent exertion the increased secretion by the adrenal cortex appears to provide an optimal amount of the hormone and nothing is gained by administrations of exogenous supplies of the substance.[30]

Epinephrine (Adrenalin). A hormone formed in the medulla

(inner portion) of the adrenal glands. When it is secreted during excitement, it directly and powerfully stimulates the myocardium and conductive tissue of the heart resulting in stronger contraction and more complete emptying of the chambers. Usually an increase in blood pressure follows resulting in a larger blood flow to the heart. The blood vessels in the smooth muscles of the skin and viscera constrict (accounting for such descriptive phrases as "white with rage") and those in the skeletal muscles relax, resulting in a greater supply of blood to the working tissues to meet the muscular demands of athletic performance.[17] This is the "fight or flight" reaction.

By lowering the threshold of the muscle to acetylcholine, epinephrine enables the smaller amounts of acetylcholine liberated during fatigue to function effectively in the transmission of neural impulses to the muscles. The blood sugar content is increased and anaerobic glycolysis in muscle is stimulated.[31] This substance has been widely used in attempts to influence the performance of race horses. It seems possible that in maximal exertions, in which the ability of the heart to circulate the blood is the limiting factor, performance capacity may be increased by injections of this hormone and the onset of fatigue may be deferred in endurance-type exercises.

Methyltestosterone. A synthetic hormone that has been found to improve muscular performance in castrates and eunuchoids.[32] In senescent men, in whom a diminution of the sex hormone production is present, intake of methyltestosterone may be effective in improving muscular performance. However, no influence was noted on the physical vigor of normal young men as a result of administering this hormone to them.[33] This is only to be expected in subjects with normal sex hormone production.

Pregnenolene. Pincus and Hoagland[34] reported that oral administration of 57 mg. of pregnenolene (a non-toxic steroid compound) for several days improved skilled psychomotor performance and decreased fatigability in normal healthy young men. They suggested that this was due to the fact that pregnenolene maintained an optimal steroid balance within the organism.

Drugs Affecting Metabolism and Nutrition

Calcium. This element is essential for the proper functioning of body tissues. Lack of calcium causes marked weakness of muscles, loss of muscle tone and an increased irritability of all types of muscle and nerve cells, known as low-calcium tetany. An individual ordinarily receives an ample supply of calcium in his diet. It is only under abnormal conditions that dietary supplements are needed and even then the administration of calcium salts is seldom the therapy of choice. Injections of this substance have been used by professional boxers in a futile attempt to improve their muscular responses.

Glycine (Gelatin). In 1940 it was reported that after the addition of gelatin to the diet of a number of subjects there was a large increase in their work output. It was postulated that this was due to the amino acid content of the gelatin.[35] Later experimenters were unable to confirm these results and it is believed that the beneficial effects observed in the earlier study were the result of training or of psychological aspects of the experiment.[36] As a result gelatin has been discredited as an ergogenic aid.

Phosphates. Phosphates furnish energy for muscular contraction and function as buffers in the blood. At one time their use was extremely popular among German athletes and it was claimed that the total work output was increased by more than 20 per cent. Bøje,[20] however, raised the question of whether the reported gains were not psychological rather than physiological, and Keys[37] concluded that there was every reason to be skeptical of any claims that high phosphate intake improved muscular performance. The phosphated sugar of Embden produced no significant difference in performance when administered to a group of cross-country runners.[38] Phosphates have a mild laxative action, and when used in daily doses of 3 gm. they apparently have no deleterious effects.

Potassium. Muscular activity is accompanied by an exchange of potassium for sodium. The loss of potassium is in general proportional to the duration and intensity of the contraction. As a result of exhausting exercise as much as 30 per cent of the cellular potassium may be lost. As potassium is lost, the intensity of muscular contraction decreases.[39] A temporary increase in the strength of contraction of normal skeletal muscle is known to follow an intravenous injection of potassium chloride and muscular fatigue is delayed.[40] However, excess potassium is rapidly excreted by the kidneys and attempts to store potassium by use of massive doses are useless.

Sodium Bicarbonate. The use of sodium bicarbonate has been suggested as a method of improving athletic performance. Dill *et al.*[41] found that an intake of this drug allowed a greater oxygen debt, although they did not notice any improvement in muscular performance. Dennig *et al.*[42] found an increase in endurance after alkali intake. Sodium bicarbonate appears to increase the rate of elimination of carbon dioxide from the body. In part this goes to make up amino acids, which in turn form cell protein.[43] Chronic usage may result in impairment of renal function and acute poisoning from massive doses of this drug is occasionally encountered.[44]

Anti-Motion Sickness Drugs. Many athletes are susceptible to motion sickness if compelled to travel any distance on trains, airplanes or other conveyances. After a five year cooperative study by the Army, Navy and Air Force of 26 anti-motion sickness compounds, it was concluded that the most effective agents were 50 mg. of Bonamine taken once or three times daily, 25 mg. of Phenergan three times daily, or 50 mg. of Marezine three times daily.[45]

REFERENCES

1. Fabing, Howard D., On Going Berserk: A Neurochemical Inquiry. *Scientific Monthly, 83:*232–237, November, 1956.
2. Morgan, Charles E., Drug Administration to Racing Animals. *Journal of the American Veterinary Medical Association, 130:*240–243, March 15, 1957.
3. Whitfield, A. G. W., W. Melville Arnott and J. A. H. Waterhouse, The Effect of Ephedrine in Asthma and Emphysema. *Quarterly Journal of Medicine, 19* (N.S.):319–326, October, 1950.
4. Karpovich, Peter V. and Creighton J. Hale, Tobacco Smoking and Physical Performance, *Journal of Applied Physiology, 3:*616–621, April, 1951.
5. Reeves, Warren E. and Laurence E. Morehouse, The Acute Effect of Smoking Upon the Physical Performance of Habitual Smokers. *Research Quarterly, 21:*245–248, October, 1950.
6. Anderson, Jackson M. and C. William Brown, A Study of the Effect of Smoking Upon Grip Strength and Recuperation from Local Muscular Fatigue. *Research Quarterly, 22:*102–108, March, 1951.
7. Kay, Hector W. and Peter V. Karpovich, Effect of Smoking Upon Recuperation from Local Muscular Fatigue, *Research Quarterly, 20:*250–256, October, 1949.
8. Jacobson, Edmund, Muscular Tension and the Smoking of Cigarettes, *American Journal of Psychology, 56:*559–574, October, 1943.
9. Fay, Paul J., The Effect of Cigarette Smoking on Simple and Choice Reaction Time to Colored Lights, *Journal of Experimental Psychology, 19:*592–603, October, 1936.
10. Henry, F. M. and J. R. Fitzhenry, Oxygen Metabolism of Moderate Exercise with Some Observations on the Effects of Tobacco Smoking. *Journal of Applied Physiology, 2:*464–468, February, 1950.

11. Hadley, Henry G., The Effect of Tobacco Upon Growth, Longevity and Metabolism. *Medical Records, 153*:350–352, May, 1941.

12. Metcalfe, Ralph H., *A Study of the Effects of Alcohol and Tobacco on Athletic Performance,* Unpublished Master's Thesis, The University of Southern California, September, 1939.

13. Nadi, Aldo, *On Fencing.* New York: G. P. Putnam's Sons, 1943.

14. Karpovich, Peter V., *Physiology of Muscular Activity.* Fourth Edition. Philadelphia: W. B. Saunders Company, 1953.

15. Allen, G. A. and G. E. Feigen, The Influence of Benzedrine on Work Decrement and Patellar Reflex. *American Journal of Physiology, 136*:392–400, May, 1942.

16. Harris, Stanley C., A. C. Ivy and Laureen M. Searle, The Mechanism of Amphetamine-Induced Loss of Weight. A Consideration of the Theory of Hunger and Appetite. *Journal of the American Medical Association, 134:* 1468–1475, August 23, 1947.

17. Goodman, Louis S. and Alfred Gilman, *The Pharmacological Basis of Therapeutics,* Second Edition. New York: The Macmillan Company, 1955.

18. *New and Non-Official Remedies.* Chicago: The American Medical Association, 1956.

19. Foltz, Eliot, A. C. Ivy and C. J. Barborka, The Use of Double Work Periods in the Study of Fatigue and the Influence of Caffeine on Recovery. *American Journal of Physiology, 136*:78–86, March 1, 1942.

20. Bøje, Ove, Doping: A Study of the Means Employed to Raise the Level of Performance in Sport. *Bulletin of the Health Organization of the League of Nations,* VIII:439–469, 1939.

21. Ivy, A. C. and F. R. Goetzl, d-Desoxyephedrine. A Review. *War Medicine, 3:* 60–77, January, 1943.

22. Haley, T. J., Desoxyephedrine—a Review of the Literature. *Journal of the American Pharmaceutical Association* (Scientific Edition), *36*:161–169, June, 1947.

23. Eckenhoff, James E. and Joseph H. Hafkenschiel, The Effect of Nikethamide on Coronary Blood Flow and Cardiac Oxygen Metabolism, *Journal of Pharmacology and Experimental Therapeutics, 91*:362–369, December, 1947.

24. Haldi, John and Winfrey Wynn, Action of Drugs on Efficiency of Swimmers. *Research Quarterly, 17*:96–101, May, 1946.

25. Nigro, A., Doping That is not Doping. *Medicina Sportiva: Studi di Medicina e Chirurgia dello Sport, 9*:451–461, October, 1955.

26. Bodansky, Oscar, Methemoglobinemia and Methemoglobin-Producing Compounds. *Pharmacological Reviews, 3*:144–196, June, 1951.

27. Karpovich, Peter V., Effect of Oxygen Inhalation on Swimming Performance. *Research Quarterly, 5*:24–30, May, 1934.

28. Miller, A. T., Jr., *et al.,* Influence of Oxygen Administration on Cardiovascular Function During Exercise and Recovery. *Journal of Applied Physiology, 5*:165–168, October, 1952.

29. Renold, Albert E., T. B. Quigley, Harrison E. Kennard and George W. Thorn, Reaction of the Adrenal Cortex to Physical and Emotional Stress in College Oarsmen. *New England Journal of Medicine, 244*:754–757, May 17, 1951.

30. Missiuro, Vladimir, D. B. Dill and H. T. Edwards, The Effect of Adrenal Cortical Extract in Rest and Work. *American Journal of Physiology, 121:* 549–554, February 1, 1938.

31. Luco, J. V., The Defatiguing Effect of Adrenalin. *American Journal of Physiology, 125*:196–204, January 1, 1939.

32. Simonson, Ernst, Walter M. Kearns and Norbert Enzer, Effect of Oral Ad-

ministration of Methyltestosterone on Fatigue in Eunuchoids and Castrates. *Endocrinology, 28:*506–512, March, 1941.

33. Samuels, Leo T., Austin F. Henschel and Ancel Keys, Influence of Methyl Testosterone on Muscular Work and Creatine Metabolism in Normal Young Men. *Journal of Clinical Endocrinology, 2:*649–654, November, 1942.

34. Pincus, Gregory and Hudson Hoagland, Effects of Administered Pregnenolene on Fatiguing Psychomotor Performance. *Journal of Aviation Medicine, 15:* 98 et seq., April, 1944.

35. Kaczmarek, Regidium M., Effect of Gelatin on the Work Output of Male Athletes and Non-Athletes and Girl Subjects. *Research Quarterly, 11:*109–119, December, 1940.

36. Karpovich, Peter V. and K. Pestrecov, Effect of Gelatin Upon Muscular Work in Man. *American Journal of Physiology, 134:*300–309, September 1, 1941.

37. Keys, Ancel, Physical Performance in Relation to Diet. *Federation Proceedings, 2:*164–187, September, 1943.

38. Johnson, Warren R. and David H. Black, Comparison of Effects of Certain Blood Alkalinizers and Glucose Upon Competitive Endurance Performance. *Journal of Applied Physiology, 5:*577–578, April, 1953.

39. Fenn, W. O., The Role of Potassium in Physiological Processes. *Physiological Reviews, 20:*377–415, July, 1940.

40. Hoff, Hebbel E., Alexander W. Winkler and Paul K. Smith, Recovery of Fatigued Muscle Following Intravenous Injection of Potassium Chloride. *American Journal of Physiology, 131:*615–618, January 1, 1941.

41. Dill, D. B., H. T. Edwards and J. H. Talbott, Alkalosis and the Capacity for Work. *Journal of Biological Chemistry, 97:*lviii, July, 1932.

42. Denning, H., J. H. Talbott, H. T. Edwards and D. B. Dill, Effect of Acidosis and Alkalosis upon Capacity for Work. *Journal of Clinical Investigation, 9:*601–613, February, 1931.

43. Greenberg, David M. and Theodore Winnick, The Transformation in the Rat of Carboxyl-labeled Acetate, Methyl-labeled Acetate, and Labeled Bicarbonate in Amino Acid, *Archives of Biochemistry, 21:*166–176, March, 1949.

44. Melrose, A. G., Acute and Chronic Intoxication Due to Sodium Bicarbonate. *Scottish Medical Journal, 2:*301–303, July, 1957.

45. Chinn, Herman I., *Evaluation of Drugs Effective Against Motion Sickness.* Report No. 55–144. Air University, School of Aviation Medicine, USAF, Randolph AFB, Texas, October, 1955.

CHAPTER X

Strength Training for Athletics

When man competes against man, the stronger individual possesses an advantage. McCloy[1] has reported that men who score high in strength also score high in general athletic ability. Hence, one of the goals of the trainer is to increase the strength of his charges.

Factors in Strength

Strength may be defined as the ability of a muscle to exert force against a resistance. The ability to exert strength depends on the actions and interactions of such factors as:

1. The amount of muscle tissue. One group of kinesiologists[2] states that the strength of muscle is about 3.6 kg. per sq. cm. of cross section area; another group[3] studying analogous muscles states that muscle strength is about 10 kg. per sq. cm. of cross section area.

2. Body configuration. Lookabaugh[4] reported that there was a moderate relationship between total strength and skeletal build, but Tappen[5] found that skeletal proportions, such as shoulder

width, had little effect upon performance in the three Olympic lifts.

4. Muscle quality. Morris[3] has discussed the wide range of strength found in corresponding muscles in different individuals. Different muscles in a single individual may also vary in strength, even though their size is the same.

5. Muscle innervation. The strength of a muscular contraction is dependent upon the number of motor nerve fibers which are activated in the muscle and the rate of discharge of the motor impulses. The strength of a dynamic action is additionally dependent upon neuromuscular coordination.

6. Environmental stimuli. The cheering of spectators and team mates and other sensory stimuli raise the threshold of sensitivity to fatigue and reinforce nerve impulses to working muscles.[6]

7. Skill. Training increases the strength of movement by eliminating extraneous motions and reduces tension in antagonistic muscles and postural muscles.[7]

8. External leverage. The use of levers and other mechanical devices, such as the vaulting pole, the throwing hammer, bat and racket, enables the athlete to exert his strength more effectively.

9. Internal leverage. The strength of a muscular action is affected by the distance from the joint at which the muscle is inserted. The further the insertion from the joint, the greater is the mechanical power.

10. Neuromuscular conditioning. Neuromuscular adaptations which take place as a result of training are believed to include increased stimuli of the anterior horn cells and reduced resistance to the passage of impulses across the synapses in the neuromuscular junctions. Thus impulses are spread more readily and more muscle fibers are brought into action.[8]

11. Nutritive state of the muscle fibers. The quantity of phosphorus compounds, glycogen and other fuels of muscular action which are available for use may limit the amount of strength a muscle can display.

12. Tension of muscle. Other things being equal, a muscle exerts its greatest power when it functions at its greatest tension.[9] The body position which elongates the muscle to be activated is the most favorable.

13. Age. The peak of muscular strength is generally attained

during the 20-30 year age range. If training is continued past this age, strength can be maintained at a high level until old age.

Physiological Basis of Strength Training

Out of the foregoing factors influencing strength, the athlete may work to increase the amount of his muscle tissue, neuromuscular adaptations and skill. Information is lacking on the degree to which human skeletal muscle can be made to grow, how much will be retained after cessation of exercise, the best type of exercise to promote muscle growth or the effect of exercise on growth in general.[10]

It is generally agreed that strength increases when repetitive exercise is performed against heavy resistance and that the slope gradient of the training curve varies with the magnitude of the stress imposed, the frequency of the practice sessions and the duration of the overload effort. In one experiment subjects gained up to 161 per cent in strength working only 5 minutes a day for 10 days, using a heavy load. When the work load was reduced 75 per cent and the repetitions were quadrupled, no perceptible gain in strength was achieved.[11]

Neither physical play nor most sports activities adequately meet the need for reserve strength, endurance and flexibility,[12] and prior to World War II trainers of athletic teams were almost unanimously opposed to the use of progressive resistance exercises (weight training). They warned that weight training would make the athletes "muscle bound" and slow, and that it was inherently dangerous. During World War II many trainers served in the physical reconditioning units of the Armed Forces. Here they gained personal experience in the therapeutic applications of progressive resistance exercise, and saw its values for themselves. Since then careful studies[13, 14, 15, 16, 17] have allayed the fears that weight training was dangerous and would make a man slow. It is now generally accepted that an individual becomes "muscle bound" only when he consistently exercises one muscle or group of muscles in a fixed position which does not permit a complete range of motion, with the result that connective tissues in the muscles become adapted to this position and become shortened. Now that these fears have been discounted, many trainers have incorporated weight training into their programs for preparing athletes for football,[18] basketball,[19] track and field,[20] swimming and diving[21] and any other sport in which additional strength would be of advantage to the athlete.

Weight Training Exercises. Athletes inexperienced in progressive resistance exercises are apt to concentrate on those parts of their body which they consider to be underdeveloped and to ignore those which they believe are up to satisfactory standards. The beginner will achieve greater overall development by following a general body-building program for several months, and then adding extra exercises to develop the muscles which he feels are not responding to a satisfactory extent. Such a general body-building program might consist of the barbell exercises described below and illustrated in Figure 9.

1. Two arms press. The weight is taken to the chest, pushed to arms' length and then lowered to the chest again. The feet should be in line, a comfortable distance apart.

2. Two arms high pull up. The bar is held against the front of the thighs, palms in. It is then pulled up to the chin, elbows being raised as high as possible.

3. Two arms curl. The weight is held against the front of the thighs, palms out. The elbows are kept at the sides and are flexed so that the weight is brought to the shoulders.

4. Two arms reverse curl. Similar to the two arms curl, except that the palms are turned in.

5. Squat. The bar is taken on the shoulders, behind the neck. The lifter then squats, keeping his heels on the floor. It is not advisable to make more than a three-quarter squat since lower back soreness sometimes occurs as a result of full squats, and some coaches and trainers are convinced that full squats tend to stretch the ligaments around the knee joint thereby weakening them and predisposing the knee to injury.[22]

6. Heel raise. Following completion of the squats, the lifter retains the weight on his shoulders and raises the heels as high off the ground as possible. One-third of the repetitions are done with the toes pointing straight ahead, one-third while with toes out as far as possible and one-third with toes in as far as possible.

7. Bent arm pullover. The lifter lies supine on a bench, in a hook-lying position, with the weight held at the chest. Keeping his elbows bent, the lifter moves the weight back overhead and lowers it as far as possible, then pulls it back to his chest. The elbows must be kept pointing up—there is a natural tendency for them to go out to the

Figure 9. General weight training program. A1, Two Arms Press. A2, Two Arms Press. B1, Two Arms High Pull Up. B2, Two Arms High Pull Up. C1, Two Arms Curl. C2, Two Arms Curl.

Figure 9 (Continued). D1, Two Arms Reverse Curl. D2, Two Arms Reverse Curl. E1, Squat. E2, Squat. F1, Heel Raise. F2, Heel Raise.

Figure 9 (Continued).   G1, Bent Arm Pullover. G2, Bent Arm Pullover. H1, Dead Lift. H2, Dead Lift. I1, Bench Press. I2, Bench Press.

Figure 9 (Concluded). J¹, Press Off Back of Neck. J², Press Off Back of Neck. K¹, Rowing Motion. K², Rowing Motion. L¹, Wrestler's Bridge. L², Wrestler's Bridge.

sides. The back must be kept in contact with the bench and not allowed to arch.

8. Dead lift. The lifter picks the weight up and stands erect. Keeping his legs straight, he bends at the waist and lowers the weight until it is approximately two inches off the floor. He then returns to the erect position and contracts the upper back muscles, as if he were trying to pull the shoulders together. It is not advisable to attempt to touch the floor with the weight since, in the bending position, the strain is borne initially by the ligaments practically without assistance from the back muscles. The tension in this position is such that it actually causes injury or may stretch the ligaments and predispose to injury.[23]

9. Bench press. The lifter lies supine on a low bench, feet on the floor, weight at the chest. The weight is pushed to arms' length.

10. Press off the back of the neck. The lifter straddles the bench with the bar on his shoulders, behind his neck. The weight is then pushed to arms' length, being kept behind the gravital vertical line of the body.

11. Rowing motion. The lifter bends over at the waist, with the weight hanging down. It may then be brought to the chest with the arms kept out and in line with the shoulders, or it may be brought to the belt with the arms kept in and close to the sides.

12. Wrestler's bridge. Starting from a hook-lying position, the lifter rocks back on his head, lifting his buttocks and shoulders from the floor. As strength increases, a bar may be held at the chest while he bridges, or it may be pressed to arms' length simultaneously with the bridge.

With the addition of dumbbells and other equipment, infinite variations in this program may be developed. Most of the equipment used in weight training is very inexpensive, durable, or even can be constructed by the manual training department of the school or by the athletes themselves.[24]

Weight Training Regimen. There are numerous systems of training, all of which are based on the theory that the quickest way to physical development is the use of weights heavy enough so that only a few repetitions can be accomplished. The beginner will usually find it best to work out on Monday, Wednesday and Friday. He executes six consecutive repetitions of each arm exercise and 12 each of the back and leg exercises. Each Monday he adds a single repetition. After he has done 12 repetitions for the arms and 24 for the legs and back for a week, he adds additional weight and starts over with the original number of repetitions. The exercises are done slowly, with a rest period of about three minutes[25] between each set of repetitions.

The amount of weight to be used is to some extent a matter of trial and error, depending as it does upon the individual's endowment of the various factors which go to make up strength. The invariable rule is that the beginner starts with light weights. Most young men are able to start training in the two arm press by using a weight equivalent to one-fourth of their body weight, ten pounds less than this should be used in the curl, ten pounds more in the bench press and half their body weight in the back and leg exercises. But even these amounts may be too heavy for some. Within two weeks after the start of training the individual's sense of balance and coordination become adjusted and he suddenly finds himself able to handle a good deal more weight than that with which he started. Ordinarily the amounts used will need to be readjusted at that time, but thereafter he can remain on his schedule.

Ordinarily a weight training program is not attempted during the time that an athlete is in active training for a sport. The energy output demanded by two training programs is usually too high to be sustained and the athlete will become fatigued and will lose weight and strength instead of gaining them. At the same time it must be recognized that if progressive resistance exercises are practiced exclusively for some period, the movement patterns required in this activity may override those of a previously-learned sport and to some extent interfere with them. This may be prevented by the frequent practice of the sport movement patterns during the periods of weight training.

Weight Training Hazards and Benefits. The participants in certain sports develop characteristic postural abnormalities. These are functional adaptations and the trainer should consider the total situation very carefully before recommending exercises designed to "correct" them. Straightening the round shoulders of the basketball player or the boxer may result in an impairment of the individual's ability to shoot baskets or to punch. The slouched position of an athlete who "hangs from his ligaments" may not be esthetic, but it requires less energy to maintain than does an erect posture. Possession of a precious bit of extra energy by a single player may well be the difference between a game won or one lost.

Figure 10. Woman gymnast, illustrating retention of feminine characteristics following years of resistive exercise. (Photo furnished by George P. Nissen.)

Weight training exercises are as beneficial for women as they are for men and may be safely practiced without fear of developing bulging, unattractive muscles. The amount of weight which an average girl can handle at the start of a program of progressive resistance exercises is very low. Some may find that even the bar alone is too heavy in certain exercises. Such individuals will require a preliminary period of training in calisthenics before starting to train with weights.

Young women who utilize resistive exercises as a part of their preparation for athletics find that instead of developing a masculine physique as they may have feared, their figure is improved, as illustrated in Figure 10. Pectoral development improves the bust line, abdominal development the waist line and the leg exercises improve the hip line, the thighs and calves. As a result of weight training the feminine figure becomes lithe and vibrant.

An abundant, well-balanced diet is essential if the subject is to make satisfactory gains in muscular development while on a program of progressive resistance exercises. As was discussed in Chapter VII, proteins should be provided in the diet of the growing athlete in order to meet his demands for both energy and growth.

Due primarily to the influence of DeLorme, trainers now recognize that the development of muscular strength is the primary weapon in their unceasing fight against joint injuries. Muscles and ligaments are the stabilizers of joints. The amount of strength found sufficient for every day living is inadequate to meet the demands of the stresses imposed by athletics, especially in contact sports. The universal and constant use of the automobile has accentuated this inadequacy even more since it contributes to the insufficient development of strength in the legs, precisely where it is needed in most athletics.

It has been estimated that one-third of all high school and junior college football injuries requiring medical attention are injuries to the ankle or knee.[26] Ligaments once torn will not return to their original state without surgical intervention. If the ligaments are not treated the burden of stabilizing the joint falls almost entirely on the muscles and this is possible only if they are well developed.

Physiological Basis of Rehabilitative Exercise

The physiological mechanisms underlying the development of muscular strength and hypertrophy by means of progressive resistance exercises have been discussed elsewhere.[27, 28] The following principles for the development of strength embody those employed in therapeutic exercise:

1. Therapeutic exercise started as soon as complete range of motion is restored counteracts the debilitating effects of atrophy which commences as soon as muscles become inactive.

2. Exercise of one limb may produce an improvement in the performance of the unexercised contralateral limb.[29] This phenomenon is known as cross education. Cross education will not occur if the injured part is immobilized and thus prevented from developing the normal proprioceptive feedback to the central nervous system.[30]

3. Exercise of a particular pattern of movement, intensity, rate or duration produces training effects which are specific to that exercise alone.

4. Unless closely supervised, individuals tend to substitute other muscle groups for those they find inefficient or painful to use.

5. Substitution is reduced if the affected muscle is first worked primarily by itself and then in full coordination with its synergists.

6. Restoration of function depends upon restoration of muscle

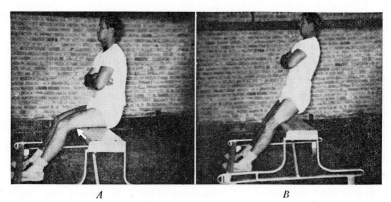

A   *B*

Figure 11. Bench technique for strengthening knee joint. *Instructions.* Subject sits on bench with the edge of the bench three to four inches above the popliteal space, as indicated by arrow in Figure 11*A*. Feet placed beneath adjustable bar. Trunk perpendicular. Subject forcefully straightens knees, raising buttocks from bench. Trunk remains perpendicular, as shown in Figure 11*B*. A backward lean increases the difficulty of the exercise. Body weight is supported by the bench at the point of contact with the posterior aspect of the thigh. (Klein, K. K.: Journal of the Association for Physical and Mental Rehabilitation, Vol. 10, 1956.)

strength, endurance and range of movement. Function may continue to improve after strength has ceased to increase, possibly resulting from an increase in the efficiency of use of available muscle strength. Functional improvement may be disappointing until coordination has been restored.

7. Corrective exercises are designed to increase the strength of weaker muscle groups, not to weaken opposing muscles.

8. Muscles grow larger and stronger only when required to perform tasks that place loads on them which are over and above previous requirements. This is the "overload principle," which is the rationale for all progressive resistance exercise systems.

9. Exercises in which muscles are made to contract slowly with maximal intensity, and in which the contraction is held for a few seconds* yield the greatest gains.

10. The daily progression of training may be hindered by continuing the exercise into exhaustion.

11. Muscular work may result in greater development if done to rhythm.

* Studies by Hettinger and Muller indicate that the primary stimulus for strength gains results from a brief sustained contraction. Erich A. Muller, The Regulation of Muscular Strength. *Journal of the Association for Physical and Mental Rehabilitation,* 11:41–47, March-April, 1957.

12. A heavy weight lifted a few repetitions will give greater strength gains than will a light weight lifted many repetitions, even though the total work load in each may be equivalent.

13. Endurance will be achieved more readily if endurance exercises are postponed until after strength has been regained.[31]

Developmental and Rehabilitative Exercises. Unfortunately, owing to limitations in time and equipment, there are serious difficulties in attempting to strengthen the muscles stabilizing the knee joints of an athletic squad by the use of weights. A "bench technique" of exercise, shown in Figure 11, has been developed by Klein[32] and is suitable for the use of large numbers of athletes at the same time.

Additional athletic exercises are shown in Figure 6. These may be referred to when special exercises are needed for the development of weak areas of the body, or for rehabilitation following injury.

REFERENCES

1. McCloy, Charles Harold and Norma Dorothy Young, *Tests and Measurements in Health and Physical Education,* Second Edition. New York: Appleton Century Crofts, Inc., 1954, p. 142.

2. Steindler, Arthur, *Kinesiology of the Human Body.* Springfield: Charles C Thomas, 1955, p. 47.

3. Morris, Carrie B., The Measurement of the Strength of Muscle Relative to the Cross Section. *Research Quarterly, 19:*295–303, December, 1948.

4. Lookabaugh, Guy, The Prediction of Total Potential Strength of Adult Males from Skeletal Build. *Research Quarterly, 8:*103–108, May, 1937.

5. Tappen, N. C., An Anthropometric and Constitutional Study of Championship Weight Lifters. *American Journal of Physical Anthropology, 8:*49–64, March, 1950.

6. Morehouse, Laurence E. and Augustus T. Miller, *Physiology of Exercise,* Second Edition. St. Louis: The C. V. Mosby Company, 1953, p. 231.

7. Morehouse, Laurence E. and John M. Cooper, *Kinesiology,* St. Louis: The C. V. Mosby Company, 1950, p. 211.

8. Darcus, H. D., Discussion on an Evaluation of the Methods of Increasing Muscle Strength. *Proceedings of the Royal Society of Medicine, 49:*999–1006, December, 1956.

9. Clarke, H. Harrison, Recent Advances in Measurement and Understanding of Volitional Muscular Strength. *Research Quarterly, 27:*263–275, October, 1956.

10. Tanner, J. N., The Effect of Weight-Training on Physique. *American Journal of Physical Anthropology, 10:*427–461, December, 1952.

11. Hellebrandt, F. A. and Sara Jane Houtz, Mechanisms of Muscle Training in Man. *Physical Therapy Review, 36:*1–13, June, 1956.

12. Morehouse, Laurence E., Unpublished paper, 1955.

13. DeLorme, Thomas L. and Arthur L. Watkins, *Progressive Resistance Exercise.* New York: Appleton Century Crofts, Inc., 1951.

14. Capen, Edward K., The Effect of Systematic Weight Training on Power, Strength and Endurance. *Research Quarterly, 21:*83–93, May, 1950.

15. Chui, Edward, The Effect of Systematic Weight Training on Athletic Power. *Research Quarterly, 21*:188–202, October, 1950.

16. Zorbas, William S. and Peter V. Karpovich, The Effect of Weightlifting Upon the Speed of Muscular Contractions, *Research Quarterly, 22*:145–148, May, 1951.

17. Karpovich, Peter V., Incidence of Injuries in Weight Lifting. *Iron Man, 11*:46–47, September-October, 1951.

18. Clausen, Dick, Weight Training for Football Players. *Athletic Journal,* XXXVI:22 *et seq.,* February, 1956.

19. O'Connor, Frank "Bucky" and Frank Sills, Heavy Resistance Exercises for Basketball Players. *Athletic Journal,* XXXVI:6 *et seq.,* June, 1956.

20. State, Oscar, *Weight Training for Athletics.* London: Amateur Athletic Association, n. d.

21. Armbruster, David A. and L. E. Morehouse, *Swimming and Diving.* St. Louis: The C. V. Mosby Company, 1950.

22. O'Keefe, Fred L., Early Conditioning for Football. *Athletic Journal,* XXVI:25–26, June, 1946.

23. Portnoy, Harold and F. Morin, Electromyographic Study of Postural Muscles in Various Positions and Movements. *American Journal of Physiology, 186*:122–126, July, 1956.

24. Rasch, Philip J. and Richard V. Freeman, Weight Training in a Neuro-psychiatric Hospital. *Journal of the Association for Physical and Mental Rehabilitation, 8*:146–151, September-October, 1954.

25. Clarke, H. Harrison, Clayton P. Shay and Donald K. Mathews, Strength Decrement of Elbow Flexor Muscles Following Exhaustive Exercise. *Archives of Physical Medicine and Rehabilitation, 35*:560–567, September, 1954.

26. *Minutes of Twenty-Fifth Meeting of National Federation and National Junior College Football Committee.* Chicago, January 3–4, 1957.

27. Rasch, Philip J. and Richard V. Freeman, The Physiology of Progressive Resistance Exercise: A Review. *Journal of the Association for Physical and Mental Rehabilitation, 8*:35–41, March-April, 1954.

28. Rasch, Philip J., The Problem of Muscle Hypertrophy: A Review. *Journal of the American Osteopathic Association, 54*:525–528, May, 1955.

29. Rasch, Philip J. and Laurence E. Morehouse, The Effect of Static and Dynamic Exercises on Muscular Strength and Hypertrophy. *Journal of Applied Physiology, 11*:29–34, July, 1957.

30. Rose, Donald L. and Ralph R. Beatty, Effect of Brief Maximal Exercise on the Quadriceps Femoris. *Archives of Physical Medicine and Rehabilitation, 38*:157–164, March, 1957.

31. Rasch, Philip J., Principles of Therapeutic Exercise. *Clinical Osteopathy, 50*:387–389, June, 1954.

32. Klein, Karl K., Specific Progressive Exercise as a Mass Technique for Preventive Conditioning and Reduction of Knee Injury Potential in Athletics. *Journal of the Association for Physical and Mental Rehabilitation, 10*:185–189, November-December, 1956.

CHAPTER XI

Massage

When an athlete suffers a blow or a strain, his automatic response is to rub the traumatized area. From this universal and instinctive reaction arose the art of massage. Galen, the first team physician, laid great stress upon its importance in athletic training. He wrote that massage before exercise opened the pores, liquified the excrements in the skin and softened the solids. The athlete was first rubbed with muslin and then with oil. The purpose of massage after exercise was to prevent and remove fatigue. The athlete, he said, should be wrapped in blankets to preserve his body heat and should be massaged quickly and gently, with liberal applications of oil. Galen cited the writings of Hippocrates (460–377 B.C.) as his authority.[1] The technique of massage today differs in no essential detail from that described by these ancient Greeks.

Scientific Studies of Massage

In spite of its long use, comparatively little of a scientific nature is known about the effects of massage. The conclusions to be drawn from the studies that have been reported in modern medical literature may be summarized as follows:

1. The initial response of the body to massage is an opening up of the capillaries and arterioles of the stimulated area. This occurs

either through stimulation of the sympathetic nervous system or through direct mechanical stimulation of the vessel walls. It may be followed by a contraction of these vessels.[2] Reflex contraction of the smooth muscle fibers in the walls of these vessels may assist in maintaining or restoring their tone.[3] Massage of skeletal muscles also serves to propel the lymph along the lymphatic channels.[4]

2. Massage produces an increase in the number of circulating red blood corpuscles and thus in the amount of hemoglobin in the peripheral capillaries. This is thought to be caused by the driving into the blood stream of a large number of erythrocytes which have been lying dormant, particularly in the splanchnic area.[2, 5, 6]

3. A local increase in the temperature of the massaged area occurs. Although friction may produce some heat, the rise in internal temperature is credited mainly to vaso-dilatation.[7] The duration of elevation of the temperature is less than that which occurs after direct heating.[8] Blood pressure and heart rate are not affected.[7]

4. Massage accelerates absorption of substances in the synovial fluid of the joints and in the intercellular fluids in the subcutaneous tissues. In experimental investigations, proteins injected into these fluids were removed through the lymphatics much faster when the injections were followed by massage.[9, 10]

5. It has not been possible to demonstrate that massage has any significant effect on metabolism. There may be an increased volume of urine after massage, but the total quantity excreted during a 24 hour period does not appear to be altered. Massage has no effect on the immediate or delayed oxygen consumption, pulse rate, hydrogen-ion concentration, carbon dioxide content, oxygen content, oxygen capacity, percentage oxygen saturation, inorganic phosphorus or lactic acid content of the venous blood, composition of the urine or rate of excretion of total nitrogen, sodium chloride, creatinine or creatine.[11, 12, 13]

6. Exercise is followed by the production of lactic acid. This cannot be produced by mechanical stimuli. This is the basis for the reasoning that massage may be superior to exercise in improving the circulation to relieve fatigue following exertion.[11] Opposed to this concept is the possible fuel value of the lactic acid in the fatigued muscles. Since four-fifths of this substance is available for reconversion into useful muscle sugar, it may be unwise to attempt to move this potential fuel from the very site at which it is most needed. Massage may be of some use in aiding an athlete to re-

cuperate from fatigue or certain types of injuries, but the physiological benefits derived will be local rather than systemic in nature.

Use of Massage in Muscle Spasms.   Storms[14] has contended that
all the circulatory benefits of massage can be accomplished more
readily by diathermy or exercise. Relief of muscle spasm is sometimes accomplished by light massage in a direction parallel to the
muscle fibers, with the force adjusted to the patient's tolerance.
However, this procedure is potentially injurious and massage is
stopped as soon as the spasm begins to soften. Continued irritation
by massage may cause it to reappear with even greater intensity.

Use of Pressure and Stretching in Muscle Spasms.   Relief of
spasm may be achieved by the application of direct pressure without
movement. This is often followed by immediate relief.[15] For example, relaxation of a cramped gastrocnemius may be obtained by

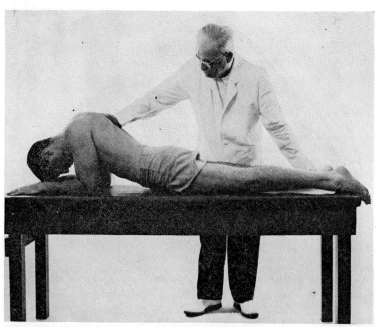

Figure 12.   Erector spinae longitudinal stretch. Subject prone, with shoulders
raised by placing humeri in vertical position. Cervical area relaxed by dropping
head forward. Operator grasps subject's near leg just above the ankle, other hand
against area of subject's back to be stretched. Pressure against thoracic, lumbar,
central or lateral position applies stretch to desired location. Operator applies
pressure gradually and gently by leaning forward, using the weight of his trunk
to apply elongation pressure.

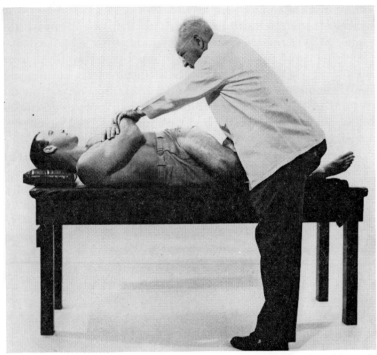

Figure 13. Erector spinae rotational stretch. Subject in relaxed position, with arms folded loosely across chest. Operator grasps behind the flexed knee and carries it to the opposite side of the table, leaving subject's ankle resting on shank of extended leg to serve as a fulcrum. Subject's shoulders are fixed against the table with a slight pressure. Operator stands with his knee on table for fixation. Rotational stretch of the erector spinae is achieved by application of a gentle downward pressure against subject's knee. Pressure is applied in a gradual and steady manner without a thrust.

pressing the thumbs forcefully into the belly of the muscle. Pressure is sustained for several seconds.

A gradual stretching of a muscle in spasm often relaxes the muscle and restores normal tone. Care is exercised not to overextend the contracted tissue, thus causing strain of the muscles. The use of stretching exercises involving momentum, therefore, is not indicated. The erector spinae muscles are often subject to spasm as a result of athletic movement. These are often difficult to relieve and require the assistance of the team physician. Two ways in which the physician may apply a stretching action to these muscles are illustrated in Figures 12 and 13.[16] Other techniques have been described by Bilik.[17] The advantageous leverage provided the operator in these techniques makes them a potentially injurious form of treatment in the hands of an unskilled individual, but they are of great value when used by a trained physician.

General Body Massage. In certain instances psychological benefits are derived from a general body massage. Aside from the reflex stimuli heretofore mentioned, the athlete may receive ego support from the masseur's exclusive attention during the massage. Because of its dubious benefits and the excessive time required to administer a general body massage, this procedure is not ordinarily considered to be a part of the busy trainer's duties.

Elementary Massage

The methods of massage used today are generally based on the techniques advocated by Hoffa,[18] McMillan[19] and Mennell,[3] as outlined by Tappan.[20] Massage can be divided into four main techniques: stroking (effleurage), compression (kneading, pétrissage), frictions, and percussion (topotement).

Stroking. Stroking consists of passing the hand slowly and rhythmically over an area of the body. This is performed in one direction only, and may be either light or deep. Its purpose is to restore or maintain the tone of the vasomotor system, and to assist the venous flow and the lymphatic circulation, thereby hastening the elimination of waste products.

Stroking is always performed centripetally. In order to make sure that there is no obstruction to the flow of the lymph from the site of the injury, the part of the body proximal to the injury is massaged first. This aids in emptying distended channels and prevents overloading when materials from the traumatized area are massaged into them. Mennell[3] has termed this the "removal of the cork from the bottle."

Compression. Compression is a kneading motion in which the muscles are pressed (vertical compression), rolled or squeezed (lateral compression) by the masseur to assist in the removal of waste products. Pressure is applied gently and with a circular motion, the hands usually working in opposite directions so that a wave-like compression movement flows through the limb. This type of massage is preceded by stroking. In squeezing, care must be used to avoid pinching the athlete's skin.

Frictions. Frictions are movements in which the masseur presses deeply on the part under treatment with the tips of the fingers, the thumb or the heel of the hand, and then makes circular movements.

It is designed to loosen scars, adhesions or other hardened tissues and to aid in the absorption of pathological deposits. Pressure should be gentle in order to avoid bruising or injuring the athlete.

Percussion.   Percussion is composed of a series of blows, usually administered by each hand alternately. It is used when the masseur desires to afford mechanical stimulation to a given area. The most common types are hacking, performed with the ulnar border of the hand, and cupping (clapping), in which the thumbs and fingers are partially flexed, so as to form a concave arch. These movements are done chiefly from the wrists, with the hands flexed only loosely. Movements which are too vigorous, too rigid or too protracted may bruise and injure the athlete.

The muscles in the part to be treated and the regions proximal to it are relaxed before massage is begun. It is almost impossible to increase the venous return if the lumina of the veins are reduced to a minimum by the contraction of the muscle tissue around them. The abdomen is relaxed in order to reduce intra-abdominal pressure on the flow of the blood from the femoral vein into the external iliac vein. The subject is placed in such a position that the force of gravity assists the massage in improving venous return.

Massage is contraindicated in cases of acute skin infections and ulcerations, acute inflammatory processes, acute infectious fevers, hemorrhage and dermatitis.

The masseur is immaculately clean and washes his hands in warm water before commencing massage. His finger nails are kept short and free from rough edges. Lubrication of the hands or of the surface to be massaged with powder, cream, alcohol, oil or some other substance is often desirable. Stroking "against the grain" of hair often proves disagreeable and it may be necessary to shave the part. The subject is kept warm, comfortable and relaxed during the entire massage.

Improperly done, massage may prove extremely fatiguing to the operator. Williams and Worthingham[21] have described techniques of body mechanics to perform the required movements in an efficient manner. The masseur uses a wide stance to provide a stable base of support for the forward and backward shift of his body in massage. The masseur takes advantage of the weight of his trunk in exerting pressure by standing close to the subject and by leaning forward and downward to transfer his weight through the arms to the hands.

REFERENCES

1. Galen, *De Sanitate Tuenda*. Translated by Robert Montraville Green. Springfield, Ill.: Charles C Thomas, 1951, pp. 72–107.
2. Carrier, E. B., Studies on the Physiology of Capillaries; V. The Reaction of the Human Skin Capillaries to Drugs and Other Stimuli. *American Journal of Physiology*, LXI:528–547, August, 1922.
3. Mennell, James B., *Physical Treatment by Movement, Manipulation and Massage*. Fifth Edition. Philadelphia: The Blakiston Company, 1945, pp. 5–53.
4. Best, Charles Herbert and Norman Burke Taylor, *The Physiological Basis of Medical Practice*. Sixth Edition. Baltimore: The Williams & Wilkins Company, 1955.
5. Mitchell, John W., The Effect of Massage on the Number and Haemoglobin Value of the Red Blood Cells. *American Journal of the Medical Sciences, 107*:502–515, May, 1894.
6. Schneider, Edward C. and Leon C. Havens, The Changes in the Content of Haemoglobin and Red Corpuscles in the Blood of Man at High Altitudes. *American Journal of Physiology*, XXXVI:380–397, March 1, 1915.
7. Kelso, Dorothy, Margaret Anne Fosse and Fae Henry, The Effect of Massage Upon Peripheral Circulation as Measured by Skin Temperature. *Research Quarterly, 5*:34–41, March, 1934.
8. Martin, Gordon M., *et al.*, Cutaneous Temperature of the Extremities of Normal Subjects and of Patients with Rheumatoid Arthritis. *Archives of Physical Medicine and Rehabilitation, 27*:665–682, November, 1946.
9. Lewis, Julian H., The Route and Rate of Absorption of Subcutaneously Injected Serum. *Journal of the American Medical Association, 76*:1142–1145, May 14, 1921.
10. Bauer, Walter, Charles L. Short and Granville A. Bennett, The Manner of Removal of Proteins from Normal Joints. *Journal of Experimental Medicine, 57*:419–433, March 1, 1933.
11. Pemberton, Ralph, F. A. Cajori and C. Y. Crouter, The Physiologic Effect of Massage. *Journal of the American Medical Association, 83*:1761–1763, November 29, 1924.
12. Cajori, F. A., C. Y. Crouter and Ralph Pemberton, The Physiologic Effect of Massage. *Archives of Internal Medicine, 39*:281–285, February, 1927.
13. Cuthbertson, David Paton, The Effect of Massage on the Metabolism of Normal Individuals. *Quarterly Journal of Medicine*, I(NS):387–400, July, 1932.
14. Storms, Harold D., Diagnostic and Therapeutic Massage. *Archives of Physical Therapy*, XXV:550–552, September, 1944.
15. Mennell, James B., *Manual Therapy*. Springfield, Ill.: Charles C Thomas, 1951, pp. 23–25.
16. Pritchard, W. W. W., Personal Communication.
17. Bilik, S. E., Essentials of Office Practice. *Medical Times, 84*:1180–1190, November, 1956.
18. Hoffa, Albert J., *Technic der Massage*. Third Edition. Stuttgart: Ferdinand Enke, 1900.
19. McMillan, Mary, *Massage and Therapeutic Exercise*. Third Edition. Philadelphia: W. B. Saunders Company, 1932.
20. Tappan, Frances M., Trends in Modern Massage Techniques. *Physical Therapy Review, 35*:560–566, October, 1955.
21. Williams, Marian and Catherine Worthingham, *Therapeutic Exercise for Body Alignment and Function*. Philadelphia: W. B. Saunders Company, 1957, p. 96.

CHAPTER XII

Reduction of Health Hazards in Athletics

Athletes are reputed to be hypochondriacs and almost super-stitious about their health[1] but, surprisingly, there is little knowl-edge of the health hazards to which they are exposed and the effect of strenuous physical exertion on their health. The only valid con-clusions that can be reached at present are that athletes with a heavy body build have a lower life expectancy than those with a lighter build, that even strenuous exercise will not damage a normal heart, and that the term "athletic heart" should be discarded, because studies of athletes[2, 3] and animal experimentation[4] generally fail to produce evidence of pathological changes in normal hearts as the result of strenuous exercise.

Illness and Longevity

Some athletes may tolerate infections poorly. This condition is considered to be related to a state of elevated metabolism due to excessive physical activity or to a depletion of the general reserve capacity as a result of over training.[5]

There is no scientific evidence that permanent harm results from the severe exertions of sport.[6] Studies of the longevity of college graduates indicate that the life span of athletes is about on a par with that of non-athletes, but that it is about two years shorter than that of the intellectuals who were non-athletes.[7] In part this may be due to the fact that the athlete typically is more adventurous and exposes himself to more hazards than do non-athletic intellectuals. The longevity studies reveal that a large percentage of former athletes die from some form of external violence.[8, 9]

There is nothing to indicate that those who participate in athletics are more healthy than are those who do not. Patty and Van Horn[10] observed 18,823 Indiana high school athletes and concluded that the incidence of illness among them was about the same as among non-athletes. Colds accounted for about 80 per cent of all illnesses among both athletes and non-athletes.

The period of time during which athletes may expect to give first-rate performance and the reasons which compel their retirement from competition have been the subjects of a Japanese investigation.[11] They found that the competitive life of their athletes ranged from eight years for field athletes to sixty-two years for fencers. Decline in physical fitness, disease and injury are the principal reasons which force athletes to abandon competition.

Injuries and Fatalities

Injuries must be anticipated in any form of maximal exertion, especially when it involves physical contact between individuals or when hard missiles are thrown or struck. Practically every sport carries with it some degree of risk, the type and nature of the injuries received being characteristic of the activity.[12] During the years 1918 to 1950 the largest number of fatal injuries among athletes in New York City were encountered in the following sports: baseball (43), football (22), boxing (21). Other individuals were killed when struck by cricket balls, golf balls and handballs. During the period 1949–1953 football accounted for 94 fatalities in the United States and at least 29 men were fatally injured in boxing.[13] Track, on the other hand, is almost free of fatalities. In twenty years of studying distance-runners, Robbins[14] learned of only two fatalities, one resulting from an occlusion of the left internal carotid artery and the other from virus hepatitis. Neither of these could have been averted by routine physical examinations.

Records maintained at Harvard[15] for nearly a quarter of a century show that the most common sports injuries are sprains, contusions, strains, fractures and dislocations, and inflammations and infections, in that order. Various other researchers or organizations periodically publish such data in the *Research Quarterly* and similar journals. *The Annual Survey of Football Fatalities* and the *Football Injuries Survey* submitted to the American Football Coaches Association* are the most elaborate examples of studies of this type. Similar data concerning high school football fatalities and injuries are reported by the Football Statistical Committee of the National Federation of State High School Athletic Associations.† Such reports often lead to modifications of the rules, equipment and facilities to increase safety in athletics.

The fact that even under such controls injury and death may occur during participation in athletics places a heavy obligation upon all individuals responsible for the welfare of the athlete. By careful study of fatality and accident surveys one may learn which accidents are the most likely to occur in a certain sport, how they occur and when they occur. This information may be employed as a guide in designing suitable playing areas, in providing proper medical examinations and attention, in utilizing proper protective equipment, selection of the most valuable conditioning routines, teaching of techniques of play which will help to offset the vulnerability of the human body to injury and in the supervising of practice sessions and competitions.

Responsibility

Two basic principles govern the treatment of injured athletes. First, a player must not be permitted to return to competition if this exposes him to more serious injury, with the danger of permanent sequelae. Second, a player must not be kept out of competition any longer than is necessary.[16] The obligation for implementing these principles is shared by four individuals: the team physician, the trainer, the coach and the athlete himself. If they are to work together efficiently and harmoniously, their separate duties and responsibilities must be clearly defined. These will vary to some extent in different local situations, but the following is offered as a general guide.

Team Physician. In order to make decisions regarding athletic fitness, the team physician needs to know not only the nature and

---

* Post Office Box 1083, Hanover, New Hampshire.
† 7 South Dearborn St., Chicago 3, Illinois.

extent of the injury or other defect, but also the physical demands of the athletic specialty in which the candidate is desirous of engaging. The responsibilities of the team physician include the following:[17]

1. Obtain a medical history and conduct a physical examination for each candidate for an athletic team. Accident prevention starts with the elimination of candidates who are physically or mentally unfit to participate in vigorous activities. Exclude from competition anyone with swollen glands, elevated temperature, dizziness, skin infection, anemia, cardiac defect, epilepsy or other similar disqualifying conditions. Individuals having defective vision, quiescent rheumatic heart disease or certain other minor defects may on occasion safely engage in some type of sports and may even play certain positions on an athletic team.[18] Since psychological trauma may occur in the youngster who is denied participation in sports, laboratory and other objective diagnostic procedures should be utilized to confirm doubtful clinical findings before disqualifying the candidate. Many athletes have performed well all of their lives in spite of organic defects. In these instances the defects did not impair function sufficiently to limit performance to a recognizable degree. Apparently training may compensate for localized or partial deficiencies by improving the functional scope of bodily responses which remain untapped in untrained subjects.[19]

2. Personally attend athletic events in which the injury hazard is high and personally treat any injuries.

3. Supervise the trainer in his administration of injury prevention, first aid and rehabilitation procedures. Although the trainer may render first aid in the absence of the physician, the assessment of the severity of the injury is made by the team physician.

4. Specifically instruct the trainer regarding the procedures to be followed in physical therapy, corrective therapy or other treatment to be given an injured player during the week.

5. Examine injured players and give written approval to the coach for their return to competition.

6. On request, counsel coach, trainer or player regarding conditioning, staleness, exercise, nutrition, protective equipment and similar matters.

Trainer. The trainer, who will be following the directions of the team physician, much of the time in the absence of the physician, requires certain technical skills and understandings regarding treatment procedures. His ability to conduct such procedures should be demonstrated to the satisfaction of the team physician. A trainer's responsibilities include the following:

1. Closely observe all members of athletic teams for symptoms which suggest referral to the team physician. Good performance in athletics does not give assurance that an athlete is in good health and should not be taken as a sign that the athlete is free from defects. Familiarization with a text on physical inspection[20] alerts the trainer to signs and symptoms of disorders which may otherwise be overlooked.

2. Administer first aid to injured players. Refer all injuries to the team physician. Some athletes, especially during the heat of competition are insensitive to injury. The following anecdotes illustrate the ability of certain athletes to transcend the limitations imposed by injuries:

a. An outstanding first-string quarterback suffered substantial fractures of two transverse processes of the lumbar spine on a Saturday afternoon game. On the following morning, after an overnight trip back to Ithaca, he limped painfully and slowly from the train. He was sent to the Infirmary, where he confidently stated to the doctor that "he would be ready for next Saturday's game." On the following day (Monday) he felt well enough to leave the Infirmary. On Tuesday he was seen jogging heavily and disjointedly around the field. On succeeding days he quarterbacked the team in practice, and, true to his word, on Saturday he was ready for the game, playing most of it with scarcely perceptible evidence of an injury-handicap.

b. A lineman after the fourth day of fall practice reported to the training room requesting that his hand be taped because of a "sprain." The trainer referred him to the team physician, who at once noted the obvious deformity of a fractured metacarpal with displacement. History revealed that the injury had, in fact, occurred ten days earlier in a baseball game, but that he hadn't paid any attention to it after its occurrence. He had to be persuaded to have a temporary cast applied.*

3. Use taping, bandaging and other protective techniques to prevent injuries or recurrence of injuries. Protective devices can sometimes be utilized which enable the player to compete without risking further damage to the injured part. The decision is made by the team physician whether an injured player utilizing such a device may compete.

4. Utilize techniques of corrective therapy and physical therapy, under the direction of the team physician, to restore injured players to competition as soon as possible.

* From Alexius Rachun, Some Guiding Principles in Handling Injuries of College Football Players. *Student Medicine*, 5:79–82, April, 1957.

5. Carry out instructions given by the team physician regarding routine procedures in the treatment of athletic injuries.

6. Maintain records of injuries, treatment given and outcome.

7. Supervise conditioning exercises, if desired by coach.

8. Maintain training quarters in an orderly and sanitary state. Care for any equipment in the quarters and see that supplies are on hand and are properly utilized.

9. See that first aid kit, stretchers, blankets or other equipment needed in case of an injury are at the scene of the competition.

10. Supervise and train student assistants.

11. See that measures designed to prevent the spread of athlete's foot or other infectious diseases are carried out.

12. Provide ego-support for the athletes.

Coach. Some years ago Savage *et al.*[21] complained that in many instances coaches sacrificed the health of their athletes in order to achieve victory. Unquestionably, such occurrences are much less common now than they were when that report was written. Coaches in general are thoroughly agreed that they must protect the health of the young men and women in their charge, not endanger it. The coach's responsibilities for the health of his athletes include the following:

1. Maintain control of the athletic squad at all times. See that sports are conducted only in suitable areas and under proper conditions. Prohibit all forms of horseplay or other activities which may result in needless injury. Insist that safety rules and regulations be followed. See that safety belts, head guards, face masks, mouth protectors, sliding pads, mats and other protective equipment are available and are utilized. Insist that spotters, life guards and other safety personnel are present when the services of such individuals are indicated.

2. Teach techniques, exercises and skills necessary to prevent accidents. Supervise or have the trainer supervise the administration of conditioning and warming-up exercises.

3. Closely observe members of an athletic squad during and after practice for conditions which indicate referral to the trainer or team physician.

4. Remove from the line-up any player who appears to be injured, excessively fatigued or not in satisfactory physical condition. Do not permit his return to practice or competition without the approval of the trainer or team physician.

5. Maintain and utilize weight chart for weight control and for indications of overwork, staleness or other undesirable conditions.

6. Insist on properly fitted equipment. See that players have proper protective clothing for cold or wet weather.

Player. To the athlete himself, making the team or winning his event may seem the most important thing in the world. While he may secretly be greatly concerned over his health, he may hesitate to bring this to the attention of the trainer or team physician for fear that it may result in his being forbidden to participate. Unfortunately, this attitude may result in a comparatively minor injury developing into a major one because of lack of proper care.

The player must face realistically the hazards of competition and when injured must accept pain as a part of total athletic experience. Through these episodes the athlete learns to minimize and to tolerate minor discomfort. However, the finest physician, trainer and coach cannot fully develop and protect an athlete unless he himself actively utilizes the resources mobilized for his benefit. The player's responsibilities include the following:

1. Obey all safety rules and regulations. Use prescribed ankle wraps, face masks, mouth protectors, head guards and other protective equipment.

2. Carry out conditioning or rehabilitation programs which are prescribed for him.

3. Report all injuries, no matter how minor, to the coach and trainer.

Principles of Safe Conduct in Athletics

Thomas Quigley,[22] Harvard team physician, has prepared a "Bill of Rights" for athletes. The athlete, he said, has the right to good coaching, good equipment and good medical care. Two points might be added: (1) these rights will prove valueless if the athlete does not cooperate to make them effective, and (2) careful organization and administration are required to insure implementation of the provisions of this bill.* It is helpful to all concerned if the athletic program is conducted within the framework of mutually acceptable operational principles. Such principles may be stated as a set of

* Some years ago it was estimated that 27 per cent of the athletic accidents among college women were preventable by better equipment controls and 29 per cent by better leadership. Among college men the figures were 10 per cent and 16 per cent respectively. Frank S. Lloyd, George G. Deaver and Floyd R. Eastwood, *Safety in Athletics.* Philadelphia: W. B. Saunders Company, 1939, p. 36.

regulations designed to insure the safe conduct of programs of sports competition:

1. Every prospective player is given a thorough medical examination prior to the first day of practice.

2. A sufficient conditioning period is required prior to competition or vigorous activities.

3. All players are thoroughly instructed in safety procedures and are required to observe them.

4. Fundamental skills are thoroughly learned before the athlete takes up more advanced movements.

5. Players are properly warmed up before being sent into a game.

6. In body contact sports, teams are matched on basis of size.

7. An injured player is immediately withdrawn from the game or practice, and is required to obtain the approval of the team physician before resuming participation.

8. The organization has a written policy regarding financial responsibility for injuries incurred in athletics. Provision is made to insure that all players, their parents or guardians as well as the coaching, training, medical and administrative staffs are thoroughly familiar with this policy.

9. Insurance is carried to provide adequate means for paying the medical and hospital care of injured athletes.

10. The length of practice sessions, the number of days between games and the total number of games played are restricted to prevent over-fatigue and injury.

Vigorous physical conditioning is a prerequisite to safe participation in sports. The pre-season training period devotes attention to exercises specifically designed to strengthen the muscle groups most liable to injury in that particular sport. The importance of developing strength in the muscles stabilizing the joints was discussed at some length in Chapter X. The proper selection of conditioning exercises, however, requires a careful consideration of their effects. In some instances exercises have been blamed for predisposing players to injury. Some students believe that full deep knee bends and "duck walks" stretch and weaken the knee ligaments.[23]

The kinesiological principles of the prevention of injury have been briefly listed by Wells.[24] Some of these principles may be profitably enlarged upon here.

Any joint is in danger of being injured if its motion is forced beyond its normal range. It is not the blow by itself that does the damage, but it is the position of the joint when the blow is received which is predisposing to the injury. The joints of the body should be used in such a way that the possibility of further action in either direction is always present. This has been termed the "factor of safety" by Goldthwait.[25]

Sudden or uncontrolled shifts of weight throw the weight of the part against the ligaments, stretching and weakening them. When a joint is to be subjected to a sudden change in motion, it should be protected by the controlled use of the opposing muscles. Athletes draw themselves together when about to receive a blow, come quickly to a stop or abruptly change direction.

When two runners of approximately equal weight collide, the one moving the faster generally suffers the least damage. The momentum of the faster man is greater and as a result the direction of his motion suffers the least change. Bones, muscles and ligaments may not be strong enough to withstand the stresses of abrupt changes in movement.

Contracted muscles are better able to resist forceful extension than are elongated muscles. At the same time they offer a greater factor of safety. In games where blocking and other forms of body contact are employed, the players should tense themselves before the impact. The idea that a drunk never gets hurt because he is relaxed is false. His threshold to pain is higher, therefore, he does not feel the hurt as sharply as does the unanesthetized individual.

The body should be in a flexed position when falling. This allows for more "give" when landing, a shorter drop and less momentum acquired in the fall. Landing should be made on the side of the thigh rather than on the ischia and coccyx. The head should be "pulled into the shoulders," and if possible the man should be rolling when he strikes the ground thus distributing his momentum over a larger area and attenuating the striking force.

Reaching with an extended arm to break a fall is particularly dangerous, because the entire force of the blow is received in an instant. This high peak force may result in a fracture at one of the weak points, usually the wrist or shoulder. If the arm is in a position of elevation above the shoulder, landing on it may cause the humerus to slip out of the joint through the triangular opening formed by the muscles beneath the armpit. In all falls the elbow should be kept below the level of the shoulder to prevent this type of dislocation. In sports in which falling is a hazard, injuries will be reduced if players are not permitted to compete until they have mastered the mechanics of falling properly. Students of judo are required to practice falling for weeks before they are allowed to engage in competition.

The danger of injury is lessened when an athlete is thoroughly warmed up, which increases the speed with which he is able to react. The possibility that the man may not be warmed up, and as a consequence may react slowly, underlies the football strategy of directing the play at a substitute lineman who newly appears on the field.[26] This may be the reason for the high incidence of fatalities (8.7 per cent) incurred by individuals who have been in a football game for less than five minutes. The only group incurring a higher incidence are players who have been in the game from 26 to 45 minutes, during which period 18.31 per cent of the fatalities occur.[27] Fatigue probably plays a large part in the occurrence of injuries during this time, but studies are needed to determine whether there were more injuries under the free substitution rule and its various modifications than under the restricted substitution rule of earlier years.

REFERENCES

1. Bannister, Roger, in Medical Aspects of Athletics. *British Medical Journal,* No. 4920:1026, April 23, 1955.
2. Editorial, The Health of Athletes. *Journal of the American Medical Association, 155:*1062, July 17, 1954.
3. Wolffe, Joseph B., The Heart of the Athlete. *Journal Lancet, 77:*76–78, March, 1957.
4. Rasch, Philip J. and Frederick Krieger, The Effect of Progressively Increased Exercise on Heart Size. *Journal of the American Osteopathic Association, 56:*286–288, January, 1957.
5. Ficarra, Bernard J., Intolerance of Athletes to Infection. *New York State Journal of Medicine, 52:*1036–1037, April 15, 1952.
6. Bannister, Roger, Stress and Sport. *The Practitioner, 172:*63–67, January, 1954.
7. Dublin, L. I., Longevity of College Athletes. Intercollegiate Association of Amateur Athletes of America, Bulletin No. 13, 1929.
8. Rook, Alan, An Investigation into the Longevity of Cambridge Sportsmen. *British Medical Journal,* No. 4865:773–777, April 3, 1954.
9. Schmid, L., How Long the Sportsmen Live. In *Sport and Health.* Oslo: Royal Norwegian Ministry of Education, 1952, pp. 100–109.
10. Patty, Willard Walter and Paris John Van Horn, The Health of High School Athletes. *Journal of Health & Physical Education, 6:*26 et seq., December, 1935.
11. Editorial, Sporting Life Spans. *Canadian Medical Association Journal, 70:*579, May, 1954.
12. Sport Injuries. *Triangle,* II:292–293, October, 1956.
13. Hazards in Competitive Athletics. Metropolitan Life Insurance Company

*Statistical Bulletin, 35:*1–3, June, 1954, and Fatal Injuries in Sports, *Ibid.,* *38:*8–10. April, 1957.

14. Robbins, Charles, Comment on Two Deaths After Races. *The Amateur Athlete, 26:*18 *et seq.,* June, 1955.
15. Thorndike, Augustus, *Athletic Injuries.* Philadelphia: Lea & Febiger, 1956, pp. 65–67.
16. Rachun, Alexius, Some Guiding Principles in Handling Injuries of College Football Players. *Student Medicine, 5:*79–82, April, 1957.
17. Novich, Max M., A Physician Looks at Athletics. *Journal of the American Medical Association, 161:*573–576, June 16, 1956.
18. Novich, Max M., Medicine in Sports. *Journal of the Newark Beth Israel Hospital,* VIII:33–43, January, 1957.
19. Jokl, Ernst, Syncope in Athletes. *Manpower,* V:8, March-September, 1947.
20. Morrison, Whitelaw Reid and Laurence B. Chenoweth, *Normal and Elementary Physical Diagnosis.* Fifth Edition. Philadelphia: Lea & Febiger, 1955.
21. Savage, Howard J., *et al., American College Athletics.* Bulletin No. 23. New York: The Carnegie Foundation for the Advancement of Teaching, 1929, p. 145.
22. Surgeon Outlines a 'Bill of Rights' for All Athletes. *Scope Weekly,* May 22, 1957.
23. O'Keefe, Fred L., Early Conditioning for Football. *Athletic Journal,* XXVI: 25–26, June, 1946.
24. Wells, Katharine F., *Kinesiology.* Second Edition. Philadelphia: W. B. Saunders Company, 1955, pp. 412–416.
25. Goldthwait, Joel E., *et al., Essentials of Body Mechanics in Health and Disease.* Fifth Edition. Philadelphia: J. B. Lippincott Company, 1952, pp. 33–37.
26. Rockne, Knute K., *Coaching.* New York: The Devin-Adair Co., 1925, p. 134.
27. Committee on Injuries and Fatalities, American Football Coaches Association, *The Twenty-Fifth Annual Survey of Football Fatalities, 1931–1956.* Hanover: American Football Coaches Association, January 7, 1957.

CHAPTER XIII

Athletic Hygiene and Care of Minor Injuries

The Athlete as a Patient

The injured athlete presents a different problem to the physician than does the patient ordinarily encountered in general practice. For the latter the physician may prescribe long periods of rest or extended periods of treatment. For the athlete, however, these periods must be considerably shortened. His career in competition is short. Every day lost from practice represents a loss in his physical condition and in the opportunity to develop his skills. Meanwhile his competitors are improving their own abilities, thereby widening the gap between them. Thus the team physician finds that he is dealing with a highly impatient individual, one who insists that he return to competition at the earliest possible moment and who is willing to risk permanent disability in order to do so. The importunings of the coach, the business manager, the alumni and others in the athlete's constellation to ready the player for active service in the next contest are difficult for even the most conscientious physician to resist.

Origins of Training Methods

Early in athletic history the trainer made his appearance as a specialist in the preparation of the athlete for competition and in

141

the care of the athlete's injuries. Today the legal aspects of his responsibilities in regard to the care which he gives an injured athlete are not always clear. If the trainer is certified in a related occupation, such as corrective therapy or physical therapy, his scope of legitimate application of therapeutic modalities is enlarged.

Working together, the trainers and the team physicians have developed methods of active rehabilitation, adhesive strappings, protective harnesses and of other devices and techniques which are common to the field of athletics. The methods presented in this chapter and Chapters XIV and XV were selected from those which are time-tested and familiar to experienced trainers, and which are believed to be best suited in aiding the athlete in returning to competition at the earliest possible moment and to protect him from further trauma while he is competing. Some of these methods are identified by the name of the individual who either originated or popularized their use. A selected bibliography of books and articles which contain source materials and descriptions of the methods shown in these chapters is included.

Because coaches and trainers are familiar with the material relating to artificial respiration, splinting, burns, sunstroke, heat exhaustion and kindred subjects covered by the Red Cross First Aid manual, it has been largely omitted from what follows.

Muscle Stiffness and Soreness

The athlete who is just beginning a season of training may find himself stiff or sore, or both, after a strenuous workout. Stiffness may persist after vigorous training even in highly conditioned athletes. It results from an acute local swelling of the working tissues, associated with the production of acid metabolites. This is the phenomenon to which weight trainers refer when they comment that a muscle has been "pumped up." The swelling may be great enough to interfere with movement and may last in some degree from a few minutes to two or three days after the exercise.

Stiffness may or may not be accompanied by soreness. Soreness may be due to minute ruptures in the muscle fibers and the connective tissues which surround them, to chemical irritation of the sensory nerve endings in the muscle fiber as a result of greater concentrations of lactic acid and other metabolites in the muscle, or to physical irritation of these nerves due to edema in the muscles. As training progresses the athlete is less likely to become sore after a vigorous workout because the connective tissue has become stronger and more elastic and other physiological modifications have provided for quicker removal of the products of fatigue.

Much discomfort can be avoided by beginning training at a rather low level of exertion and progressing to more severe levels by gradual stages. In addition, the experienced athlete warms up gradually and thoroughly before making any vigorous effort. Once he has finished his workout he puts on a sweat suit, a bathrobe or some other garment designed to protect him from chilling. A dry warm towel draped over the head and wrapped around the neck gives an added protection and it is almost invariably worn by professional boxers. The colder the weather, the more important it is for the athlete to warm up and to keep warm after his workout.

If he does become stiff, light stretching and mild rhythmic exercise will give relief, as the pumping action of the muscle contractions will aid in carrying the fluid from the working tissues. Massage may prove beneficial for the same reason, and many athletes massage the muscles of their arms and legs after a workout in an attempt to prevent stiffness. Hot baths, heat lamps or similar methods of improving circulation give relief to stiff muscles.

The athlete who suffers from soreness requires rest in order not to further damage the torn fibers. Heat and gentle massage of adjacent areas will aid in restoring normal function and in relieving irritation.

Care of the Feet

No athlete can function at maximal capacity if he is being borne by uncomfortable, aching feet. Proper foot care is basic to fielding a well-conditioned athletic team and constitutes one of the fundamental problems in athletic training.

Foot care starts with the selection of properly designed and fitted shoes and socks. The trainer should provide that every individual under his care is properly outfitted in this respect. If the team is operating on a limited budget, savings should be made in some other way than by the purchase of cheap, poorly made shoes. These will almost certainly lead to serious troubles.

Shoes which are too small may cause a tingling or numbness of the feet. This condition also occurs in cyclists who use a toe clip which is too small. Marathon runners and other distance athletes must remember that their feet may swell under the continued pounding to which they are subjected, and that shoes which are comfortably snug at the start of a race may be painfully tight before the finish. This is particularly apt to happen on hot days. Shoes which are too large or ill-fitting may cause blisters, calluses or other irritations.

In fitting shoes it is important to measure both feet in the standing position, since one foot is often a size or more larger than the other, and since many athletes have flexible feet which expand a size or more on weight bearing. When one foot is found to be larger than the other, it is better to fit the larger foot. In fitting the shoe the ball of the foot should coincide with the widest part of the shoe. Selection of a last which gives proper alignment and support to the foot assures normal foot function and freedom from discomfort and pain.

The feet must be kept clean by frequent washing with warm water and soap. They must be carefully dried, particularly between the toes, and dusted with talcum or fungicidal foot powder. The socks must be changed and washed frequently, so that they are kept clean, soft and pliable. Socks which shrink or which stretch out of shape must be discarded. Use of such socks can prove as damaging as the use of improperly fitted shoes.

The toe nails must be kept clean and cut short, since long toe nails may be bruised or torn during running. Cutting them straight across has been thought to prevent ingrowing toe nails.

If the feet are unduly tender, they may be toughened by the use of alum water baths, tincture of benzoin or any one of the several other skin tougheners.

Blisters. ETIOLOGY. Blisters of the feet and hands tend to occur routinely at the start of an athletic season. As a result of friction, the epidermis becomes separated from the dermis and the intervening space is filled with serum or blood.

CARE. The quickest way to get rid of blisters is to open them under sterile conditions and cut the overlying dead skin away from the blistered area. This area may then be painted with an antiseptic solution and covered with gauze firmly secured with tape. Some trainers paint the blistered area with tincture of benzoin. Blisters in themselves are not serious, but once opened they are liable to infection. An unhealed blistered area should be padded during practice and competition.

Calluses. ETIOLOGY. Calluses are thick horny layers of skin built up to protect the hand or foot against mechanical irritation. They commonly occur on the sides of the heel, the ball of the foot, the plantar surface of the great toe and over the distal ends of the metacarpals. The benefit of the callus is lost when it becomes torn or split and it must then be removed.

CARE. The foot may be first soaked in hot water to soften the calluses. The callused area may then be painted with an antiseptic solution and the callus shaved or scraped away with a sterile scalpel. The cause must be removed to prevent recurrence. If the shoes fit properly, the athlete should be observed for abnormalities of gait which may need correction.

Corns. ETIOLOGY. Like calluses, corns are a response to mechanical irritation, usually pressure from a shoe which is too tight in the toes. Hard corns ordinarily form on the dorsal surfaces of the toes or on the lateral aspect of the fifth toe. The outer horny layers of the skin are stimulated to an abnormal growth. This forms a cone-shaped mass which impinges on the small nerves in the body of the skin, producing pain. Soft corns are produced in the same manner, but form between the toes (usually between the fourth and fifth) where the greater amount of moisture present keeps the corn macerated and soft.

CARE. The first step is to remove the pressure which is causing the corn. The feet may then be soaked daily and the softened material on the top of a hard corn scraped off until the corn becomes level with the surrounding skin. Some trainers use sandpaper to level the corn. It may then be protected by the application of a piece of adhesive tape. An absorbent cotton pad may be used to separate toes which have a soft corn growing between them. The corn may then be painted with a salicylic acid solution and the dead surface material removed.

Epidermophytosis (Athlete's foot). ETIOLOGY. Poor foot hygiene, especially failure to dry between the toes after showering, is very apt to result in the appearance of a condition characterized by severe itching, minute blisters and scaling of the skin between the toes. This is popularly known as "athlete's foot," and may spread to the hands or other parts of the body. It is believed to result from the action of a fungus, possibly Trichophyton mentagrophytes. It is a matter of dispute whether this parasite is exogenous or is always present but does not become bothersome until the proper conditions exist in the host, and whether it is contagious or not.

CARE. Moisture between the toes seems to afford optimal conditions for the growth of this parasite. Care begins with proper drying of the feet, particularly between the toes, after washing. At the first signs of athlete's foot the infected areas may be coated with Whitfield's ointment, 1 per cent methylene blue alcoholic solution or some other fungicide. This treatment is continued daily until the condition disappears. It is, however, likely to reappear at any time. The socks should be boiled to prevent possible spread of the disease. The use of mats of any kind on the floors of dressing rooms is undesirable, since these may become contaminated and are hard to disinfect, whereas cement floors can be washed down at any time. The use of foot baths for the prevention of athlete's foot is of dubious value.

Bunion. ETIOLOGY. Bunions result from wearing shoes or socks which are too short or pointed toe shoes which restrict toe action. The great toe becomes deviated outward toward the little toe, the bursa at the base of the toe becomes swollen, inflamed and painful. The soft tissue may then become calcified, causing malalignment of the great toe and its metatarsal bone.

CARE. Care begins with the removal of the cause of the pressure. During the stage of acute pain it may be necessary to cut away the sides of the shoe covering the bunion. In the early stages a felt pad placed between the great toe and its neighbor may assist the great toe to straighten out. After the bursae have become calcified and malalignment has resulted, surgical intervention may be indicated.

Ingrown Toe Nail. ETIOLOGY. Shoes which are too short, socks which are too tight or improper trimming of the toe nails may cause the nail to grow into the flesh of the toe. If the athlete cuts off the corner of the nail, the situation becomes worse since the flesh in front of the nail folds back and over it, so that the nail grows into the tissue.

CARE. In mild cases the toe may be soaked in hot water for 30 minutes. The buried edge may then be lifted and a small wad of absorbent cotton which has been dipped in an antiseptic solution may be forced under the nail to protect the tissue from it. This treatment must be repeated regularly until the nail grows out over the flesh. In acute cases inflammation and severe pain result. This situation can be remedied only by surgical means.

Soccer Ankle. ETIOLOGY. The athlete complains of pain at the attachment of the ankle joint capsule along the tibial margin and the neck of the astragalus. This is probably due to osseous outgrowths in that area as a result of repeated minor strain of the capsular attachments and of repeated compression injuries of the bones against each other when the ankle is forcibly dorsiflexed or plantarflexed. The condition is especially common among soccer players, but is also found in gymnasts.

CARE. Conservative treatment, consisting of immobilization of the foot, heat and whirlpool baths, may be tried. It is doubtful whether the condition can be helped if the athlete continues to participate in his sport during medical treatment.

Tennis Heel (Stone bruise, pounded heel). ETIOLOGY. This condition results from trauma caused by the unaccustomed use of the feet on hard surfaces. The lesion occurs at the posterior insertion of the plantar fascia and the plantar muscles into the anterior edge of the calcanean tubercles, usually the medial one.

CARE. Use of a sponge rubber pad under the heel, raising the heels of the shoes from a quarter to a half inch or the use of thick rubber heels on the shoes may prove beneficial. The sponge rubber heel pad is trimmed in an elongated wedge shape at the anterior portion to avoid a concentration of pressure. Adhesive strapping to support the longitudinal arch and to relieve the tension on the plantar surfaces may afford relief of symptoms but does not affect the duration of the disability. A bruise of this type is actually a "charley horse" and may be treated accordingly.

Foot Examination. Foot injury occurs in a number of forms and the athlete has difficulty in distinguishing among them. He may complain that his foot hurts, that he feels a pain on weight bearing or it may be observed that he walks with a limp. In examining the injured foot, the trainer compares it in all aspects with the uninjured one to detect abnormal appearance or mobility. Using caution and gentleness, he grasps the heel to detect tenderness of the calcaneus at the periphery and on its plantar surface. Tenderness at the periphery is suggestive of bursitis or a calcaneal spur, tenderness at the plantar surface indicates a stone bruise, or periostitis. Next, the trainer examines for tenderness, indicating strain, sprain or fracture, at the longitudinal arch, the outer border of the foot, the metatarsal arch and at each toe. Dorsiflexion of the foot will bring the extensor tendons into prominence and aid in determining the presence of edema of the foot. If any of the above signs are elicited, or if the complaint persists, the attention of the team physician is secured.

Skin Care, Abrasions, Incisions and Punctures

Adhesive Strapping. Application of adhesive strapping is preceded by two preparatory steps designed to avoid discomfort for the athlete.

1. The part of the body to be strapped is shaved, carefully avoiding any razor nicks to the skin.
2. The skin is then washed and dried. Alcohol or tincture of benzoin is applied and this is allowed to dry before applying tape.

In applying a tight strapping care must be exercised not to exceed the athlete's tolerance, for if he finds it uncomfortable he will likely remove it and leave himself unprotected.

To minimize discomfort in removing tape, the adhesive is pulled off parallel to the body surface, with the tape back to back, and not at a right angle. After the tape has been removed a light massage over the area will stimulate circulation. The skin must be washed with soap and water before another strapping is applied.

Occasionally a trainer will find an athlete who is allergic to adhesive tape and whose skin breaks out in a rash when it is applied. This may be treated by application of a bland antiseptic ointment. It may be necessary to apply a gauze bandage to the injured part and then tape over it. This will not give as strong a support as will tape applied directly to the skin, but it may be the only means of strapping an athlete who is allergic to adhesive.

Tearing Tape. The roll of tape is held in the palm of one hand and the tape is gripped by the thumb and index finger near the roll. The free end is draped over the index finger of the opposite hand and is held in place by the thumb, the thumbs of the two hands being placed close together to prevent wrinkling of the tape. The hand holding the roll is then snapped away from the trainer, while the other hand is held firm to resist this movement. This technique is illustrated in Figure 14.

Gym Itch. ETIOLOGY. There are two types of gym itch. One is a simple dermatitis due to chafing between skin surfaces or between the skin and tight clothing. It usually appears in the genital regions or the axilla in the form of a red rash. Failure to dry properly the affected parts after showering, or excessive sweating aggravates the condition. The second type is caused by a species of ringworm (Tinea cruris). The parasite burrows into the skin and forms reddish, scaly patches which tend to spread. Ringworm is highly contagious.

CARE. In the case of dermatitis the inflamed skin should be carefully dried and coated with a bland antibiotic ointment. A pad may be placed between the two folds of skin to prevent further irritation. If the trouble is caused by a uniform which fits too tightly, a larger size must be obtained. The ringworm may be treated by application of Whitfield's ointment, one-half strength.

Boils. ETIOLOGY. Boils are infections caused when some break in the skin permits staphylococci to enter the tissues. They typically occur around a hair follicle. A painful, red, conical mass rises on the skin. In a few days the center turns yellow, owing to an accumulation of pus. These infections are especially common among wrestlers, very frequently occurring on the back of the neck where the skin has been scratched by their opponents' fingernails, and among football players whose necks have been irritated by shoulder pads.

CARE. Hot poultices may be applied to assist in drawing the boil to a head. Antibiotic ointment may be applied and covered with gauze and tape. The trainer should make no effort to open the boil before it has come to a head. At that time the surrounding skin may be cleansed with an antiseptic, an incision made over the head of the boil and the core carefully removed with a pair of sterile tweezers. Any attempt to squeeze the core out may rupture the capsule in which it is enclosed and permit the organisms to spread into the blood stream. The team physician may instruct the trainer in the

Figure 14. Technique for tearing adhesive tape. See text for description.

use of ethyl chloride spray to lessen the pain during the removal of the core. There is danger of a boil cavity healing over while infectious material remains within it. A dressing of antibiotic ointment will aid in preventing this.

Cellulitis.   ETIOLOGY.   Cellulitis is a generalized term implying an inflammation of the subcutaneous tissues. It appears as a flat, red, painful swelling.

CARE.   Athletes showing signs of cellulitis must be referred to the team physician. Cold packs may be applied until he is able to give it his attention.

Lime Burns.   ETIOLOGY.   Unslaked lime, a caustic substance, is occasionally used by mistake on athletic fields. It produces burns when brought into contact with skin wet with perspiration.

CARE.   Lime burns on the body should be washed with soapy water or with boric acid solution and coated with a bland ointment. If lime gets into the eye, the eye must be irrigated with pure distilled water until all particles of this substance have been removed. An application of ophthalmic antibiotic ointment furnished by the physician may then be placed in the eye.

Miliaria (Prickly heat).   ETIOLOGY.   Athletes engaged in strenuous training during warm seasons of the year may suffer from prickly heat. When the free flow of excretory sweat to the surface is impeded by the plugging up of the distal sweat pore, degeneration of the epidermal sweat-duct unit results. This appears as an itching, reddish area, usually located where shoulder pads or some other piece of protective equipment caused excessive sweating and chafing of the skin.

CARE.   The body may be dusted with talcum powder before practice and washed off with alcohol following practice. The condition will usually disappear as soon as the weather turns cooler.

CHAPTER XIV

Athletic Strains
and Contusions

Mechanics and Physiology

A strain is an over-stretching or rupture of a muscle or tendon, resulting from an external force or from a temporary imbalance between the force exerted by a muscle and the amount of relaxation of the antagonist. In the latter instance it is the working muscle which suffers the injury. Trauma of this type frequently occurs when the athlete is making a supreme effort without having properly warmed up. Trainers ordinarily refer to such injuries as "pulled muscles." The muscle fibers are actually torn, and herniation may occur. This results in damage to the capillaries, with a consequent hemorrhage and the formation of hematoma. Certain strains are typical of given activities.

Strains are usually accompanied by severe pain and an immediate loss of function in the muscle involved. Injuries of this type often prove extremely difficult to manage satisfactorily. In healing the torn muscle tissue is replaced with weaker fibrous scar tissue which is prone to further injury. Fear of this may result in psychological inhibitions which prevent the athlete from making maximal efforts.

First Aid. The general treatment for muscle strains is similar to that employed for contusions. Compression bandages and cold are first applied in an attempt to limit the amount of hemorrhage and consequent formation of hematoma. If the strain has taken place in one of the deeper muscles, this treatment may not prove sufficient, since the cold and pressure may fail to penetrate to that level.

Rehabilitation. Conservative treatment consists of complete rest to afford the torn fibers an opportunity to heal. If the rupture is complete, surgical intervention will be necessary. Heat is helpful during recovery, and diathermy may be employed by the team physician to reach deep muscles. If massage is used at all, it should be very gentle. The athlete is forbidden to place any strain on the muscle until it is certain that healing is complete. When possible, the limb is protected against further injury by appropriate adhesive strapping.

In complete contrast to this procedure is the active treatment endorsed by certain British physicians. Assuming a thigh injury, they recommend that the athlete be walked around until the spasm has worn off and that he then be persuaded to trot. The following morning he is made to take a gentle run, raising this to three-quarter speed in the evening. On the fourth day he resumes running at full speed. No strapping of any kind is permitted. The literature does not contain a sufficient number of reports on the effects of this form of treatment to permit an evaluation of this procedure.

In the following paragraphs care of strains typical of common athletic injuries will be briefly discussed. It will be assumed that first aid in the form of compression bandages and cold packs has been rendered, and that this will be followed by conservative rehabilitation procedures.

Tennis Leg. ETIOLOGY. This injury usually occurs when a tennis or basketball player suddenly twists or stretches his body while his legs are in an extended position. There is some disagreement as to the actual site of the lesion. Some writers believe that it is a rupture of the plantaris muscle alone while others believe that the gastrocnemius and soleus muscles may also be involved. All of these muscles serve as heel raisers. Hard nodules may sometimes be felt in the calf as a result of this injury.

CARE. After a twenty-four hour period has elapsed, the injured part may be given light massage and whirlpool treatment. The athlete should be encouraged to walk, even though this causes some pain. Adhesive strapping of the type shown in Figure 15 may give relief.

Sprinter's Strain. ETIOLOGY. Powerful contraction of the quadriceps and failure of the leg flexors to relax quickly enough or sufficiently may result in a strain of the hamstring muscles, usually the semitendinosus or the semimembranosus. This injury usually occurs during sprinting and the runner may drop to the track.

CARE. Following the application of heat and rest, an adhesive strapping as shown in Figure 16 may be applied. A ½ inch felt pad in the heel of the shoe will give additional relief.

High Jumper's Strain. ETIOLOGY. Certain styles of high jumping require the jumper to twist one leg and to rotate the body, placing a strain on the outward rotators of the thigh which originate from the pelvic bones and are attached to the femur.

CARE. Because this is an injury to deep muscles, there is little protection afforded by adhesive strapping. Diathermy may prove useful, but the principal treatment consists of rest from any form of twisting or rotating of the muscles involved. Recovery may require several weeks.

Groin Strain (Rider's strain). ETIOLOGY. Horse riders contract the adductor muscles of the femur in order to keep their seat. If the rider becomes unbalanced or is thrown, these muscles may be

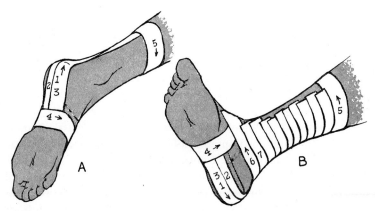

Figure 15. Adhesive strapping for tennis leg. *A,* Athlete is placed in prone position. Three two-inch strips of adhesive tape (Nos. 1–3) are pulled up over heel to back of lower calf. Tape is molded at sides of Achilles tendon. Two-inch anchors (Nos. 4–5) are applied at lower and upper ends. *B,* Athlete turns to supine position and one and one-half inch strips of tape (Nos. 6–16) are successively applied parallel to sole of foot. These overlap about one-half. Wrinkling is avoided.

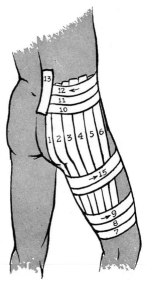

Figure 16. Adhesive strapping for sprinter's strain. Player stands with knee of injured leg in slight flexion. Six strips of two- or three-inch tape are placed just above the back of the knee and pulled upward to the level of the crest of the ilium (Nos. 1–6). Lower ends of straps are anchored (Nos. 7–9). Strips Nos. 10–12 are fastened forward of the hip and pulled to midback. These are anchored at each end by vertical strips, as No. 13. Strips 14 and 15 are applied to prevent tape from loosening and are put on loosely to avoid interference with neural and circulatory functions.

strained. Similar injuries may be suffered in vaulting over the long horse, in landing on the parallel bars in the cross riding seat position or in slipping while running on an athletic field.

CARE. Usually this injury is not too severe and the muscle will return to normal within a week. A wrapping for injuries of this type is illustrated in Figure 17. A spica wrap using elastic bandage applied in the same position will hold a heated analgesic balm pack in place, as described under Contusions.

Lower Back Strain. ETIOLOGY. Lower back strains generally result from a twist or from requiring a sudden effort from the lower back muscles. They commonly occur among weight lifters and generally result from improper technique in lifting or from failure to warm up properly before starting to lift. The individual will complain that if he bends forward he experiences great pain on attempting to come erect. If placed on his back, he will find it painful to attempt to raise the extended leg, with the pain greater on the side which is the more affected.

CARE. These injuries are very slow to heal and the athlete may be incapacitated for a month. During the first 24 hours after injury an ice bag may be applied to the site of the pain for fifteen minutes during every hour. Thereafter heat is helpful and is best administered by use of a Sitz-bath. Immobilization of the back will give considerable relief. For this purpose an adhesive strapping as shown in Figure 18 is useful. The victim will find that there is no position in which he can lie down in comfort, but that a firm mattress is less uncomfortable than is a soft one since it supports the body in an elongated position. A board may be placed under the mattress to

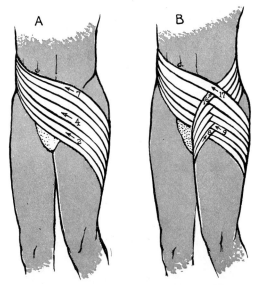

Figure 17. Adhesive strapping and elastic wrapping for groin strain. *A*, Player stands with injured leg slightly flexed at hip and knee, thigh rotated inward. Genitals and pubic hair covered by 12-inch square piece of Canton flannel. Seven overlapping strips of two-inch tape (Nos. 1–7) are applied, starting at the rear of the thigh, and pulled around the outside of the thigh, upward across the front of the thigh, over the pubic pad, across the opposite hip, and finished past the middle of the back. This aids in maintaining internal rotation, thus reducing movement of the adductor muscles of the thigh. *B*, Ten additional overlapping strips of two-inch tape (Nos. 8–17) are started from the back of the thigh and the first is pulled around the inside of the thigh, upward around the hip, finishing on top of the first layer. The next strip is started around the outside of the thigh, and the ten overlapping strips are thus alternated.

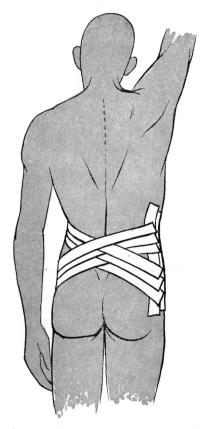

Figure 18. Adhesive strapping for lower back injury. Player stands with arm raised. Two vertical overlapping strips of two-inch tape are applied to the player's sides to serve as a base. Diagonal strips of two-inch tape are applied in an overlapping basket-weave manner. This strapping permits forward and backward movement of the trunk, but restricts lateral and rotatory movement. An anchoring strip may be applied over the ends of the diagonal tape.

prevent it from sagging. Many weight lifters wear a wide fitted belt when they resume training.

Rib Strain. ETIOLOGY. A twisting of the torso while the pelvis is held firm, as in the guillotine hold in wrestling, may cause strains of the intercostal muscles. They may also be injured by trauma, as in football.

CARE. These injuries are painful on movement, but are seldom serious. Treatment consists primarily of immobilization of the ribs.

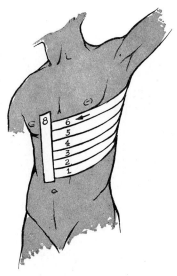

Figure 19. Adhesive strapping for rib strain. Player stands with arm raised. Overlapping two-inch strips (Nos. 1–6) are applied with firm pressure from rear to front, following the contour of the ribs, covering the affected area and crossing the midline of the spine and the chest to immobilize the ribs. Ends of the tape are covered with an anchor strip (No. 7).

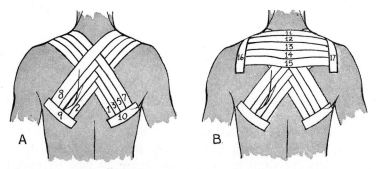

Figure 20. Adhesive strapping for trapezius strain. *A,* Overlapping strips of two-inch tape (Nos. 1–8) are placed diagonally from beneath the shoulder blade to the top of the opposite shoulder in basket-weave fashion to decrease the mobility of the upper back. Lower ends are anchored by strips Nos. 9 and 10. *B,* Horizontal strips of two-inch tape (Nos. 11–15), serving both as anchors for the upper ends and for further immobilization, are applied from the base of the neck downward in overlapping manner. These horizontal strips are also anchored (Nos. 16–17).

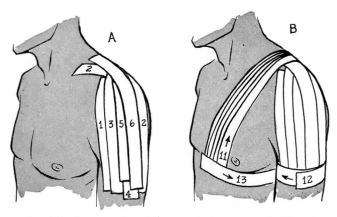

Figure 21. Adhesive strapping for supraspinatus strain. *A,* The player holds his upper arm tightly to his side. A strip of two-inch tape (No. 1) is placed anteriorally at mid-biceps and applied with firm tension upward over the shoulder, pulling the upper arm toward the upper torso to support the weight of the arm. Strip No. 2 is attached slightly posterior to the upper arm in the same manner and is finished anterior to the shoulder. Strips 3 and 4 are placed medially and overlapping Strips 1 and 2. Strips 5 and 6 are pulled straight upward and inward toward the neck. *B,* Overlapping strips (Nos. 7–11) are pulled upward from the chest and are continued over the shoulder to the middle of the back. Anchor (No. 12) is applied in a loose manner so as not to restrict circulation in the arm. Anchor 13 is applied below the nipple.

For this purpose adhesive strapping of the type depicted in Figure 19 is helpful.

Trapezius Strain. ETIOLOGY. Wrestlers frequently complain of a "stiff neck." The head is usually turned to one side and severe pain results when attempts are made to move it. The injury ordinarily results from overflexion of the neck, as in resisting a Nelson hold. It may also occur to gymnasts who fail to tuck their head in properly when doing a forward roll.

CARE. These injuries are best treated by the application of heat using an analgesic pack, and by rest until function is regained. The type of adhesive strapping shown in Figure 20 may be used to decrease motion and minimize pain. This same strapping may be used for almost any other strain of the muscles of the upper back. These upper back strains are often annoying, but seldom serious.

Supraspinatus Strain. ETIOLOGY. Strains of the supraspinatus result from forced abduction and from blows to the tip of the shoulder. They are fairly common in weight lifting and football.

CARE. In acute strains the arm may have to be placed in a sling to relieve the muscle from its weight. Routine care consists of diathermy and gentle massage. The muscle may be supported by an adhesive strapping such as is shown in Figure 21.

Anterior Deltoid Strains. ETIOLOGY. Anterior deltoid strains frequently occur in boxers and fencers, both sports in which this muscle must function to keep the arm extended in resistance to blows from an opponent. It may also be injured in somewhat the same way in football or other body contact sports. Localization of the pain makes the site of the injury easy to determine.

CARE. The treatment of this muscle and the manner of strapping it are the same as is used in supraspinatus strains.

Glass Arm. ETIOLOGY. Two theories have been advanced to explain the syndrome known as "glass arm": (1) It is an irritation of the tendon of the long head of the biceps or of the thecal tunnel through which the tendon descends, caused by whipping the tendon against the outer border of the tunnel; (2) it is a strain of the insertions in the humerus of the teres major and minor muscles and a setting up of a myositis or irritative lesion locally, which is aggravated by constant use. This injury often occurs among baseball pitchers in throwing "roundhouse" out-curves which produce irritation and pain felt in front of the shoulder about two inches below the head of the humerus.

REHABILITATION. No effective method of repairing this injury has yet been developed. Absolute rest, heat and daily massage, followed by very gradual throwing exercises may be employed. At the first sign of the "glass arm" syndrome the pitcher must modify his method of throwing to prevent debilitating injury.

Epicondylitis Humeri (Tennis elbow, pitcher's elbow, fencer's elbow). ETIOLOGY. From the standpoint of athletics injuries, epicondylitis humeri is a syndrome characterized by pain over the distal end of the anterior surface of the lateral condyle of the humerus. Gripping or resisted movements of the wrist accentuate the pain and cause it to radiate down the forearm to the wrist and hand. Carrying a weight or palpation around the elbow may also cause pain. Weakness results and the athlete may complain that he is suffering from "neuralgia" or "rheumatism" in his arm.

This syndrome is common in tennis, badminton and squash players, boxers, fencers, golfers, polo players and baseball pitchers. It appears to result from the repeated forceful pronation and supination of the extended arm required in these activities. There is no general agreement as to the pathology involved and more than a score of theories have been advanced. It is clear that various types of trauma have been lumped under this heading. Perhaps the most common form of injury is a tear between the tendinous origin of the extensor carpi radialis brevis and communis and the periosteum of the lateral epicondyle.

care.   Rest is important in the care of this injury. The condition will normally disappear after six to nine months of rest from the movements which cause pain. In severe cases a cock-up splint or other form of immobilization may be utilized. Rehabilitation procedures will depend largely upon the team physician's opinion of the type of injury suffered. Heat, manipulation, massage, diathermy, electrical stimulation, ultrasonics, immobilization and surgery have been used with varying degrees of success. Strapping the upper third of the forearm to restrict contraction of the radial extensors ordinarily gives relief. When the player returns to the team the coach should make a careful analysis of the way he uses his racket or club or throws the ball, since a contributing cause to this disability may be an unnecessary strain placed on the elbow by improper movements or by the use of a racket the handle of which is the wrong size. Most often the handle will be found to be too large for the player to grasp comfortably.

Tenosynovitis (Peritendinitis crepitans).   etiology.   This condition is an inflammation of a tendon and its sheath. It usually occurs in the toes, feet and ankles as well as in fingers, hands and wrists. The chief complaint is one of pain on movement of the affected muscles. Swelling may be present and crepitation may result from voluntary movement of the muscles.

care.   Treatment consists of rest and heat. Excellent results have been reported from the use of diathermy three or four times daily.

Cramps.   etiology.   A cramp is a spasm of a muscle, usually of the foot, calf or thigh, due to an incoordinated muscular movement or to the muscle being subjected to exposure to heat or cold. Cramps may also result from dietary deficiencies, particularly of calcium, sodium, vitamin B_1 and salt.

care.   Muscle spasm may be relieved by applying pressure or a stretching action. Attention must be given to the diet so that missing elements are supplied.

Stitch in the Side.   etiology.   A stitch in the side is a spasm similar to a cramp. The cause is not fully understood. It has been variously attributed to excessive demands upon the diaphragm by untrained runners, overeating, insufficient abdominal development to support the viscera and constipation.

CARE. A stitch can sometimes be relieved by stretching, squeezing or kneading the affected part. Attention to training, exercise of the abdominal muscles and proper dietary habits may prove successful in eliminating the cause of this disability.

Muscle Contusions (Charley horse). ETIOLOGY. A direct severe blow to a muscle or organ causes a contusion. The capillaries in the area are torn and there is an immediate hemorrhage into the surrounding tissues. The pressure of the exudates on the sensory nerve fibers produces pain, and the reflex response of motor nerves causes contraction of the muscle fibers. In a short time pain, redness, swelling, heat and immobility result. A muscle injury of this type is termed a myositis. The most frequent site of occurrence is the quadriceps, particularly the extensor femoris. Contusions of the quadriceps are known colloquially as "charley horse."

FIRST AID. Immediate first aid should be directed towards limiting the amount of hemorrhage by the application of a compression bandage and ice packs for thirty minutes.

REHABILITATION. After 24 hours heat may be used to accelerate the absorption of the hematoma. Massage should never be used over the contused region. It may, however, be applied to the surrounding tissues to assist in disposing of the waste materials. A heated analgesic balm poultice may be used to stimulate the circulation. A half inch thick layer of the balm is spread over the thigh. This is covered with a layer of absorbent cotton, which is taped into place. The whole pack is then firmly wrapped with an elastic bandage.

PROTECTION. The injury occurs primarily in football and prevention depends principally upon the thigh pads being properly fitted so that trauma of this type does not occur.

Hematoma Auris (Cauliflower ear). ETIOLOGY. Contusion of the ear is a common injury among boxers and wrestlers. A superficial hematoma may form between the skin and the cartilage as the result of a blow or rough pressure on the external auditory meatus. Hematoma formation and the necrosis of the underlying cartilage form a keloid, a solid, wrinkled mass colloquially termed "cauliflower ear."

FIRST AID. A compression bandage and ice packs are immediately applied to the ear and left in place for 30 minutes.

REHABILITATION. If the ear remains swollen in spite of first aid, the team physician will usually aspirate it. If a solid mass has formed in the ear before it is seen by the doctor, it can be removed only by surgical means.

PROTECTION.   In amateur boxing and wrestling headguards may be worn in both practice and competition. Professional athletes may use them in practice. Use of these forms of protection will eliminate these injuries in amateur athletics and will assist in preventing them in professional athletics. If headguards are not available during practice sessions, a thin layer of petroleum jelly may be applied to the ears, so that blows and pressure will slide off them before damage is done. Absorbent cotton may be placed behind and on top of ears which have been injured and they may then be taped to the sides of the head.

Epistaxis (Nosebleed).   ETIOLOGY.   Nosebleed is a rather common condition in athletics and generally results from some of the nasal blood vessels being ruptured by a blow to that organ. The injury is disconcerting but seldom serious.

FIRST AID.   The team physician will first satisfy himself that the bleeding does not result from a fracture of the nose or of the skull. The athlete should then sit or stand up. Ice or cold water may be applied to the back of the neck. A common treatment is stuffing the nasal passages with cotton plugs saturated with Adrenalin solution. When these are removed, the athlete is cautioned not blow his nose since that would dislodge the clotted blood and bleeding will recommence.

REHABILITATION.   Ordinarily no further attention will be required. In some cases bleeding may break out afresh and it may be necessary for the physician to cauterize the ruptured blood vessels.

Brain Concussion.   ETIOLOGY.   A blow to the head may result in unconsciousness and the athlete is said to have suffered a "knockout." Momentary unconsciousness does not cause demonstrable brain damage. Several theories have been advanced to explain the mechanism of the loss of consciousness and the mental confusion which follow a knock-out. The one most generally accepted is that oblique blows to the lower jaw cause a forceful rotation of the head. Shear strains set up in the brain tissue as a result of this rotation are believed to be the essential cause of both concussion of the brain and cerebral contusions. In direct blows the contre coupe effect is produced by the rebounding shock waves within the brain mass. In many instances the injury received when the back of the head strikes the mat or floor is more serious than is received from the blow causing the knock-down. The duration of the period of amnesia after recovery of consciousness bears a direct relationship to the severity of the damage inflicted upon the brain. It is, of course, only in boxing that a knock-out is the objective of the game, in other sports its occurrence is accidental.

FIRST AID. A competitor who has been knocked-out must not be moved until he has been examined by the physician. Occasionally severe injury may be present, and this may be dangerously aggravated by unskillful attempts to move the fallen athlete. When the player regains consciousness, the physician will test for signs of amnesia by asking him a few questions to reveal his memory for recent events—where he is, what he is doing, the date, etc. If the concussion is a mild one, the athlete will recover quickly, and aromatic spirits of ammonia or some other stimulant may be used to help him regain complete consciousness. In any event, the player should be removed from the game and placed under observation. If, after a short rest, he makes a complete recovery and there are no contraindications, such as nystagmus, dizziness, or headache, the team physician may permit him to return to the game.

REHABILITATION. In cases in which consciousness is lost for more than a momentary period, the athlete is placed in bed and kept under observation. X-ray studies will be made of the skull to determine the possibility of fracture and neurological examinations will be conducted to determine the extent of the injury. Even minor brain trauma may cause alterations of the personality and loss of memory. Repeated or severe injuries of this type result in deteriorated cerebral functions, such as thickened speech and incoordination observed in "punch drunk" boxers. Injuries of this kind are irreversible and an athlete susceptible to being knocked-out should give up all participation in body contact sports.

PROTECTION. Protection against such injuries is afforded by the wearing of headguards in sports in which their use is permitted.

The design and use of equipment for protecting the head, face and teeth are discussed in Chapter XVI.

An athlete who has suffered repeated knock-outs is given a skull x-ray. There is some indication that individuals with skull bones thinner than average are particularly susceptible to blows to the head. Such individuals should not be permitted to participate in body contact sports.

Handball Palm. ETIOLOGY. Contusion of the palm occurs in handball or similar games in which a ball or some other object is repeatedly struck with the open palm. The athlete will complain that the palm is painful to any form of pressure. In most cases this is due to contusion of the soft tissues but occasionally tenosynovitis may result.

FIRST AID. Soaking the hand in cold water may afford temporary relief. Rest from the activities which cause the soreness is the only form of treatment which will prove of lasting benefit. Massage is apt to make the condition worse. Heat may be useful in the later stages of recovery.

PROTECTION. The athlete should toughen his hands gradually before engaging in protracted bouts of handball or similar games and should wear proper gloves. Once such an injury has been suffered it is apt to recur unless the palm is padded prior to play.

Solar Plexus Trauma. ETIOLOGY. A powerful blow to the abdomen may force the muscles back against the network of nerves, termed the solar plexus, and produce a momentary paralysis of the diaphragm. The athlete remains conscious, but is weak, in pain, unable to breathe or talk.

CARE. Loosening of the belt or of any other restrictive clothing and instructing the man to take short quiet breaths, using his upper chest, will aid him in recovery. If the player does not recover and becomes cyanotic, it may be necessary to commence artificial respiration in the prone position. Bending the knees and pumping the legs up and down is an ineffective form of treatment.

PROTECTION. It is practically impossible to devise padding which will afford protection to this area. Any athlete participating in body contact sports must provide his own protection by the use of vigorous exercises to strengthen the abdominal muscles.

Testicular Trauma. ETIOLOGY. A blow to the testicles is exceedingly painful and temporarily incapacitating. With rest the intense pain may soon be diminished, but examination of the scrotum should be made. Hydrocele or enlargement of the veins of the spermatic cord, termed varicocele, may result from the trauma. Examination may reveal that a testicle has been driven into the abdominal cavity. These conditions require medical attention.

CARE. Relief from pain can be afforded by the application of ice packs until the physician arrives. Pelvic inclination while the athlete lies supine, obtained by grasping the athlete's belt and slowly lifting and lowering him, appears to provide some relief.

PROTECTION. Protection to the male genitalia in body contact activities and in ball games may be provided by the use of a metal cup inserted in the athletic supporter.

Hematuria. Hematuria (blood in the urine), also known as athletic pseudonephritis, is frequently observed in athletes after strenuous exercise, particularly that which involves body contact, and may occur during preseason conditioning exercises. Ordinarily it promptly clears up with rest and does not denote renal disease. Episodes of gross hematuria or hematuria in conjunction with upper respiratory infection should be promptly reported to the team physician.

CHAPTER XV

Athletic Sprains, Dislocations and Fractures

A sprain is the partial or complete rupture of the ligaments holding a joint together, caused by a forcing of a joint past the point of ligamentous restriction of range of motion. They are one of the most common athletic injuries and the trainer will have frequent occasion to care for them.

ANKLE SPRAINS

Anatomy and Kinesiology

The ankle is a ginglymus (hinge) joint formed by the articulation of the lower ends of the tibia and fibula with the astragalus. The only movement possible in the ankle is flexion and extension. The anatomic arrangement of the ankle is such that it is poorly supported by muscles and ligaments, particularly on the anterolateral aspect. It is stabilized by a number of ligaments, the most important of which are the tibiofibular and the collateral ligaments. The tendons of the muscles of the gastrocnemius and soleus (the tendon of Achilles), the peronei, the tibialis and others form a sort of stirrup which supports the joint. Thus the tone of these muscles affects the stability of the ankle joint. In the erect position the entire body weight is transmitted through the ankle to the foot; hence the ankle supports more weight than does any other joint in the body. As a result it is peculiarly susceptible to injury, especially sprains.

Etiology

The most common injuries of the ankle are sprains caused by excessive pressures resulting in abnormal inversion or eversion of the foot. Abnormal inversion causes a stretch or rupture of the fibulocalcaneal and fibulotalar portions of the external collateral ligaments. These sprains may be accompanied by the pulling off of a fragment of the fibula or a portion of the calcaneus. Sprains caused by eversion of the foot are frequently accompanied by fracture and frequently tear the internal collateral and the tibiofibular ligaments. It is important to determine which type of injury has occurred, since care and treatment is based on supporting the ankle in its normal position until it has healed.

Symptoms

Examination is made objectively and by using passive movement. All aspects of the injured ankle are compared with the uninjured one to detect abnormal appearance, position or mobility. Rapid swelling, deformity in the shape or resting position of the ankle are suggestive of sprain, fracture or dislocation.

In walking, the injured athlete may be unable to sustain pressure on the forefoot. Harsh crepitations (grating sensation), which may be audible, are indicative of a fracture. A soft crepitation is indicative of epiphyseal separation. When signs of loss of function, abnormal mobility or crepitation are present the athlete is referred immediately to the team physician.

The symptoms of both sprains and fractures of the ankle joint are immediate pain, localized tenderness, swelling, sensitivity to and limitation of movement, muscle spasm, redness, deformity and, later, discoloration. A sprain is generally characterized by pain below the joint and fracture by a more intense pain above the joint, with a sudden stab of pain on passive movement. However, any severe injury requires x-ray to determine whether a fracture exists.

First Aid

The immediate care of ankle injury generally proceeds in the following sequence: (1) The athlete is withdrawn from the game to prevent possible aggravation of the injury. (2) A layer of absorbent cotton is first placed around the joint and the joint is temporarily wrapped with a crepe or elastic bandage extending from the bottom of the foot to about nine inches above the ankle. The toes are left exposed and their color frequently inspected to ascertain that blood circulation is not halted by the pressure of the bandage. If the athlete complains of pain, the bandage may be too tight. It should be removed and reapplied with less pressure. (3) Cold compresses are applied to the injured area for thirty minutes to control internal bleeding and to prevent effusion. (4) The injured leg is elevated to prevent edema. (5) Muscle setting exercises are done in which the muscles of the leg and foot are rhythmically contracted and relaxed to exert a pumping action without moving the ankle joint; these exercises aid in the dispersal of accumulating fluid.

Heat, massage, weight bearing and exercise involving movement and resistance are not commenced within the first thirty-six hours after injury unless the team physician so indicates. Attempts to relieve pain by rubbing with ointments or liniments are contra-indicated, as they may increase or prolong internal bleeding.

Rehabilitation

Although the athlete with an injured ankle may be kept off his feet during repair, he needs to keep as active as possible in other ways in order to prevent muscular atrophy and debilitation of his overall strength and endurance. A general set of resistance exercises may be prescribed by the physician for the athlete to do while he is in bed or in a wheelchair; these should be supervised by a corrective or physical therapist.

When the athlete returns to the squad after about ten days, the team physician may suggest certain special ankle strengthening exercises for the trainer to supervise. A device such as is shown in Figure 22 is useful for this purpose. Exercises are described in Chapter X.

Figure 22. Progressive resistance apparatus for strengthening the ankle. (Logan.)

To promote healing, removal of exudates and dispersal of hematoma, the physician may instruct the trainer to provide heat and gentle massage. Both modalities are conveniently furnished by a whirlpool bath. If the whirlpool bath is used, the athlete assists its action by moving the ankle rhythmically in its full range of motion in all possible directions during the latter portion of the bath.

Protective Wrapping

Athletes engaging in body contact sports in which the ankle is subject to injury can protect themselves by using a simple ankle

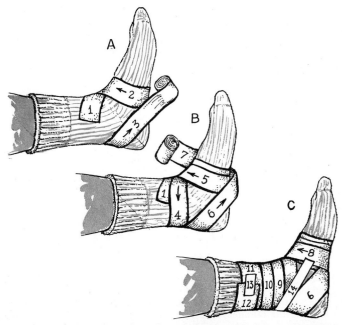

Figure 23. Louisiana or double figure-of-eight ankle wrap. *A,* Cotton webbing wrap is applied over the sock, starting at the medial malleolus, continuing forward and passing underneath the longitudinal arch (Nos. 1–2). It is then carried upward, across the external malleolus, and diagonally downward underneath the arch (No. 3), commencing the heel lock. *B,* Continuing from 23*A,* the bandage is carried around the foot (No. 3) and brought across the internal malleolus (No. 4) and then brought diagonally downward across the outside of the heel, completing the heel lock. This process is repeated (Nos. 5–7), carrying the strips medially. *C,* The wrap is completed by carrying the strip from the outside of the heel upward across the inner border of the longitudinal arch (No. 8) and then wrapping in circular overlapping fashion above the ankle (Nos. 9–12). It is anchored by a strip of one-inch tape (No. 13). Finally a strip of one-inch tape (No. 14) is applied diagonally to prevent slipping of the bandage at the heel.

wrap during practice and competition. The wrap consists of a 96 inch long strip of two inch wide woven cotton webbing made with non-ravel ends. Using a technique such as that shown in Figure 23, the wrap may be applied either directly against the skin or over the sock. The sock helps to prevent abrasion and blisters and allows the wrap to be drawn firmly. Care is exercised to smooth out all wrinkles in the sock as the wrap is applied. In applying the wrap a firm upward pull on the lateral side serves as an external support to assist the stirrup-like stabilizing action of the ankle ligaments.

After instructing the athletes in the application of the ankle wrap, the trainer assures proper utilization of the technique by occasional checks made throughout the season. Clean wraps are issued frequently and winding spools are located conveniently in the training and locker rooms.

Adhesive Strapping

Adhesive tape is used to protect weak ankles from injury and to prevent recurrence of injury to ankles weakened by former sprains ·

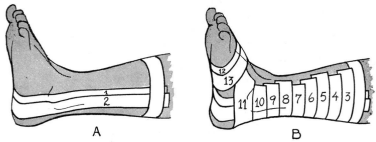

A   B

Figure 24. Lonn Mann adhesive strap for the ankle. (After Dolan.) *A,* The foot is held in dorsiflexion and slight eversion, as two strips of two-inch tape are applied vertically covering the malleoli (Nos. 1–2). The tape is drawn up snugly to bring the calcaneus into secure contact with the talus and fibula. For this purpose the tape is placed well back toward the heel; it is not intended to support the arch. The vertical strips are anchored at the top by a circular strip. *B,* Overlapping circular strips (Nos. 3–11) starting at the lower end of the belly of the gastrocnemius are applied, extending to about an inch above the sole of the foot. The tape should be applied without drawing it tight, since undue pressure in this area can easily block the nervous and circulatory functions. To assure preservation of these functions the ends of the tape are not brought together at the front. Two pieces of two-inch tape (Nos. 12–13) are placed around the instep to give support to the structure of the foot. Both pieces are started from the inside of the foot and are drawn gently upward across the outside. If desired a figure-of-eight wrap or strap may be applied over-all to provide further support and to hold the strapping in place.

Figure 25. Gibney strapping for ankle. *A,* The foot is dorsiflexed and everted. Overlapping vertical and lateral strips are applied in basket weave fashion from the rearward portion of the heel forward (Nos. 1–6). Tension is applied to the outside of the foot as the vertical strips are drawn into position. Two-inch tape is shown above, but one or one and one-half inch tape can be used if stronger support is desired. *B,* For additional support a figure-of-eight may be added (No. 7). Two anchoring strips (Nos. 8–9) secure the tops of the vertical strips.

or fractures. Three types of ankle strapping are shown. The technique depicted in Figure 24 is applicable to weak ankles in general. Figures 25 and 26 show techniques for protection against recurrence of more severe strains of the lateral or medial ligaments.

SHIN SPLINTS

Anatomy and Kinesiology

The shin is composed of the tibia and fibula bone shafts. The tibia is the large medial bone of the foreleg which articulates with the femur and transmits the weight of the body to the foot. Fatigue fractures of this bone occasionally occur in male ballet dancers. The fibula is positioned laterally to the tibia and carries no direct body weight. Lying between the two bones is the interosseus membrane, which provides stabilization of the tibia and fibula. The interosseus membrane and the periosteum covering the bones serve as attachments for the muscles of the soleus and six flexor muscles of the foot and toes.

Etiology

The interosseus membrane and periosteum are poorly provided with blood vessels. Thus, when poorly warmed up they are easily injured and, once injured, are slow to heal. Infections or irritation of these membranes easily spread to bone tissue and the two

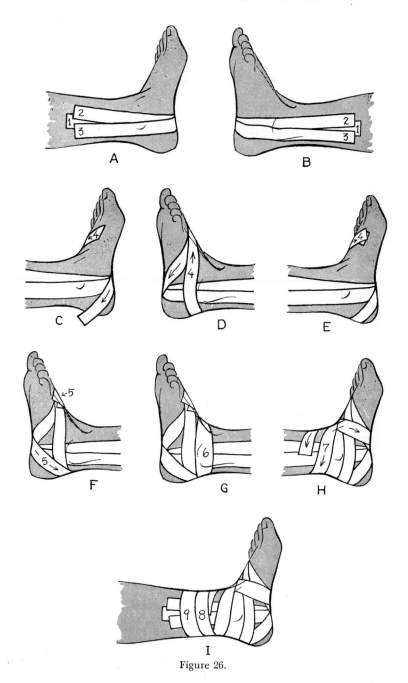

Figure 26.

deteriorate together. If the athlete runs on a hard surface, or if he commences fast sprints before he conditions his muscles and tissues by easy jogging and gradual extension into rapid running, the constant pull of the muscles against the interosseus membrane and periosteum tears the muscle origins away from the membranes, or tears the periosteum away from the bone. This damage, termed irritative myositis, occurs especially at the origin of the tibialis posticus, where it arises from the posterior and medial surface of the upper two-thirds of the tibia.

Symptoms

Pain is felt in the shin on weight bearing, especially when the athlete rises on his toes, or if he runs on a hard surface. The shin is tender to the touch, particularly on the posterior border of the tibial shin surface on the inside of the leg. In serious cases the pain of shin splints is persistent.

First Aid

Rest seems to be the only sure method to obtain relief. Pain and tenderness is lessened by heated analgesic balm compress applied from ankle to patella. Worn as an overnight compress, the analgesic can be covered with flannel and wrapped snugly with a wide elastic bandage.

Figure 26. Drake ankle strapping. *A,* The foot is placed in eversion at a 90 degree angle to the lower leg. Three overlapping strips of two-inch tape (Nos. 1–3) are applied vertically across the malleoli, extending about four inches above the malleoli. *B,* External view of vertical strips, showing the medial placement of the first strip, anterior placement of the second strip, and posterior placement of the third strip, as on the inside of the ankle. *C,* A heel lock is commenced (No. 4) starting across the top of the instep and continuing around the outside of the foot, then under the heel and diagonally and upward across the inside of the heel. *D,* External view of ankle, showing continuation of the heel lock passing across the lower border of the malleolus (No. 4).

E, Internal view of ankle, showing completion of the first of the heel lock strips (No. 4). *F,* The second heel lock strip is applied from the outside of the ankle just above the malleoli, extending across the instep, under the heel and diagonally upward on the outer border of the heel, carried across the inner malleoli, and completed across the instep (No. 5). *G,* A circular strip (No. 6) is carried around the ankle at malleoli level. *H,* A partial figure-of-eight (No. 7) is applied to provide stability to the external border of the foot. *I,* Two overlapping circular anchors (Nos. 8–9) secure the vertical strips.

Rehabilitation

Continued overnight use of the analgesic compress appears to speed recovery from shin splints. Light massage over unaffected areas promotes circulation and offers some relief. Daily treatments with a whirlpool bath heated to 108° F. promote healing. When activity is again commenced, the athlete runs on grass or other soft surfaces to avoid the constant jarring which damaged the tissues in the first place. Flexible Ripple soles on practice shoes will reduce landing shock and prevent sharp jerking action of the muscles against the membranous bone covering. The athlete should commence running very gradually, starting with an easy jog—striking the ground with the foot nearly flat. Speed is progressively increased after several days and if shin irritation does not recur, the athlete can gradually work into fast sprints and onto hard surfaces.

Preventive Measures

Protective padding made of foam rubber 6 inches long and two and one-half inches wide placed over the shin bone and bound down by an elastic bandage reduces the jarring, pulling and jerking actions. A piece of foam rubber in each heel reduces shock in running and raises the heels, thereby limiting the stretch of the soleus muscles. If one leg is shorter than the other, a heel pad placed in the shoe of the short leg promotes better balance and may reduce the strain in running. Flexible Ripple soles on training or practice footgear absorb shock and increase stability, thereby reducing the factors contributing to shin splint.

KNEE SPRAINS

Anatomy and Kinesiology

The knee joint is formed by the articulation of the femur and the tibia. The patella, a sesamoid bone embedded in the quadriceps tendon, is the third component of the joint. While the knee is basically a ginglymus joint, its movements are considerably more complicated than simple flexion and extension, since these motions occur in association with a rotation of the tibia. The knee articulation is cushioned by two semi-lunar menisci. The joint is stabilized by a number of powerful ligaments, the most important of which are the lateral and medial collaterals which run perpendicularly, and the cruciate ligaments which cross the joint obliquely. The quadriceps, the hamstrings, the gastrocnemius, and other muscles assist in stabilizing the knee joint.

Etiology

Most knee injuries result from direct trauma. With the knee in a flexed position, a blow producing forced abduction or external rotation will cause a rupture of the medial collateral ligament. This is the most common knee injury in skiing and often occurs in football when the partially flexed knee is struck from the side during a tackle or a block. A severe injury of this type may also result in the displacement or chipping of the medial meniscus. A blow from the inside will produce similar types of injuries, but these are less frequently encountered in athletics. Damage to the crucial ligaments, as often occurs from clipping in football, results from a marked displacement of the tibia. A direct blow to the patella may cause a dislocation or a fracture of that bone, but dislocations and fractures of the knee joint itself are quite rare in athletics. Infrapatellar bursitis (housemaid's knee) may be caused by contusion of the bursa underlying the patella, as when the knee strikes the ground in football line play.

Symptoms

If the medial collateral ligaments are injured, pain will be felt on the inner side of the knee and tenderness will be localized at a point over the ligaments. Signs of injury to the lateral ligaments will be similar, except that the pain will be felt on the outer side of the joint. If the medial meniscus has been torn, "locking" will often result and the patient will be unable to extend the leg. In cases of rupture of the cruciate ligaments, the tibia displays an increased range of movement. The team physician may test for this by using the "drawer sign." With the knee flexed at 90 degrees, the tibia displays an abnormal amount of mobility when passively moved back and forth with the distal end fixed. Fracture of the patella commonly results in swelling of the joint and the break often may be palpated. Within 24 hours after damage to the knee joint, the increased secretion of synovial fluid will result in "water on the knee." If the patient sits with his leg extended and the muscles relaxed, the patella will be felt to "float" on the underlying accumulated synovial fluid. With the application of pressure it can be forced through the fluid and into contact with the other bones of the joint, but will rise again when the pressure is released.

First Aid

The player suspected of having suffered a knee injury should be immediately removed from the game. Injuries to this joint almost invariably prove difficult to rehabilitate and it is essential that additional trauma be avoided. First aid treatment is directed towards controlling hemorrhage by reducing the blood supply to the injured part. One inch sponge-rubber pads may be placed on the joint and then tightly wrapped to produce local pressure. To lower the temperature at the site of the injury and to produce vasospasm, the knee is placed in ice water or surrounded with a cold compress. After thirty minutes of this treatment the water or compress may be removed, the limb dried and the joint covered with absorbent cotton. A six inch square of sponge rubber, with the center cut out so that the patella may protrude through it, may be used to cover the joint, which is then wrapped with a moderately firm compression bandage. No weight bearing is permitted at this stage.

Rehabilitation

X-ray views and observations of the joint reactions will be necessary to determine the nature and severity of the injury. The physician may prescribe quadriceps setting exercises as soon as he has made his diagnosis, or immediately after surgery, if the latter is necessary. These exercises are necessary to prevent atrophy and will usually be administered by a corrective therapist or a physical therapist.

After the team physician approves the athlete's return to the squad, rehabilitation exercises for the knee joint will be given by the trainer. At this stage progressive resistance exercises, as described in Chapter X, will usually be the treatment of choice. Normally these are given two or three times a day and consist of ten repetitions each time. It is essential that the knee be extended to a full range of motion on each repetition, since exercises performed with a partially flexed knee will not produce complete recovery of strength. Active exercises also aid in the removal of the exudates and other debris from the injured area. This process may be assisted by the use of massage and heat. Whirlpool baths offer a combination of these modalities. With an injury of average severity, a period of 10 days or more may elapse before the athlete is pronounced fit to rejoin the team. During this period he should endeavor to maintain his physical condition by performing vigorous exercises with the non-injured limbs.

Adhesive Strapping

Upon return to active participation in sport, the injured knee must be protected from further damage by the use of adhesive strapping. An ordinary elastic bandage does not provide sufficient tension to furnish the necessary support, and the effectiveness of hinged knee brace devices is somewhat limited. A technique for strapping the knee to protect the collateral ligaments is illustrated in Figure 27. The strapping depicted in Figure 28 is utilized to protect the cruciate ligaments.

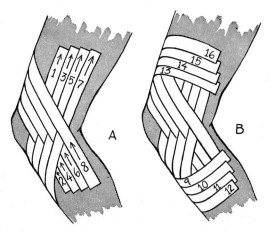

Figure 27. Double X method of knee strapping. *A*, Player stands with knee in semi-flexed position. Diagonal overlapping strips of tape (Nos. 1–8) are alternately applied on both sides of the knee in basket-weave fashion. If applied on only one side of the knee, it is termed the Single X method. *B*, Circular anchor strips (Nos. 9–16) are used to secure the ends of the diagonal strips. The taping may be covered with a four-inch elastic spiral bandage, anchored with strips of one-inch tape.

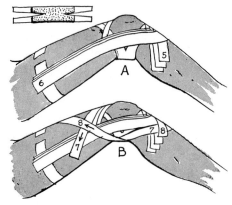

Figure 28. Duke Simpson strapping for unstable knees. (After Thorndike.)
A, A felt base is prepared by splitting an eighteen-inch strip of adhesive tape
upon which is placed a ten-inch strip of two-inch-wide felt padding. The tape
and felt are then split six inches at each end, providing four four-inch adhesive
tails. The felt pad is placed behind the semi-flexed knee and the tails are spread
to cross the knee above and below the patella. A two-inch anchor strip is applied
well up on the thigh. Vertical overlapping strips (Nos. 1–6) are applied in basket-
weave fashion from lower to upper leg. *B,* Spiral strips (Nos. 7–8) are then applied
from lower to upper leg, crossing the felt pad at the rear of the knee. Anchor
strips are applied at the thigh and lower leg ends of the strips.

RIB SPRAIN

Anatomy and Kinesiology

The arching curvilinear design of the rib, together with its flexibility and intercostal fastenings to neighboring ribs, make this
seemingly fragile bone highly resistant to damaging forces. Thus,
the ribs form an effective barrier to prevent physical injury upon
the vital heart and lungs.

Etiology

When the ribs receive a crushing force sufficient to cause a fracture
or separation, the attending damage to surrounding ligamentous and
other soft tissues usually extends from front to back. In the unusual
circumstance when one rib alone is fractured by a special set of
forces which localize the injury, there is very little pain or discomfort, and the unsuspecting athlete may continue playing a game
with only an occasional twinge on certain movements.

Symptoms

The site of rib fracture can be located by complaints of tenderness over the damaged area and by palpating for discontinuity in the rib line. X-ray views are always necessary to determine whether or not a rib splinter has entered the pleural cavity.

First Aid

Immobilization of an injured rib is difficult because the heart and the lungs cause the ribs to move in and out, and up and down. Strapping is restricted to the injured half of the rib cage, as shown in Figure 19. In this manner the undamaged side can work, while the injured side rests.

RUPTURE OF INTERNAL ORGANS

Anatomy

Organs such as the intestines, spleen, liver, gall bladder and kidney are suspended loosely in the abdominal cavity. Blows to the trunk or sudden twists of the body sometimes tear these organs loose from their attachments, or may even rupture the organ. Simultaneous tearing of blood vessels causes internal hemorrhage.

Etiology

The force need not be great to cause such injuries; considerable damage can be sustained if the organ happens to be in a certain position or in a certain condition at the time the blow is struck. An accidental blow by the elbow during dancing has caused rupture of the liver. Blocking with the flank or using the lower ribs as the point of contact has caused the rupture of an athlete's spleen.

Symptoms

Characteristic of internal organ damage is an immediate reaction —mild shock, tenderness and perhaps some pain. These signs may disappear altogether and the athlete may seem to have recovered. Later, from an hour to four days, or even six months, signs of weakness, pallor, faintness, nausea, vomiting and shock suddenly appear. An explanation for the delayed reaction is that the hematoma which had formed within the ruptured organ has degenerated and internal bleeding now floods the abdominal cavity; the athlete is now in a critical condition.

Rehabilitation

Early recognition of internal injury by the trainer and coach depends on careful attention to complaints of abdominal tenderness, unexplained shock, or vague pain in the upper chest, flank, or shoulder region. Surgery within an hour of the rupture of an internal organ can be effective in saving the athlete's life.

Protection

Athletes preparing to engage in sports in which blows to the trunk may be anticipated need to strengthen the musculature of the abdomen and back before exposure. Exercises for this purpose are shown in Chapter X. The stomach, spleen, intestines and bladder increase in size and weight after a meal, and in this condition are more susceptible to injury. The observance of the rule to eat a light, quickly digestible meal not later than two hours before exercise permits these organs to return to their resting size within that period. The athlete before exercise should defecate and urinate and relieve himself of stomach or rectal gases. Organs filled with fluid or gas are more liable to be ruptured by a sharp blow than are empty ones.

FRACTURE OF THE CLAVICLE

Anatomy

The brittle clavicle is held loosely at either end by ligaments which permit raising and lowering of the glenoid fossa in wide arm movements. It lies unprotected just under the skin where it is frequently exposed to blows and shocks in contact sports. The clavicle is frequently subjected to undisplaced fractures because of its unusually thick periosteum.

Etiology

Fractures of the clavicle are produced by a blow on the tip of the shoulder or by a fall on the extended arm or elbow. Fractures usually occur at the narrowest point. The susceptible area is the junction of two curves and there are no muscle attachments at this point to act as a protective splint against injury.

Symptoms

The signs of fracture of the clavicle are deformity, abnormal mobility along the prominences of the clavicle, crepitation, pain, shock, inability to move the arm on the side of the injury, head sometimes tilted to the affected side and the athlete holding his hand under his elbow to support the arm. The area of injury is tender along the line of the bone, and it is sometimes possible to feel displaced bone fragments. X-ray is important to ascertain the extent of the damage, since splintered fragments of the bone may have injured surrounding tissues, including the lungs.

First Aid

If the clavicle is fractured, the team physician is called. Meanwhile support may be applied in the form of a bandage formed by two slings, one under the elbow and up over the opposite shoulder to support the arm, and the other around the arm and body, with the addition of a flexible pad under the armpit.

Rehabilitation

A week after fracture of the clavicle, while support is still worn, it is important to exercise gently all joints of the arm from shoulder to fingers to prevent stiffness. After three weeks the physician may recommend light resistance exercises, such as those described in Chapter X, to redevelop the muscles of the shoulder girdle. Since the biceps muscle tendon acts as a ligament to the shoulder joint and the tendons of the other muscles around the joint are responsible for maintaining the joint, it is important to exercise these muscles.

Protection

Before the development of the cantilever type shoulder pad in 1930, fractured clavicles were frequent during football seasons. The design of shoulder harness which provides effective protection is discussed in Chapter XVI.

STERNOCLAVICULAR SPRAIN

Anatomy

The sternoclavicular joint is formed by the medial end of the clavicle and the upper and lateral aspect of the sternum.

Etiology

Sternoclavicular sprains are produced by a sudden backward wrench of the shoulder, as in wrestling, which loosens and partially tears or dislocates the joint.

First Aid

Since fracture of the clavicle may complicate this injury, the athlete should not be permitted to move his shoulder until he is seen by the team physician.

Adhesive Strapping

Support of this joint while the injury is healing may be obtained by placing a pad over the medial end of the clavicle and fastening it with adhesive strapping, as shown in Figure 29.

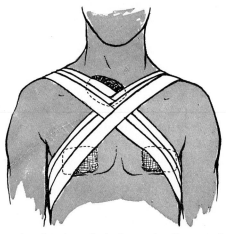

Figure 29. Strapping for sternoclavicular strain. Gauze pads are placed over the nipples and a rubber pad is placed over the medial tip of the clavicle. Pressure is applied to the pad by diagonal overlapping strips of adhesive placed in a basket-weave pattern, with the strips extending from the tops of the scapulae across the chest and sides.

ACROMIOCLAVICULAR SEPARATION

Anatomy

The acromioclavicular joint is made up of the inner margin of the acromion process of the scapula and the outer end of the clavicle. The joint is held loosely together by two short coracoclavicular ligaments. The acromioclavicular joint represents the "awning" that projects outward over the head of the humerus, and is often referred to as the point of the shoulder.

Etiology

In football and other body contact sports the acromioclavicular joint is occasionally pushed beyond the limits of its connection and the ligaments are torn or stretched—a condition known as knock-down or tackle shoulder, but more precisely defined as an acromio-clavicular separation. Acromioclavicular sprains are also produced by a violent glancing blow on the tip of the shoulder, at the joint between the clavicle and the acromion process. This sometimes occurs in ice hockey, or by falling with considerable force on the shoulder.

Symptoms

In this injury any movement which calls for rotation of the shoulder joint elicits pain. The athlete is unable to lift his arm to shoulder level and there is a marked loss of force. There may be a localized swelling over the acromion process. There is a point of tenderness at the acromioclavicular joint. A lump above the normal level of the acromion may be caused by the clavicle having been forced above the acromion at the point of junction. The injury is sometimes complicated by a fracture of the acromion process, which can be determined only by x-ray.

First Aid

When a shoulder separation occurs the area is covered with cold compresses for 30 minutes to reduce the hemorrhage caused by the

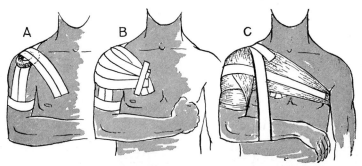

Figure 30. Duke Wyre strapping for acromioclavicular separation. *A,* The pur-pose of this strapping is to support the weight of the arm in order to decrease the pull of the arm at the side to an acromioclavicular separation. Two over-lapping strips of two-inch tape are drawn from the middle of the arm over the shoulder to the middle of the back. A felt doughnut is placed on top of the shoulder joint. Overlapping strips are placed on the scapula, drawn over the doughnut and pulled down hard against the chest. *B,* The arm is held tightly against the body and overlapping strips are drawn from the middle of the back over the deltoid to the chest, where they are anchored. An anchor is also applied to the ends of the vertical strips on the upper arm. *C,* A four-inch elastic spica bandage is wrapped around the upper arm and beneath the other arm in a figure-of-eight. A strip of two-inch tape is applied over the bandage to hold it in place. A strip of two-inch tape is used to make a sling to support the arm.

tear. The elbow is placed in a sling for support and a bandage is applied as shown in Figure 30 to bring the humerus tighter into its socket, taking the weight of the hanging limb off the ligaments of the joint.

Rehabilitation

If x-ray discloses no broken bones, the team physician may instruct the trainer to apply heat twice a day, forty-five minutes in the morning and again in the afternoon. Supplementing this treatment, upon arising and again before retiring, the athlete may stand under a shower with the shower head removed, allowing a forceful stream of hot water to douche the tip of the shoulder for about ten minutes. The shoulder usually responds well to such rehabilitation procedures and the athlete can ordinarily return to participation within two weeks.

Adhesive Strapping

Taping assists the action of the ligaments and decreases the pull of the arm, which weighs 15 to 20 pounds. The basket-weave method of strapping shown in Figure 31 is employed for supporting the separation and providing protection.

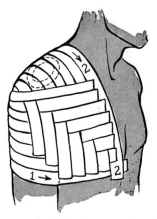

Figure 31. Basket weave strapping for acromioclavicular separation. After applying the doughnut as shown in Figure 30A, the tape is applied in basket weave fashion, starting with a horizontal strip binding the arm to the trunk, following with a vertical strip across the shoulder and continuing medially, applying firm pressure against each overlapping strip, until the entire joint is encapsulated.

SHOULDER SPRAIN

Anatomy

The shoulder is a shallow ball and socket joint articulating be-tween the head of the humerus and the glenoid cavity of the scapula. Held away from the trunk by the projecting clavicle, the shoulder joint is loosely bound together by its ligaments and muscles which provides great freedom of motion in all directions. The joint is held in place by a capsule formed by the tendons of the four muscles which act to rotate the humerus: the subscapularis tendon across the anterior aspect of the head of the humerus, the supraspinatus tendon across the upper aspect, the infraspinatus tendon across the upper and posterior aspect and the teres minor tendon on the posterior aspect. The tendon of the long head of the biceps muscle rides through a groove in the upper end of the humerus. These tendons act to hold the shoulder joint intact.

Etiology

Rupture of the tendons of the shoulder capsule occurs in athletes during football tackling and blocking, in wrestling as the result of a sudden backward wrench of the shoulder and occasionally during body contact in basketball rebounding. Quick movements, as in javelin throwing, also may cause overstretching of the capsule. The superiorly situated supraspinatus tendon is the one most commonly irritated in "sprained" or "pulled" shoulder injuries.

Symptoms

Little can be discovered by examinations made through athletic uniforms and equipment. Shoulder injuries can be detected in-directly by observing the way a player carries or uses his shoulder, or how he favors it. Upon examination of the shoulder capsule, sprain will be found to produce swelling, localized tenderness over the joint and a marked loss of function and force. After an accident of this type any movement should be reduced to a minimum.

First Aid

Sprain of the shoulder capsule calls for support by a sling placed under the elbow, and a bandage around the trunk and upper arm to bring the head of the humerus tight into its socket, similar to the method shown in Figure 30.

Rehabilitation

Continuous mild heat may be applied by the use of an analgesic compress held in place by a spica bandage. Each time the compress is removed, massage may be applied around, but not to, the injured joint.

After about a week, when swelling is reduced, exercise can be commenced by gripping a hand exerciser or a tennis ball. The shoulder and neck exercises in Chapter X can be employed until both arm and shoulder recover their normal strength. The period of convalescence varies from four to twelve days, averaging nine days, depending on the degree of injury. The athlete is not permitted to participate in vigorous sport until all functions return to normal.

Adhesive Strapping

To prevent recurrence of shoulder sprain, adhesive support can be provided using the method shown in Figure 21.

SHOULDER DISLOCATION

Anatomy and Etiology

Dislocation of the shoulder, in which the head of the humerus slips out of its junction with the glenoid fossa, is frequent in body contact activities because of the extreme mobility of the shoulder, the mechanical disadvantage under which it works whenever the extended arm or elbow is struck and because of the use of the shoulder as a striking surface. The shoulder can be displaced either forward (anterior or subcoracoid dislocation) or backward (posterior or subspinous dislocation). In a forward dislocation, which is the more common in athletics, the head of the humerus is in a position to rupture the brachial artery, vein and nerves. As a further complication, the head of the humerus may be fractured and the tendon of the long head of the biceps muscle often becomes completely detached from its groove, sometimes necessitating surgical intervention. Frequent dislocation of the shoulder joint indicates a rupture of the tendinous capsule. A shoulder subject to recurrent dislocation is commonly referred to as a "trick shoulder."

Symptoms

Signs of dislocation are pain, shock and tenderness. The normal contour of the shoulder is lost and it may be possible to feel the head of the humerus in its abnormal position. The elbow is unable to touch the side of the body and the athlete cannot touch his hand to his opposite shoulder.

First Aid

If the shoulder appears to be dislocated the team physician is called immediately. The nonmedically trained coach or trainer must not attempt to reduce a shoulder dislocation because of the potential danger of damaging nerves, arteries and veins. Furthermore, the attention of the physician is needed because of the possibility of fracture of the humerus or displacement of the biceps tendon. Surgical repair of recurrent shoulder dislocation is considered necessary for permanent correction.

Rehabilitation

Exercises following surgical repair of the shoulder joint are important to rebuild atrophied muscles. Some of the exercises described in Chapter X may be suggested by the surgeon or team physician for use in the later stages of rehabilitation.

Remedial exercises are given in a progressive fashion, starting with a very mild program. An easy way to move an injured shoulder is for the athlete to allow the arm to hang limply at his side; then, by flexing his body forward from the waist, the arm flexes automatically. It is returned to its original position by straightening the trunk. Next, with his body bent forward and the arm dangling as before, the arm is swung gently from side to side, thus achieving abduction and adduction. Finally, these movements are combined by assuming the same trunk-flexed position and gently circling the arm from the shoulder. During exercise the trainer assists the athlete in avoiding compensating motions of the shoulder joint, in which the scapula is moved, to spare the injured joint. It is important to move the arm through a full range of movements to prevent atrophy.

Protection

Shoulders easily dislocated can be protected by a restrictive harness which prevents the athlete from raising his arm higher than 85 degrees. This harness, shown in Figure 32, protects the shoulder without severely inhibiting arm action and can be worn effectively by football passers.

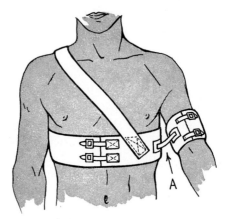

Figure 32. Restrictive harness for dislocated shoulder. Check-rein indicated by arrow A limits range of motion of affected shoulder joint. (Logan.)

SHOULDER BURSITIS

Anatomy

Three bursae lie under the deltoid muscle at the tip of the shoulder. The subdeltoid and subacromial bursae are brought together and act as one when the arm is next to the body. They are separated when the arm is abducted. The subcoracoid bursa acts independently of the other two.

Etiology

Nearly all shoulder injuries involve inflammation of the bursae, described as subdeltoid bursitis or subacromial bursitis. Pain arises from the joint when the athlete raises his arm, especially when putting on a T-shirt.

First Aid

Ice bags alone or mild analgesic balm will alleviate the pain while awaiting medical treatment.

Rehabilitation

During the latter part of the course of therapy for bursitis, simple exercises such as those offered in Chapter X may be suggested by the physician.

TRAUMATIC ELBOW

Anatomy and Etiology

The elbow is a ginglymus joint in which the ulna and radius articulate with the humerus in such a manner as to provide only flexion and extension. Hyperextension of the elbow, in which the momentum of the forearm causes the head of the radius to be thrust against the projecting olecranon process of the humerus, often produces traumatic injuries. Repeated light shocks, as in fastball pitching in baseball, cause an irritation of the periosteum covering the two bones and make movement painful, thus seriously limiting performance. Continued trauma of this type is almost certain to result in formation of osteoblasts, which produce calciferous deposits.

First Aid

For this injury first aid is limited to cold compresses to reduce the swelling. After swelling is reduced, an analgesic compress may be applied to the elbow for the relief of pain and soreness.

Protection

Use of the check-rein type adhesive strapping described in Figure 33 will protect the elbow from further irritation.

HYPEREXTENDED ELBOW

Etiology

Sprains of the elbow may result from falling on the extended arm or from straight arming an opponent in such a way that the ligaments surrounding the joint are overstretched or ruptured. The origins of the flexors or extensors of the fingers and wrist may also be strained. The injury may not be bothersome at the time, but later on swelling occurs and movement of the joint becomes painful. If the player is asked to flex and extend his fingers and wrist with the elbow flexed at a 90 degree angle, pain will be felt in the muscle attachments.

First Aid

The elbow may be flexed to a 90 degree angle and compression bandages and ice water or cold compresses applied for 30 minutes.

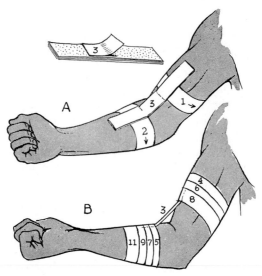

Figure 33. Check-rein for hyperextended elbow. *A,* The arm is encircled with a two-inch base strip of tape just above the elbow (No. 1) and another just below the elbow (No. 2). These are covered with two more strips of tape. Six layers of tape ten inches long by one and one-half inches wide are placed on top of each other, adhesive side up. A three-inch by one and one-half-inch strip is placed on top of these, adhesive side down, as shown in *A* and *B* in the figure. This check-rein is placed on the arm, adhesive side down (No. 3). *B,* The ends of the check-rein are secured by three or more overlapping anchor strips (Nos. 4–11). Care should be taken that neither the base strips nor the anchor strips are so tight as to interfere with neural or circulatory functions.

Rehabilitation

X-rays are taken to determine whether chips of bone have been torn off the elbow. Heat may be applied, but it is better not to use massage. When the player returns to practice a restrictive bandage, such as is shown in Figure 33, may be used to prevent recurrence of the injury and the physician may prescribe some of the exercises shown in Chapter X for rehabilitation.

JAVELIN THROWER'S ELBOW

Anatomy and Etiology

The javelin is often delivered in such a manner that a violent hyperextension occurs without a force-attenuating follow-through motion. In this action the head of the radius strikes the olecranon process with such force that damage occurs. The damage can be of several types. The most serious is a fracture of the olecranon process which can extend from a small chip or hairline fracture to a complete shattering of the process. Other damage can include crushing of the periosteum, dislocation of the elbow joint, rupture of the ligaments and tendons about the joint and a fracture of the humerus. The athlete suffers severe pain and there is local tenderness and restriction of movement.

First Aid

Care consists of a cold compress applied to the injured area and splinting to restrict motion. While awaiting medical attention, the arm is splinted in the position in which it is voluntarily carried by the athlete. If flexed, it is placed in a sling.

Rehabilitation

When the physician indicates that exercise can be begun, the trainer can conduct arm muscle setting exercises. Forearm musculature can be exercised by gripping a hand exerciser or a tennis ball. When the cast is removed range of motion is restored by administering exercises requiring the full extent of movement. The physician may wish to recommend some of the exercises shown in Chapter X.

Protection

Protection from re-injury can be afforded by the check-rein type of adhesive strapping described in Figure 33.

WRIST SPRAIN

Anatomy

The wrist joint is formed by eight small carpal bones articulating proximally with the radius and ulna and distally with the metacarpals of the hand. All eight carpals are supported by two small ligaments, one anterior and one posterior. The blood supply to these bones is carried through vessels imbedded in these two ligaments. If both ligaments are torn, nourishment to the carpal bones is permanently cut off. If one ligament survives an injury, the circulation to the carpals remains adequate. Older athletes with seed-like carpals were onetime sufferers from complete ligamentous damage.

The lunate is the carpal bone most frequently fractured. If the bone is held together in one piece by its periosteal covering, healing proceeds rapidly and no disability ensues. However, if a chip of the bone floats free, it may become wedged in between the other bones causing irritation and limitation of motion.

Symptoms

Signs of wrist sprain are swelling, pain and local tenderness. X-ray is required to determine whether fracture is present.

First Aid

Care consists of applying cold compresses, splinting or taping to restrict motion.

Rehabilitation

Hand and wrist exercises can usually be commenced early during healing.

Protection

The wrist can be protected from recurrence of the injury by adhesive strapping such as that shown in Figure 34.

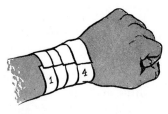

Figure 34. Adhesive taping for wrist support. Athlete clenches his fist. This increases the size of the wrist and minimizes possibility of strapping interfering with neural or circulatory functions. The wrist is then encircled with four overlapping strips of two-inch tape.

THUMB SPRAIN

Anatomy and Etiology

The thumb, separated as it is from the rest of the hand and fingers, is in an advantageous position to oppose the fingers for grasping and manipulating actions, but it is in a precarious position to receive blows or to resist forces. As a result, the thumb is frequently hyperextended in athletics in movements of fending, catching and snagging. A common type of damage is jamming, caused by striking the extended thumb.

Symptoms

Signs of sprain are swelling, redness, pain and tenderness in the affected area. Fracture or dislocation can be observed visually or by running the finger over the line of bony prominences of the thumb. Pain at the base of the thumb may indicate fracture of the scaphoid, a bone with very poor healing properties because of its poor circulation.

First Aid

Care consists of cold compresses, splinting and holding the hand in an elevated position with the help of a sling.

Rehabilitation

The hand is soaked in hot water for two hours each day. While the thumb is being soaked, movement in all directions to the extreme range of motion will prevent adhesions, a condition known as "glass thumb."

Protection

In athletic events where liability to thumb injuries is great, a protective gauze bandage can be applied in the form of a modified spica, shown in Figure 35. Taping of a recently injured thumb is shown in Figure 36.

TENNIS THUMB

Etiology

Tendinitis with calcification in the flexor pollicus longus is sometimes termed as tennis thumb because of its frequent incidence among tennis players.

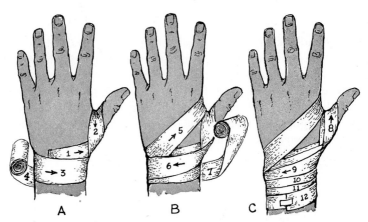

Figure 35. Bandaging for thumb sprain. *A,* The athlete spreads his fingers and holds his thumb in a semi-relaxed position. The end of a two-inch gauze roller bandage is placed on the back of the wrist (No. 1) and a spica bandage is formed by leading the gauze around outside of the thumb, up over the thumb (No. 2) and around the wrist (Nos. 3–4). *B,* The bandage is continued around the back of the hand (No. 5) up over the thumb, drawing the first metacarpus medially. Bandage is continued around the wrist (No. 6) and carried into a second spica around the thumb (No. 7). *C,* After completing the second spica (Nos. 8–9), three turns (Nos. 10–12) are taken around the wrist and the bandage is secured by a strip of one-inch tape.

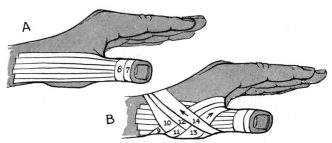

Figure 36. Taping for sprained thumb. *A,* One-inch strips of tape are applied from the base of the thumbnail to below the base of the thumb, beginning medially (Nos. 1–6). Two circular strips of one-inch tape anchor the distal ends (Nos. 7–8). *B,* Using one-inch tape, figures-of-eight are applied, avoiding pulling the tape too tightly which may cause constriction.

Symptoms

It appears originally as a pale lump under the thumb of the playing hand. At first it does not cause pain and does not interfere with tennis performance. As it increases in size and becomes reddened on the volar aspect, it becomes tender and causes discomfort while gripping the racket. Flexion and extension at the interphalangeal and metacarpophalangeal joints becomes limited and painful.

First Aid

Care consists of rest and immobility. Massage and movement are harmful. Relief from pain may be obtained by diathermy.

Rehabilitation

Following medical correction and rehabilitative exercise of the hand, the athlete can resume tennis competition.

HAND WRAP

Anatomy and Etiology

The structure of the hand is designed for grasping. The arrangement of these bones, tendons and connective tissue is such that the hand is not an appropriate instrument for striking, as in boxing, or for straight-arming, as in football. The unprotected hand is easily damaged when put to such uses because of the loose articulations of the joints of the hand and of the wrist, and because of the thin construction of the bones of the palm, thumb and fingers. Strains, sprains, fractures and dislocations are almost unavoidable when the athlete uses his hand as a striking implement against heavy resistance.

Protection

Bandaging the hand can increase its tolerance to striking forces. The object of the hand wrap is to bring the loose articulations of the hand together so that, in effect, each bone acts as a protective splint to its neighbor. Extra layers of gauze over the knuckles will provide a protective pad to lessen the forces applied to the ends of

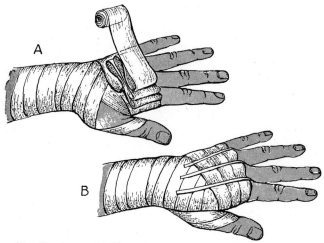

Figure 37.   Hand wrap for boxers. *A,* A two-inch gauze roller bandage is slotted near the end. The thumb is inserted into the slot and the bandage is carried clockwise around the wrist three or four times to reinforce the wrist joint. The circular wrapping is continued to the base of the thumb and a figure-of-eight around the thumb, as in Figure 35, secures the base of the thumb to the hand. A turn around the palm and across the knuckles is followed by the formation of a pad, using about eight layers of gauze. *B,* The pad is secured by three circular turns around the hand. These are fastened in place by strips of one-half inch adhesive tape drawn over the back of the hand, between the fingers and down the palm. When applied snugly, the bandage forms the hand and wrist into a single unit.

the metacarpals. Directions for applying a protective hand bandage are presented in the legends accompanying Figure 37.

BASEBALL FINGER

Etiology

Avulsion of the extensor tendon from its insertion on the distal phalanx often results from being struck on the finger tip with a baseball. Thus, this condition is often referred to as baseball finger.

Rehabilitation

Medical treatment of this injury requires about six weeks, during which time the proximal interphalangeal joint is held at about 60 degrees of flexion, while the distal interphalangeal joint is held in hyperextension by an acrylic resin splint.

REFERENCES

Books

1. Dolan, Joseph P., *Treatment and Prevention of Athletic Injuries*. Danville: The Interstate Printers and Publishers, 1955.
2. Featherstone, Donald F., *Sports Injuries Manual*. New York: Philosophical Library, 1956.
3. Larsson, L. E., *et al.*, *Acute Head Injuries in Boxers*. Copenhagen: Enjar Munksgaard, 1954.
4. Lloyd, Frank S., George G. Deaver and Floyd R. Eastwood, *Safety in Athletics*. Philadelphia: W. B. Saunders Company, 1939.
5. Logan, Gene A. and Roland F. Logan, *Techniques of Athletic Training*. Los Angeles: Franklin-Adams Press, 1952.
6. Thorndike, Augustus, *Athletic Injuries*. Fourth Edition. Philadelphia: Lea & Febiger, 1956.
7. Woodard, Christopher, *Sports Injuries*. London: Max Parrish, 1954.

Articles

1. Aldes, John H., Ultrasonic Radiation in the Treatment of Epicondylitis. *GP*, XIII:89–96, June, 1956.
2. Baer, Rudolf, *et al.*, Experimental Investigations on Mechanisms Producing Acute Dermaphytosis of Feet. *Journal of the American Medical Association, 160:*184–190, January 21, 1956.
3. Bennett, George E., Shoulder and Elbow Lesions of the Professional Baseball Pitcher. *Journal of the American Medical Association, 117:*510–514, August 1, 1941.
4. ————, Shoulder and Elbow Lesions Distinctive of Baseball Players. *Annals of Surgery, 126:*107–110, July, 1947.
5. Boone, Alex W., Earl Haltiwanger and Robert L. Chambers, Football Hematuria. *Journal of the American Medical Association, 158:*1516–1517, August 27, 1955.
6. Bosworth, David M., The Role of the Orbicular Ligament in Tennis Elbow. *Journal of Bone and Joint Surgery, 37A:*527–533, June, 1955.
7. Brain Injury in Boxing. *British Medical Journal*, No. 4903:1535, December 25, 1954.
8. Brashear, Robert G., The Neglected Athlete. *Journal of the Tennessee State Medical Association, 46:*371–373, October, 1953.
9. Burrows, H. Jackson, Fatigue Infraction of the Middle of the Tibia in Ballet Dancers. *Journal of Bone and Joint Surgery, 38B:*83–94, February, 1956.
10. Catching Cold from Showers After Exercise. *Journal of the American Medical Association, 163:*1419–1420, April 13, 1957.
11. Cave, Edwin French, Treatment of Ankle Injuries. *GP*, XV:85–93, March, 1957.
12. Coffey, T. H., Pitfalls in the Treatment of Athletic Injuries. *New York State Journal of Medicine, 56:*2377–2382, August 1, 1956.
13. Courville, Cyril B., The Mechanism of Coup-Contrecoup Injuries of the Brain. *Bulletin of the Los Angeles Neurological Society, 15:*72–86, June, 1950.
14. Cruickshank, C. D. and M. D. Trotter, Separation of Epidermis from Dermis by Filtrates of Trichophyton Mentagrophyte. *Nature, 17:*1085–1086, June, 1956.

15. Cyriax, J. H., Pathology and Treatment of Tennis Elbow. *Journal of Bone and Joint Surgery, 18:*921–940, October, 1936.
16. Dawson, C. DeWitt, An Intensive Program for Use in Knee Surgery and Pathology. *Archives of Physical Medicine and Rehabilitation,* XXXIV:750–755, December, 1953.
17. DeLarue, Norman C., The Treatment of Athletic Injuries. *Canadian Medical Association Journal, 70:*408–416, April, 1954.
18. Discussion on Injuries in Sport. *Proceedings of the Royal Society of Medicine, 49:*445–454, July, 1956.
19. Dobson, Richard L. and Walter C. Lobitz, Jr., Some Histochemical Observations on the Human Eccrine Sweat Gland. II. The Pathogenesis of Miliaria. *A.M.A. Archives of Dermatology, 75:*653–666, May, 1957.
20. Gardner, Kenneth D., Jr., 'Athletic Pseudonephritis'—Alteration of Urine Sediment by Athletic Competition. *Journal of the American Medical Association, 161:*1613–1617, August 25, 1956.
21. Gonet, L. C. L., Tennis Elbow: A New Conception. *Annals of Physical Medicine,* IV:70–73, May, 1957.
22. Hillman, Francis E., New Techniques for the Treatment of Mallet Fingers and Fractures of Distal Phalanx. *Journal of the American Medical Association, 161:*1135–1138, July 21, 1956.
23. Hobart, Marcus H., Athletic Injuries. *Journal of the American Medical Association, 107:*488–491, August 15, 1936.
24. Holbourn, A. H. S., Mechanics of Head Injury. *Lancet,* No. 6267:438–441, October 9, 1943.
25. Kaplan, Harry A. and Jefferson Browder, Observations on the Clinical and Brain Patterns of Professional Boxers. *Journal of the American Medical Association, 156:*1138–1144, November 20, 1954.
26. Kirby, F. J., Foreign Bodies in the Elbow Joint—"Baseball Pitchers' Elbow." *Journal of the American Medical Association, 95:*404–405, August 9, 1930.
27. Lannin, Donald R., Knee Injuries in Athletics. *Journal Lancet, 76:*287–289, October, 1956.
28. London, Russell I., The Industrial Back. *Journal Lancet, 76:*65–68, March, 1956.
29. Loque, John T., Acrylic Cast for Baseball Finger. *U. S. Armed Forces Medical Journal,* V:757–758, May, 1954.
30. Lord, Richard E., Intramedullary Fixation of Metacarpal Fractures. *Journal of the American Medical Association, 164:*1746–1749, August 17, 1957.
31. McDougall, A., Footballer's Ankle. *Lancet,* No. 6902:1219–1220, December 10, 1955.
31a. Morehouse, Laurence E., Influence of a Flexible Outsole on the Dynamics of the Walking Gait. *International Record of Medicine, 170:*452–457, August, 1957.
32. Moseley, H. F., Disorders of the Knee. *Ciba Clinical Symposia, 5,* November-December, 1953.
33. Moseley, H. F., Traumatic Disorders of the Ankle and Foot. *Ciba Clinical Symposia, 7,* November-December, 1955.
34. Murray, Clay R., Treatment of Injuries to the Knee Joint. *New England Journal of Medicine, 236:*265–269, February 20, 1947.
35. North, John Paul, Tennis Elbow. *International Abstract of Surgery.* In *Surgery, Gynecology and Obstetrics, 67:*176–179, August, 1938.
36. Novich, Max M., Medicine in Sports. *Journal of the Newark Beth Israel Hospital,* VIII:33–42, January, 1957.

37. Ochsenhirt, Norman C., Clifford D. Chambers and Murray B. Ferderber, Prevention and Management of Athletic Injuries. *Archives of Physical Medicine and Rehabilitation,* XXXIV:153–161, March, 1953.

38. O'Donoghue, Don H., Prevention and Treatment of Acute Ligament Injuries in Athletics. *GP,* XVI:75–81, August, 1957.

39. Oldfield, Michael C., "Tennis Thumb" Tendinitis with Calcification in Flexor Pollicis Longus. *Lancet,* No. 6665:1151–1152, May 26, 1951.

40. Penn Relay Medical Plan Spikes Spike Injuries. *Scope Weekly,* 2:15, May 29, 1957.

41. Quigley, T. B., James Cox and Joseph Murray, A Protective Wrapping for the Ankle. *Journal of the American Medical Association, 132:*924, December 14, 1946.

42. Rasch, Philip J., John F. Fahey and Robert Magrill, The Role of the Athletic Commission Physician. *Journal of the American Osteopathic Association, 56:*657–662, July, 1957.

43. Rasch, Philip J., Lucius Faires and M. Briggs Hunt, The Effects of a Combat Sport (Amateur Wrestling) on the Kidneys. To be published in *Research Quarterly,* March, 1958.

44. Raycroft, J. E., The History and Function of the Athletic Team Doctor. *Journal Lancet, 54:*271 et seq., May 1, 1934.

45. Reid, Stephen and William Schiffbauer, Role of Athletic Trainers in Prevention, Care and Treatment of Injuries. *Journal Lancet, 77:*83–84, March, 1957.

46. Rugby Football Injuries. *British Medical Journal,* No. 4906:154–155, January 15, 1955.

47. Scherbart, J. Donald, The Pathology of Cerebral Concussion. *Journal of the American Osteopathic Association, 56:*206–209, November, 1956.

48. Selman, David and Clifford Gualano, Effects of Football Playing on the Composition of the Urine. *New York State Journal of Medicine, 55:*3120–3122, November 1, 1955.

49. Waris, Wille, Elbow Injuries of Javelin-Throwers. In M. J. Karvonen, editor, *Sport Medicine.* Helsinki: Finnish Association of Sports Medicine, 1953, pp. 214–222.

50. Waxman, A., and H. Geshelm, Boxer's Bursitis. *California Medicine, 69:* 203–204, September, 1948.

51. West, E. F., Tennis Elbow. *Medical Journal of Australia,* I:330–331, February 19, 1938.

52. Williams, J. A., Skiing Injuries in Novices. *Lancet,* No. 6907:96–98, January 14, 1956.

53. Woolnough, J., "Tennis Heel." *Medical Journal of Australia,* II:857, November 27, 1954.

CHAPTER XVI

Protection from Impact Forces in Athletics

The devices developed to protect individuals from injury reflect the philosophical approach of a culture to combat, and indicate the level of its art and science.[1] Until recent decades, protective equipment in athletics had shown but little progress beyond the crude leather headgear, gloves, arm guards and footgear worn in ancient contests. Today the rapid advance in the application of engineering principles to package design and the discovery of new protective materials, together with efforts to reduce the increasing number of fatalities and personal injuries in automobile and airplane travel, are fostering the development of the science of protection of the human body from external impact forces. In engineering the man is considered as a package in action. The athlete's protective equipment must shield him from injury, but must not interfere with his speed or agility, and the weight and bulk of it must not tax his energy or cause chafing or restriction of movement. Furthermore, the protective device worn by an athlete must not jeopardize the safety of his opponent.

Human Tolerance to External Impact Forces

Analysis of factors contributing to the survival of individuals falling from heights up to one hundred and fifty feet showed that the body withstood forces of 100 g* or more.[2] It is estimated that under ideal conditions a force of 200 transverse g† might be tolerated.[3] Muscles, fat, skin, ligaments, cartilage and other soft tissues of the body serve as shock absorbing materials to protect against fracture of the bone. Each tissue has its own impact tolerance limit, that of bone being the highest. The neck of the femur will begin to fail under a suddenly applied load of 15.8 inch pounds of energy.[4] A static load of 400–700 pounds may be tolerated before similar failure begins, and a maximum load of about 1300 pounds or more may be applied before fracture of the neck of the femur results.[5]

Bone is strengthened by mineral deposits within its collagenous tissues. The collagenous development enables the adult to withstand greater stress than does a child, although in old age the bones become more brittle. Men have greater resistance to fracture than women because their bones are more dense and their skeletons are more massive. Years of hard physical labor tend to increase the density of bone.[6]

Factors Affecting Severity of Impact Forces

In some instances human beings have survived the impact of thousands of pounds of jarring forces; on the other hand blows of only slight force have been sufficient to cause a fracture or dislocation. The effect of impact on the body is determined by several factors:

1. Magnitude. The force at the peak of its intensity. Lessening of magnitude by prolonging the period of energy absorption diminishes severity.

2. Duration. The time of exposure to the impact force. In general, forces of higher magnitudes can be tolerated only if the duration of the force applied to the whole body is brief.

3. Direction. Positive g forces, acting parallel to the long axis of the body from foot to head can be tolerated better than negative g forces, acting from head to foot.

* 1 g is equal to the weight of the body caused by the force of gravity at the earth's surface. Thus, a 100 g force produced by a 150 pound man striking the earth would be 15,000 pounds.

† Transverse g designates that the force vector acts perpendicularly to the long axis of the body, i. e. from chest to back, or from back to chest.

4. Distribution. Spreading of force over a large area of the body reduces severity. Concentration of force in a small area increases damaging effects.

5. Speed of Application. A segment of the body is better able to resist an impact if the force is applied gently at first and then gradually increased. A gradually increasing push is better tolerated than is a sharp blow of the same energy.

6. Hardness of Body Surface Struck. Surfaces of the body which yield under contact absorb and distribute the force of the blow and render the blow less injurious.

7. Anatomical Location. Less damage is likely to occur if the major loads during impact are borne by the strongest parts of the body.

8. Anatomical Position. A joint at an extreme range of motion is in jeopardy if the blow extends the joint beyond normal range of motion subjecting the tight ligaments to a tearing sprain. Thus, it is not only the force of the blow which determines the extent of the injury, but also the position of the joint in relation to its limit of motion when it is struck.

Tests of Shock Absorbing Materials

Shock absorbing properties of protective materials are determined by an accelerometer which records the forces developed as a striking object is decelerated by the protective material being tested. The test assembly consists of a hammer at the end of a pendulum which strikes the test specimen. G forces are recorded by using an accelerometer strain gauge connected by wires to an amplifier, oscilloscope and camera. The arrangement is shown in Figure 38.

The "ball bounce" test also indicates the relative shock-absorbing properties of a material. In this test a steel ball is dropped from a measured height onto the material and the height of the rebound is recorded. A lesser rebound indicates a greater shock-absorbing quality. Calculations employing the weight of the ball, the distance of the drop and the height of the rebound make it possible to compute the amount of energy dissipated by the material. To be significant, the drop energy of the ball is proportional to that which might be expected to occur in a given athletic situation.

Extreme cold is found to impair the shock-absorbing quality of some materials, notably of highly plasticized vinyl materials. The porous construction of others permits absorption of perspiration,

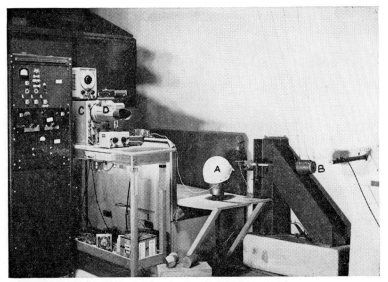

Figure 38. Apparatus for determining accelerative forces attenuated by protective materials. The test helmet (*A*) is struck by a hammer (*B*). An accelerometer affixed to the head-form is connected by an electrode lead to an amplifier and oscilloscope (*C*) which records the accelerative force as the hammer strikes the test material. A high speed strip camera (*D*) makes a permanent record of the oscilloscopic picture. (Protection Inc.)

thereby increasing the weight of the material and simultaneously reducing its shock-absorbing quality. Porous material also presents a cleaning and sterilizing problem, since the substance retains moisture and traps debris.

Heat resistance is a desirable quality in athletic protective material. The equipment is at times dried in heated ovens which tends to deteriorate some materials. Flame resistance is an additional desirable quality.

Specifications for Protective Equipment

In order for athletic protective equipment to be completely effective it should possess the following essential features:

1. Ability to absorb shock without rebound.
2. Designed to distribute the impact forces to the **stronger parts** of the body.
3. Flexible and nonrestrictive.
4. **Light weight.**

5. Nonabsorbent of perspiration.

6. Energy absorbing properties not affected by changes in temperature or by age of material.

7. Does not endanger an opponent.

8. Heat and flame resistant.

An ideal impact protective equipment for use in sports combines two characteristics: (1) energy absorption offering protection against severe blows and (2) cushioning to minimize discomfort from minor blows. These are provided by two classes of material, one which does not compress unless a force of an intensity potentially injurious to the body is applied, and the other which is easily compressible and conforms readily to the part of the body which it covers. Materials of the first type comprise relatively rigid or non-resilient foamed plastics, such as cellular polystyrene, cellulose acetate or polyesters. Those of the second type include foam rubber and soft foamed synthetic plastics.

When subjected to compressive loads, this combination of materials compresses only slightly until the load reaches a value at which deformation of the non-resilient cellular structure begins. An efficient material will then deflect through two-thirds of its original thickness without much further increase in applied force.[7] The high energy absorbing materials have a disadvantage in that they do not recover after heavy blows. This can be overcome by having new sections on hand to replace the damaged ones.

A practical material for athletic use would be one which would have the shock absorbing characteristics described above, but in addition would have the property of slow (about 1 second) recovery to its original shape and efficiency. Thus, the material would be ready for a repeated blow. Cork is an effective energy absorbing material, but it loses its energy absorbing efficiency under repeated blows. Material of expanded cellular polyvinyl chloride has fairly good energy absorbing qualities, but hardens when cold and softens in heat. Rubber has a dangerous rebound quality. Wool felt in appropriate thickness is a good shock absorber when new, but it absorbs moisture and tends to harden in service.

Head Protection

Threshold of Skull Fracture. The impact energy necessary to fracture human skulls was determined in a test with 46 cadaver heads from which the tissues had not been removed. The mean value was found to be 616.5 inch pounds, which represents the equivalent of dropping a head weighing 12.5 pounds on a steel plate from a distance of 49.32 inches.[8] Serious injury or death can result from impact forces far below the threshold of skull fracture.[9] It is axiomatic that there is no injury to the head so slight that it may not be fatal, and few injuries so serious that recovery may not be possible. Studies with experimental animals have shown that unconsciousness may result from blows to the head which do not produce demonstrable morphologic changes in the brain.[10] The seriousness of this problem in athletics is evident from the fact that 51.03 per cent of all known fatalities occurring in football between 1931 and 1956 resulted from head injuries.[11]

Damage to the head depends more on the characteristics of the object struck than on the impact velocity. When gelatin-filled plastic artificial heads with strength characteristics similar to those of human heads were catapulted against various surfaces, it was found that on a hard, flat, non-deflecting plate fractures occurred at velocities of 18 to 20 feet per second. When energy-absorbing surfaces were used, fractures did not occur until the velocities approached 100 feet per second.[12]

Tolerance to Head Impact. Two hundred thirty-five blows to the heads of eleven volunteers wearing helmets were delivered by a pendulum weighing 9.44 pounds, as shown in Figure 39. Blows to the top, front and back of the head up to 38 g (acceleration of 1220 feet per second) produced no symptoms of concussion, but resulted in local bruising, neck pains and general discomfort. There was no serious interference with cerebral activity or neuromuscular co-ordination.[13]

All helmets of the sling suspension type moved at impact bringing the head of the subject against the shell. Hard shelled helmets with sling suspension vibrated upon impact. The distortion of the face upon impact (shown in Figure 39) reveals considerable tension upon soft tissues. Bulging of the palpebrae near the lateral canthus of the left eye and near the medial canthus of the right eye shows the displacement of the eyes with resulting tension upon the oblique ocular muscles, indicating also probable tension upon optic nerves.

Types of Headgear. In the 1874 football game between Harvard and McGill, the Harvard players wore crimson headkerchiefs bound around their heads, while the McGill squad wore turbans. In 1890 the Yale players started the practice of letting their hair grow all

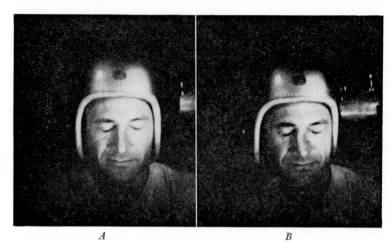

A   B

Figure 39. Photographs of subject taken just prior to and after a blow by 9.44 pound pendulum at a velocity of 6 feet per second. Note displacement of soft tissues of the face as the skull is driven sideward by the force of the hammer. (Protection Inc.)

summer to provide head padding for the coming football season. With ear and nose harness and turtle neck sweater, the player of the nineties shown in Figure 40 was ready for football combat. Early in the twentieth century many devices designed to protect the head were tried and discarded. These included a pneumatic head harness made of soft rubber with an inflated crown and one composed of straps of leather lined with heavy wool felt padding provided with large openings for ventilation. After World War II the plastic football helmet with web suspension was developed along the principles

Figure 40. Player of the 1890's using long hair and ear and nose harness as head protection for football. (Rawlings Sporting Goods Company.)

of the helmets worn by aviators. Web suspension offers ventilation but provides inadequate protection against lateral blows.

Helmet Effectiveness. In order to determine the degree of protection afforded by different types of helmets against massive compression, human cadaver heads were subjected to test impacts of 500 foot pound force applied to the temple area. The skulls were x-rayed and the helmets were disassmbled and examined. The helmet containing a liner of composition padding made up of the firm and soft materials described above was the most effective in preventing skull fractures.[14]

In a second and more definitive study of dynamic impact, helmets of different varieties were subjected to tests using the apparatus shown in Figure 38. All helmets except those with a padded non-resilient liner showed a tendency to "bottom" upon impacts. In bottoming, the liner is totally compressed and there is no more shock-absorbing action between the head and the helmet shell. Sling suspensions, resilient liners and slow rebound liners bottomed under high lateral dynamic impact forces.[15]

Projections, such as fasteners for face shields or chin straps, serve to concentrate most of the striking force onto one small area, preventing distribution of force and allowing development of forces of highest magnitudes. Location of the fastening devices at the temple area focuses the impact force upon the weakest portion of the skull. Loose or weak chin straps permit the helmet to shift during impact decreasing its protective quality. Loose fitting helmets develop motions of force of their own during impact which add to the damaging effect. Helmet shells afford but little protection without "non-resilient" liners. Shells without liners, or with highly resilient liners, permit the impact forces to be transmitted directly to the head. Once a shell has cracked it loses its energy-distributing capacity and is no longer an effective protective device.

Helmet Fitting. To assure a proper fit, each player is assigned a personal helmet with the padding conforming to all contours of the head. The line of the front of the helmet comes immediately above the eyebrows, as shown in Figure 41. The ear portion of the helmet covers the mandibular joint. The rear portion of the helmet fits below the base of the skull to protect as much of the cervical vertebral area as possible without restricting the movement of the head and neck.

The chin strap is fitted snugly and is kept tight at all times during

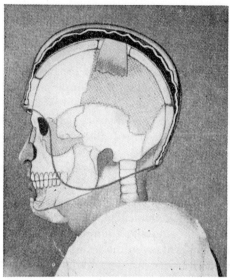

Figure 41. Football helmet. This cut-away view shows the relation of the various portions of the helmet to the susceptible areas of the skull and face. (Rawlings Sporting Goods Company.)

play to keep the ear portion of the helmet in place over the mandibular joint, to keep the rear of the helmet down to protect the base of the skull and cervical vertebrae and to prevent the helmet from shifting out of position. A cup type chin strap holds the helmet in position without exerting undue pressure on the jaws. With a properly fitted helmet the athlete is able to move his head in all directions without any independent rotation of the helmet. Jolting blows from any direction against the outside of the helmet will not displace it. The head and the helmet are as a single unit.

Face Protection

Molded plastic face bars of cantilever construction are attached to the helmet to protect the eyes, nose, teeth and jaws. The face bar is padded for shock absorption. The face protector is wide enough to cover the lower half of the nose and mouth, but the space between is large enough to permit unobstructed breathing and speech. These protectors can crack at the site of attachment to the helmet and wearers can be injured if the bars break or the mask becomes loose. In many cases these masks have to be custom fitted if they are to be useful.[16, 17]

Mouth Protectors

In 1950 the University of Missouri made a survey of 4000 athletes in 62 colleges and universities. This survey revealed that a total of 733 teeth had been lost, broken or chipped in a single season.[18] Approximately 54 per cent of all high school football injuries are facial and dental. Most—perhaps all—of the dental injuries could have been prevented had the players been required to wear mouth protectors.[19]

The demand for mouth protectors came from boxers about 1927. These are designed to hold the jaws apart and to act as shock absorbers. They also help to prevent upward displacement of the condyle in its articulating fossa which often results in concussion or even cerebral hemorrhage, lateral displacement of the mandible leading to dislocation or fracture of this bone and split lips or cheeks and chipped teeth.[20] A satisfactory device of this type must include the following features:

1. Maximum protection.
2. No enroachment on the air passage when the athlete is forced to breathe through his mouth.
3. No interference which makes speech difficult or impossible.
4. Comfort in wearing.
5. Ability to remain in place.[21]

These advantages can be obtained only from custom made mouth protectors in which the rubber is molded to the exact contours of the teeth and orthodontic devices. Stock mouth protectors do not afford the same amount of protection; athletes find them clumsy and uncomfortable, and often refuse to wear them.

The necessity for observing strict sanitary precautions in the use of mouth protectors is obvious and creates a definite problem. Each athlete is furnished with a container for storage of his mouth protector and neither the protector nor the container should be loaned to other players.

Shoulder Pads

In sports such as football, in which the athlete is required to hurl himself against an opponent in blocking or tackling, the player must

Figure 42. Shoulder pad. One half of the football shoulder pad is in place and the position of the bones and joints which the pad protects are shown on the opposite shoulder. (Rawlings Sporting Goods Company.)

have confidence that the equipment he is wearing will protect him from injury. The shoulder pad is designed to give firm protection to the bones and ligaments which make up the acromioclavicular and sternoclavicular joints. It is constructed of movable parts to allow free movement of the shoulder or upper arm.

In order to protect while remaining flexible, the shoulder pad is made up of three parts: an arch, a cap and a flap. The arch is the basis for the shoulder pad. The upper and front portions of the arch protect the clavicle, sternoclavicular joint and upper ribs, as shown in Figure 42; the rear portion protects the scapula. To anchor the pad, the contour of the arch is molded to duplicate the shape of the body so that the rear portion hugs the back of the shoulders. If the opening of the arch is too wide, it permits rocking and slipping motions which expose parts of the shoulders to injury. The slow-recovery padding of the arch extends along the clavicle to a point beyond the edge of the shoulder. The greater amount of padding is centered over the acromioclavicular joint. The neck opening is large enough to permit free movement of the head and neck and to prevent chafing and the ridges do not pinch the neck when the arms are raised upward.

The cap and flap of the shoulder pad provide protection to the fragile acromioclavicular joint while permitting a wide range of motion. The cap is fastened to the arch so as to remain in place over the acromioclavicular joint, protecting it from blows at all

times. The padding of the cap extends over and fits snugly against the deltoid muscle, protecting it from the jarring blows of blocking and tackling.

The flap of the shoulder pad is also fastened to the arch. It is centered directly in front of the acromioclavicular joint and is prevented from shifting out of position by a web anchor.

The entire shoulder pad is adjusted by laces in front and back and by the underarm straps to fit tightly. These straps are placed far enough below the armpits to prevent chafing. Removal is accomplished by detaching the front lacing so as not to alter the fit.

Hip Pads

Although the hip joint is composed of sturdy bones deep-seated in the body and protected by thick layers of muscle, there are several points which need protection in contact sports such as football. These are the crest of the ilium, lying close to the surface of the body, the ball and socket hip joint, the sacrum and coccyx.

The contoured girdle made of slow-recovery padding material contains fiber pieces designed and located to protect the vulnerable areas. The hip fibers protect the exposed edge of the crest of the ilium. The femur fibers fit over the side of the hip joints and protect the ball and socket articulations. The spine fiber at the rear protects the sacrum and coccyx. Form fitting padding in the rear upper area of the hip fibers protects the kidneys. The relation of the protective pads to the vulnerable areas of the hip is shown in Figure 43.

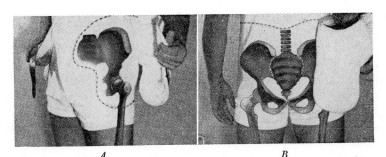

A   *B*

Figure 43. Hip pad. *A,* Hip pad opened to show position protecting the iliac crest and the hip joint by the hip fiber and the hip joint fiber. *B,* Hip pad opened further to show protection to the sacrum and coccyx offered by the tail fiber. (Rawlings Sporting Goods Company.)

Shoes

In addition to providing traction, athletic footgear is designed to protect the foot from cuts and bruises, to provide support to the foot and to permit full function during events requiring speed and fast change of direction.

The upper portion of the athletic shoe is constructed of either kangaroo or cowhide leather. Kangaroo leather is lighter, has a higher tensile strength, is more durable and will stretch less than cowhide. Football and baseball shoes are of welt construction, with one-piece oak-tanned leather outsoles, either sewed to the sole with nylon thread lock-stitched on full cut patterns, or bonded to the sole without stitching. They may be waterproofed.

Fitting of shoes is done by determining several dimensions while the athlete is standing. The heel-to-ball fit is ascertained by first checking that the heel is well seated and then noting the position of the ball of the foot in relation to the widest portion of the shoe. The athletic shoe is constructed to provide flexion of the sole one inch behind the ball-line to allow full foot action at the metatarsophalangeal articulation. The shoe fits loosely around the toes to provide free toe action. The heel of the shoe conforms to the shape of the heel in a snug fit to prevent friction and side-slipping. The instep of the shoe supports the longitudinal arch from the narrow shank upward. Even before the shoe is laced the athlete feels the leather of the upper far under the longitudinal arch.

For fitting athletic shoes, other precautions have to be taken. Because one foot may be significantly larger than the other both are fitted. If each foot cannot be fitted individually, that pair is selected which fits the larger foot. An extra sock may make up the size difference of the smaller foot. The socks to be worn in play are worn during fitting. The surfaces of the inside of the shoe must be free from seams and creases. Any projections are liable to cause blisters.

In many types of athletic shoes in which the manufacturer has provided only one or two widths, the lacing adjustment is set wide enough apart so that the athlete with a slim foot will not draw the upper parts of the shoe together. The upper leather is drawn snugly around the foot by lacing one pair of eyelets at a time, drawing the laces with equalized pressure at each eyelet. During activity the foot size may be reduced or may be enlarged. Such changes can be accommodated by lacing adjustments. Broken laces are replaced immediately; a knot easily causes a blister.

In football shoes cleats are placed on the outside of the shoe to coincide with the flexion section an inch behind the ball-line of the foot. This juxtaposition is shown in the x-ray photographs in Figure 44. Also shown are the front three cleats which form a wide base triangle of contact for effective toe action. Heel cleats are placed directly under the base of the calcaneus, the rearward weight-bearing portion of the foot. They are placed laterally and wide apart, as far to the outside of the outsole as possible for the sake of stability.

The cleats themselves may be of hard rubber, aluminum, nylon or nylon with metal tip. Most high school coaches find aluminum the most satisfactory but a large percentage believe that their use should be banned as potentially dangerous to opponents.[22] Oblong cleats are the most substantial but the conical ones give better traction.

Some experimentation has been done with rubber soled canvas topped shoes for use in high school football. These are reported to be light and comfortable, and their use is believed to eliminate some injuries. However, on prolonged wear complaints of breaking off of

Figure 44. X-ray photo of foot in football shoe. Heel and ball cleats are placed under weight-bearing portions of foot; forward cleats form base for toe action in running and lunging. (Rawlings Sporting Goods Company.)

the cleats, lack of arch support, insufficient ankle support and other difficulties become common.[23]

The Ripple sole, whose multiple rearward angulated wedges furnish shock absorption and increase stride length, has been used successfully in long distance walking and running, in golf and mountain climbing, and as a training shoe in track. Its flexibility feature makes it especially adaptable also to basketball, tennis and other sports played on hard surfaces.

REFERENCES

1. Stendahl, Alfred and Cyril B. Courville, Development and Use of the Helmet as a Means of Protection Against Craniocerebral Injury. *Bulletin of the Los Angeles Neurological Society, 19:*1–17, March, 1954.
2. DeHaven, Hugh, Mechanical Analysis of Survival in Falls from Heights of Fifty to One Hundred and Fifty Feet. *War Medicine, 2:*586–596, July, 1942.
3. Spector, William S., editor, *Handbook of Biological Data.* Philadelphia: W. B. Saunders Company, 1956, p. 464.
4. Evans, F. Gaynor, H. R. Lissner and Herbert E. Pedersen, Deformation Studies of the Femur Under Dynamic Vertical Loading. *Anatomical Record, 101:* 225–242, June, 1948.
5. Evans, F. Gaynor and H. R. Lissner, "Stress-coat" Deformation Studies of the Femur Under Static Vertical Loading. *Anatomical Record, 100:*159–190, February, 1948.
6. Morehouse, Laurence E. and John M. Cooper, *Kinesiology.* St. Louis: The C. V. Mosby Company, 1950, p. 26.
7. New Helmet Protection Theory Advanced. *Aviation Week,* January 24, 1949, pp. 18 and 20.
8. Lissner, H. R., E. S. Gurdjian and J. E. Webster, Mechanics of Skull Fracture. *Proceedings of the Society for Experimental Stress Analysis, 7:*61–70, 1949.
9. McFarland, Ross A., Human Factors in Air Transportation. New York: McGraw-Hill Book Company, Inc., 1953, p. 558.
10. Miller, G. Gavin, Cerebral Concussion. *Archives of Surgery, 14:*891–916, January, 1927.
11. Committee on Injuries and Fatalities, American Football Coaches Association, *The Twenty-Fifth Annual Survey of Football Fatalities, 1931–1956.* Hanover: American Football Coaches Association, January 7, 1957, p. 19.
12. Wahl, N. E., *et al.* Head Impact Investigation. Contract No. N-ori-119, Rept. OG-537-D-9. Office of Naval Research, Department of the Navy, Washington, D.C., May 21, 1947.
13. Lombard, Charles F., *et al.,* Voluntary Tolerance of the Human to Impact Acceleration of the Head. *Journal of Aviation Medicine, 22:*109–116, April, 1951.
14. Snively, George G., Skull Busting for Safety. *Sports Cars Illustrated, 3:*22 *et seq.,* July, 1957.
15. Borgeson, Griff, *Comfort or Survival? Sports Cars Illustrated, 3:*16 *et seq.,* October, 1957.
16. *1956 Summary of Football Equipment Survey.* National Federation mimeographed report, 1957.
17. *Summary and Report of An Experiment by Wisconsin Interscholastic Athletic Association.* National Federation mimeographed report, 1956.

18. Vanet, Randy, Gridiron Challenge. *Dental Survey, 27:*1258–1260, September, 1951.
19. Editorial, Mouth Protectors for Football Trainees. *Journal of the American Dental Association, 52:*358–359, March, 1956.
20. Cathcart, Jack F., Football's Ounce of Prevention. *Journal of the Association for Health, Physical Education and Recreation, 24:*8 *et seq.,* October, 1953.
21. Watts, George, Archie Woolard and Carl E. Singer, Functional Mouth Protectors for Contact Sports. *Journal of the American Dental Association, 89:*7–11, July, 1954.
22. *1955 Summary of Football Equipment Survey.* National Federation mimeographed report, 1956.
23. *Composite Report of 1956 Football Shoe Experiment.* National Federation mimeographed report, 1957.

CHAPTER XVII

Training Room Design, Equipment and Operations

The training room in which the team physician, the trainer, and his assistants perform their duties in the care of athletic teams is designed to provide efficient service to large numbers of athletes at one time. The typical trainer spends 60 per cent of his time on prevention and 40 per cent on care of injuries.[1]

The training room is immediately adjacent to the locker room and the athletic equipment supply room where towels and ankle wraps are issued. A small examining room provides privacy and convenience for the team physician when he is on duty and at other times serves as a private office for the trainer. In this room is a locked cabinet for surgical equipment, pharmaceutical supplies and medical records. An adjustable table, an ophthalmological examining chair, sterilizer, and a mobile dressing table complete the minimal furnishings of this room.

The trainer and his assistants are provided each day with clean white duck trousers and T shirts. Monogrammed jackets and caps are provided for outdoor use.

216

Interior Materials and Colors

The training room walls and floors are usually of cement, which can easily be cleaned and disinfected. The ceiling is covered with perforated acoustic tiles to minimize noise. For ease of seeing and eye comfort, the acoustic tiles are of white, ivory, cream or buff color to provide reflective values of 80 to 99 per cent. They have matte finish to prevent glare. Upper walls are painted with waterproof paints in light colors, such as pale green, buff, gray or blue, for high reflectivity. Lower walls, or dado, are slightly darker in color than the upper walls. Medium shades of green, brown, gray or blue are used.

Woodwork, such as door jambs, window frames, molding and built-in cabinets, may be covered with a glossy paint for ease in cleaning and may match either upper or lower wall colors. If a contrasting color is used for woodwork, it is white, ivory, cream or gray.

Flooring has only about 15 to 30 per cent reflectivity, but is not dark. A bare concrete floor is easy to maintain and has a good acoustic quality. If a covering is used, asphalt, thick linoleum or vinyl asbestos tile laid over cement, tile or wood floors is acceptable. Cement floors provide an unyielding surface, are fatiguing and are slippery when wet. Rubber mats over work areas reduce fatigue and slipping but increase the work of cleaning. Shoes with flexible Ripple soles provide firm support to the foot, reduce fatigue and keep the trainer's feet dry.

Furniture is light in color. If a natural wood finish is used, it is stained a light tone.

Color Code. Certain colors and color combinations have been accepted as code to identify material and equipment. When employed in the training room they may improve efficiency and safety.[2]

Red—Fire protection equipment.

Green—Safe materials, such as water.

Blue exterior with orange interior—Electric controls.

Purple—Valuable materials; caution against waste.

Yellow—Maintenance equipment.

Blue—Protective materials, such as antidotes for poisons.

Red letters on white background—Poisons.

Black letters on green background—Compressed gases.

Black letters on red background—Inflammable liquids.

Black letters on white background—Acids.
Green cross on white background—First aid equipment.

Lighting

Good lighting requires an adequate intensity of illumination, an even diffusion of light, the avoidance of glare and shadows and proper attention to contrast.[3] Unilateral window lighting in the training room is most desirable, preferably from windows facing north. Outriggers attached to the building are used to screen out direct sunlight and also can be arranged to provide indirect natural light by reflection. Ceiling shadow is reduced by extending windows to ceiling height. Central glare from a large window is eliminated by using venetian blinds or two-roller shades. Frosted glass is used to insure privacy. Equipment in the training room is placed so that the window light is from the left of the trainer as he performs his usual operations. This arrangement assumes the trainer to be right-handed and would be reversed if he were left-handed.

For the work of the trainer and physician illumination intensity needs to be 75 to 100 foot candles, without glare or shadows.[4] This is best provided by indirect lighting which offers general, evenly diffused illumination. In this method, 90 to 100 per cent of the light is directed toward the ceiling and the upper walls from which it is reflected fairly evenly about the room.

Fluorescent units give a diffused light but cause some glare and shadows. The use of baffles aids in scattering the light and reduces some of the glare.

Equipment Arrangement

Since the trainer is responsible for the training room, he must be able to see what is being done in all parts of the room. His view is not obstructed by cabinets or other tall equipment in the center of the room. Such equipment is arranged along the walls as shown in Figure 45. If a separate examination room is provided within the training room, a one-way glass will permit the physician or the trainer working in this room to observe conditions in the training room and at the same time will give privacy in the examining room. A training room which is nearly square permits a shorter viewing distance than an elongated rectangular room. It also enables better talking links making shouting unnecessary and shortens the distance in moving from one area to another.

The question whether one or two doors should be provided is usually answered by an analysis of traffic. If two doors invite the use of the training room as a convenient short cut from one part of the building to another, the undesirable traffic usually outweighs the advantage of the extra door.

The equipment in the training room is arranged to form aisles about five feet wide for channelling of traffic. Working space around the tables, workbench and cabinets allows about three feet of unobstructed area.

Storage for regularly used supplies and equipment is provided at the site of use. For example, a shelf for tape is built into the end of the taping table. Large uncovered waste receptacles are placed in areas where packages are opened and bandages are removed. Electric outlets are installed at a height of 37 to 41 inches above the floor and about 8 feet apart around the training room.

Tables for massage, exercise and heating are 7 feet long, 30 inches wide and approximately 30 inches high. The taping table has the same surface dimensions but is approximately 36 inches high so

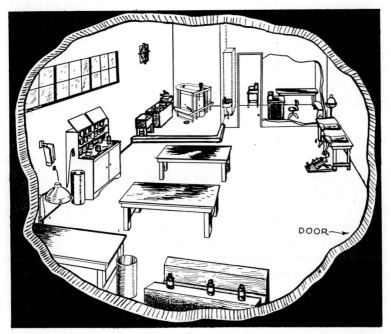

Figure 45. Training room layout.

that the trainer can work without bending forward. All tables are padded with foam rubber and are covered with waterproof material to allow for frequent washing.

Sinks are approximately 36 inches high and 24 inches wide. If sink cabinets are provided, a kickroom 4 inches high and 4 inches deep is allowed at the base.

A supply cabinet equipped with a work counter is used for the preparation of bandages and dressings and for a storage of supplies and records. The overall height of the cabinet does not exceed 76 inches. The work counter is 36 to 39 inches high and projects 4 inches over the storage cabinet beneath. The front edges of the shelves above the work counter are recessed 10 inches from the projecting edge of the counter. Kickroom is provided at the base.

Hydrotherapy Area

All equipment using water is assembled in the hydrotherapy area, which has provision for drainage. If a curb is constructed surrounding the hydrotherapy area it is sufficiently massive to be easily observed. A one inch curb is more apt to cause accidents due to tripping than a 4 inch one. A clean towel supply and receptacle for wet towels located within the hydrotherapy zone allows the athletes to dry themselves while standing in the drainage area, avoiding thereby unnecessary dripping of water in the dry area of the training room.

Installation of all electrical equipment in the hydrotherapy area is done by a competent electrician. Improper wiring or grounding could lead to fatal accidents.

Ventilation

A ventilating fan forces stale air out of the training room and provides a gentle movement of air without causing a draft. Located near the ceiling in the wall of the hydrotherapy area, it helps to lower the humidity in the room and eliminates odors. In order to avoid excessive noise, the tip speed of the ventilating fan does not exceed 55 feet per second and the air outlet velocity does not exceed 1500 feet per minute.[5] The fan casing is rigid and damped and a silent motor is used.

Water Cooling Box

The extensive use of cold water and cold compresses in early care of injuries makes necessary some form of refrigeration in the training room. An ideal solution is a large cooler, such as is ordinarily used for bottled soft drinks, which maintains the water in the tub at a 35° F. temperature. It can be used to soak towels for cold compresses or the injured limb can be immersed in the cold water for prescribed periods. Athletes with skin infections are not permitted to use the tub for immersion. For sanitary purposes, the tub is emptied at the end of each day and rinsed with an antiseptic solution.

Whirlpool Bath

A whirlpool bath large enough to accommodate several athletes at one time is located in the hydrotherapy area. The tub, at least 40 inches long, 20 inches wide and 25 inches deep, holds 75 gallons or more of water maintained by a thermostat at 104° F. Athletes with skin infections are not permitted to use the tank unless it is emptied, cleaned and sterilized after such use. Athletes use the whirlpool bath only after a thorough soaping and water shower. If the whirlpool bath is used throughout the day it is emptied, cleaned and sterilized at least every four hours. Addition of chlorine solution to the bath water provides antisepsis.

The whirlpool bath may be fitted with a metal or enamel painted wooden platform on one side upon which the athlete can sit while bathing his leg. A low stool permits another athlete to sit alongside with his arm immersed.

Moist Compress Heater

When moist heat is prescribed, a convenient method is to use a compress containing gel filler heated in a tank at 170° F., and then wrapped in a towel for application. This provides 30 minutes of effective moist heat. The tank, with a capacity for 12 compresses, is located in the hydrotherapy area.

Heat Lamps

If heat lamps are employed in the training room, the type with a metal filament is selected because it is limited to the less dangerous infra-red portion of the spectrum. The skin is usually moistened with Ichthyol or some other type of ointment to promote heat penetration and to prevent skin irritation. Exposure to the heat lamp is carefully scheduled by the team physician and supervised by the trainer. A timing clock operated by the trainer or an automatic exposure meter is useful to prevent overexposure.

Diathermy, ultrasonics and other special electronic devices are used only by qualified therapists under the physician's immediate supervision. They are highly dangerous in the hands of unskilled manipulators.

Exercise Equipment

Equipment for reconditioning exercises after injury is located near the tables or mats where it is to be used. Equipment not used frequently may be stored in a cabinet with harnesses and other special equipment. Iron plates and weights for the dumbbells, barbells and similar equipment, and springs for the ankle and knee strengtheners are stored in a wooden box or a rack.

Foot Care Bench

Two seats are arranged facing a foot rest, with a powder box between, as shown in Figure 45. Seats are padded and each accommodates two athletes. They are 42 inches long, 12 inches wide and 20 inches high. The foot rest is 12 inches wide and 16 inches high, with four skin toughening spray can receptacles. Powder boxes are 6 inches deep and 16 inches wide This bench is located either in the locker room or training room.

Experience has shown that the use of the foot care bench by the younger athletes has to be supervised because of the temptation to scatter the powder and use the sprays in a playful manner. Such misuse not only creates a maintenance problem but also is potentially dangerous should the foot spray or powder get into the eyes.

Music

Recorded background music in the training room promotes feelings of well-being, helps to relax and assists in relieving fatigue. Music will also boost the morale of the trainer and his assistants, especially when the season is well advanced and the work becomes monotonous. The addition of music results in better care of the athlete. Speakers are placed away from the examination room, which is reserved for quiet operations.

A television set helps to amuse the athletes under whirlpool or other prolonged treatment, but it tends to attract loiterers and lowers the efficiency of the training room.

EQUIPMENT AND SUPPLIES NEEDED

For fitting out the training room, travel and field kits, the equipment and supplies are listed in Tables 9 and 10. These lists contain only the minimal requirements and the team physician and trainer will add other items customarily used in their practice.

Table 9. List of Minimal Equipment

Adjustable examining table
Ankle wrap roller
Bandage cutter using detachable razor blade
Bookshelf
Braces
Containers for supplies
Desk and chair
Field kit
Foot care bench
Forceps
Heat lamps—300 watt infra-red with metal filament
Massage and heat tables
Medical and surgical cabinet, with lock
Mobile dressing table
Moist compress heater
Open supply shelves
Ophthalmological examining chair
Physician's scales
Plinths
Safety razor
Scalpel, with detachable blade
Scissors—bandage, surgical, nail
Sitz bath
Splints
Sterilizers
Thermometer
Towels
Traveling bag
Tweezers
Wash basin and towel rack
Waste containers
Water cooler for cold compresses
Weights, bars and boots for progressive resistance exercises
Whirlpool bath

Table 10. List of Minimal Supplies

Absorbent cotton
Adhesive tape, 1″, 1½″ and 2″ widths
Adhesive tape remover
Adrenalin, 1:1000 solution
Analgesic balm
Ankle wraps, woven cotton webbing, 2¼″ x 96″, with non-ravel ends
Antiseptic liquid
Antiseptic ointment
Aromatic spirits of ammonia ampules
Boric acid ointment
Cold compresses
Disinfectants, germicidal and fungicidal
Elastic bandages, 2″, 3″ and 4″ widths; length 5½ yards stretched
Felt, ½″ thick
Foot powder
Gauze roller bandages, 2″ width
Heat compresses
Ichthyol ointment
Liniment
Pads
Petroleum jelly
Record cards
Salicylic acid solution
Salt tablets
Sponge rubber, ½″ thick
Styptic astringent
Swab sticks
Talcum powder
Tape remover solution
Teeth protectors
Tincture of benzoin, alum, or other skin toughener
Triangular bandages
Weight charts
Whitfield's ointment, 1% methylene blue alcoholic solution, or other fungicide

WORK METHODS AND MOTION ECONOMY

An apprentice trainer can use to good advantage the principles of work simplification that trainers have found by experience to be the most efficient. A few of these are listed below and other suggestions for the prevention of fatigue[6] and the use of proper body mechanics[7] may be found in the literature.

1. Employ continuous curved motions and a rhythmic pattern of such motions, instead of straight line movements involving sudden and sharp changes of direction.
2. Interrelate successive movements so that one movement carries easily into the next, each ending in a position favorable for the beginning of the next movement.
3. Eliminate hesitations or temporary cessation from movement.
4. Lay emphasis on form rather than accuracy at the beginning of the learning of a new combination of movements even if this results in a poor showing at the beginning of the apprenticeship.
5. When fingers alone can accomplish a task, do not use wrist or arm motions.
6. Simplify the operation by placing the tools, materials and controls in positions which require the least movement and muscular effort. Eliminate searching and selecting.
7. Arrange the height of the work places and chairs so that alternate sitting and standing at work are easily possible.
8. Secure rest periods through frequent movements of relaxation during work, five minute breaks hourly, and vacation periods away from work between seasons and during holidays.

REFERENCES

1. *The First Aider, 24*:68, January 2, 1955.
2. Woodson, Wesley E., *Human Engineering Guide for Equipment Designers.* Berkeley: University of California Press, 1954, pp. 1–80.
3. *Lighting and Health.* Health Practices Pamphlet No. 18. National Safety Council.
4. Mennell, James B., *Manual Therapy.* Springfield, Ill.: Charles C Thomas, 1951, p. 18.
5. *Handbook of Human Engineering Data.* Second Edition (Revised). Medford: Tufts College Institute for Applied and Experimental Psychology, 1952, Part VI, Chapter IV, Section II.
6. *Practical Methods for Reducing Fatigue.* Safe Practices Pamphlet No. 50. National Safety Council, Inc., 1940.
7. Rasch, Philip J., Practical Body Mechanics for Hospital Workers. *Journal of the Association for Physical and Mental Rehabilitation, 5*:8–13, March-April, 1952.

Index